Rhetoric in American Anthropology

D1500761

Pittsburgh Series in Composition, Literacy, and Culture

David Bartholomae and Jean Ferguson Carr, Editors

Rhetoric in American Anthropology

GENDER, GENRE, AND SCIENCE

Risa Applegarth

UNIVERSITY OF PITTSBURGH PRESS

Portions of chapter 1 originally appeared in Risa Applegarth, "Rhetorical Scarcity: Spatial and Economic Inflections on Genre Change," *College Composition and Communication* 63, no. 3 (2012). Copyright © 2012 by the National Council of Teachers of English. Reprinted with permission.

Portions of chapter 2 originally appeared in Risa Applegarth, "Field Guides: Women Writing Popular Anthropology," in *Women and Rhetoric between the Wars*, ed. Ann George, Elizabeth Weiser, and Janet Zepernick (Carbondale: Southern Illinois University Press, 2013). Reprinted with permission.

Permission to quote from unpublished manuscript materials was generously extended by the American Philosophical Society; the Bancroft Library, University of California, Berkeley; Dr. Mary Catherine Bateson; Dr. Philip Deloria; and the Zora Neale Hurston Trust and Victoria Sanders & Associates, LLC.

Published by the University of Pittsburgh Press, Pittsburgh, Pa., 15260
Copyright © 2014, University of Pittsburgh Press
All rights reserved
Manufactured in the United States of America
Printed on acid-free paper
10 9 8 7 6 5 4 3 2 1

Library of Congress Cataloging-in-Publication Data

Applegarth, Risa.
Rhetoric in American Anthropology: Gender, Genre, and Science / Risa Applegarth.
pages cm — (Pittsburgh Series in Composition, Literacy, and Culture)
ISBN 978-0-8229-6295-3 (paperback)
1. Ethnology—History. 2. Anthropology—Philosophy. 3. Anthropologists' writings.
4. Women anthropologists. 5. Feminist anthropology. I. Title.
GN308.A66 2014
301.01'4--dc23
2013049420

For my mother, Joy
and for my partner, Matthew

Contents

Acknowledgments

I T SEEMS especially appropriate to begin this book about disciplinary practices in a professional community by recognizing the generous communities of scholars, mentors, colleagues, and friends who have sustained me throughout this project. First, Jane Danielewicz and Jordynn Jack have provided for years precisely the kind of mentorship I hope to offer my own students, challenging and encouraging me in equal measures, and offering generous support while trusting me to pursue my own interests to their best ends. Jane and Jordynn, along with Erika Lindemann, Valerie Lambert, and my two earliest mentors, Claudia Brown and Carol Rutz, have together forged a community of women intellectuals who have inspired me across all the stages of my education.

The ideas in this book have also been improved by a generous community of colleagues at the University of North Carolina at Greensboro (UNCG) and elsewhere. My writing group, who knows my writing habits—my love of dashes, my overuse of pairs—better than anyone else, deserves more than half the credit for any good idea I ever have. I want to express my deepest appreciation to Erin Branch, Heather Branstetter, Sarah Hallenbeck, and Chelsea Redeker, whose intelligence has made my writing life a joy and whose friendship has sustained and energized me for years. Thanks are due as well to my anthropologist friend Tom Guthrie, who provided feedback on portions of the manuscript. Several of my colleagues at UNCG also provided feedback on the manuscript, and many more have engaged me in conversations that have stretched and clarified my thinking; I am indebted especially to Claudia Cabello-Hutt, Elizabeth Chiseri-Strater, Michelle Dowd, Jennifer Feather, Holly Goddard Jones, Jennifer Keith, Cybelle McFadden, Christian Moraru, Nancy Myers, Mark Rifkin, Kelly Ritter, David Roderick, Hepsie Roskelly, Amy Vines, and Stephen Yarbrough. Long-standing conversations with friends and colleagues in genre studies and in feminist historiography, especially Dylan

Dryer, Jessica Enoch, Melanie Kill, Valerie Kinsey, Sharon Kirsch, Whitney Myers, and Lindsay Rose Russell, have improved this project and made this field a most congenial intellectual home. I am indebted to Josh Shanholtzer and to the excellent production and marketing staff at the University of Pittsburgh Press, who together guided this project through the process of publication with enormous thoughtfulness and generosity, and to two reviewers who offered incisive suggestions for revision that improved both this book and my thinking in important ways.

I benefited enormously from the help of many archivists and librarians over the course of this project. I would particularly like to thank Inga Calvin, curator of the Ann Axtell Morris and Elizabeth Ann Morris Family Papers, for her generous assistance over several years, and the librarians at the National Anthropological Archives in Washington, D.C. and the American Philosophical Society in Philadelphia. This research was supported by a Thomas S. and Caroline H. Royster Jr. Fellowship from the University of North Carolina at Chapel Hill, a Dissertation Fellowship from the Department of English at UNC Chapel Hill, a New Faculty Research Grant and a Summer Excellence Research Grant from UNCG, and a Mark Friedlaender Faculty Excellence Award from the Department of English at UNCG.

Long-standing debts are owed to my remarkable family and to the dear friends whose support, humor, and love have provided the shape to my life. Leslie Eager, Kelly Ross, Autumn Eakin, and Jillian Ball have shared countless meals, movies, books, and conversations with me over the years, ensuring that my work could never become my only occupation. My mother, Joy Maxine Sparks, is my model in every way; I owe every opportunity I have had in my life to her curiosity, creativity, and warmth. To Dakota, Chenoa, Robert, and Avery, and to Mary, Dick, Thomas, and Andrew, I extend my deepest gratitude for your encouragement, generosity, and humor. Finally, I happily thank Matthew Loyd, the best partner, sharpest thinker, and dearest friend I can imagine, for his magical ability to make each day and every year better than the one before.

Rhetoric in American Anthropology

Introduction

Gender, Genre, and Knowledge
in the Welcoming Science

Anthropology, a new science, welcomed the stranger. As a science which accepted the psychic unity of mankind, anthropology was kinder to women, to those who came from distant disciplines, to members of minority groups.

—Margaret Mead, *The Golden Age of American Anthropology*

WITH ITS reputation in the late nineteenth and early twentieth century as a "welcoming science," anthropology attracted a disproportionate number of women and Native American researchers into its ranks.[1] Margaret Mead, the most famous anthropologist of the twentieth century, suggested in 1960 that it was anthropology's status as a "new science" that made her discipline more welcoming to women and minority groups than other sciences.[2]

Not only its newness but also its research methods contributed to anthropology's relative openness to women and people of color; founded upon firsthand observation as the key mechanism for creating knowledge, and committed to constructing a complete account of human history, anthropology seemed to positively *require* women's participation as it emerged in the late nineteenth and early twentieth centuries. Following on the successful public careers of such nineteenth-century anthropologists as Zelia Nuttall, Alice Fletcher, Erminnie Smith, and Matilda Coxe Stevenson, the increasing number of white women (and, to a lesser extent, women and men of color) who entered into higher education in the 1910s and 1920s swelled the ranks of the new science of anthropology.[3] Scores of women earned credentials, conducted research, served in professional organizations, and shaped their developing discipline during the 1920s and 1930s, including not only Ruth Benedict and Margaret Mead, the century's most widely read anthropologists, but also Elsie Clews Parsons, Gladys Reichard, Ella Cara Deloria, Ruth Underhill, Ruth Bunzel, Clara Lee Tanner, Zora Neale Hurston, Esther Schiff Goldfrank, Ann Axtell Morris, Erna Gunther, Hortense Powdermaker, and many others.[4] During the same period, increasing numbers of men and women of color studied anthropology in universities and pursued anthropological field research, including Hurston and Deloria, as well as Edward Dozier (Tewa Pueblo), William Jones (Fox), Gladys Tantaquidgeon (Mohegan), Louis Eugene King, Arthur Huff Fauset, and others.[5] These women and men of color often conducted their research among the Native American and African American communities with which they identified, using their insider status to access and make public enormous amounts of cultural material.

Yet the burgeoning "culture of professionalism" that developed rapidly in the early twentieth century wrought institutional transformations that rendered the lives of these researchers contradictory in many ways. Professionalism shaped scientific and social scientific fields during this period by heightening such values as specialization and insularity. Each field of study was conceived as a unique enterprise with "its special qualities and language, its special distinction as an activity of research and investigation" and consequently with a degree of imperviousness to critiques from outsiders.[6] Amid a rising tide of professionalism, fields that had previously shared significant overlap and garnered significant involvement from amateurs—including the fields that became professional sociology, education, political science, linguistics, and anthropology—worked urgently to distinguish themselves from one another and to distinguish professional research from work undertaken by amateurs. The categories *amateur* and *professional* were in many ways mutually constitutive, insofar as "the immeasurably important phenomenon of professionalization" depended upon the material and discursive "marginalization of specific groups and interests."[7] Specifically, as Philippa Levine argues, "the elite conditions we now associate with professional standing" were generated by limiting "entry to these avenues of employment through more stringent training and qualification"—limitations that "provided both a sense of community and of status for those within."[8]

These efforts can been seen through the lens of what Thomas Gieryn has called "boundary work," that is, as the material and discursive labor of scientists to distinguish between their practices—and the objective knowledge those practices seem to ensure—and some "less authoritative residual non-science." Such distinctions reinforce the "link between 'science' and knowledge that is authoritative, credible, reliable, and trustworthy" and guard the power and prestige afforded to those who produce it.[9] Consequently, the rich tradition of amateur scientific research came under reorganization across many fields in the late nineteenth and early twentieth centuries, as professional members of developing fields such as archaeology, geology, astronomy and other disciplines worked to solidify their control over research directives, their coordination of collective activities, and their authority to shape public perceptions of their field.[10] In some cases, as in geology, amateur members were specifically excluded from national scientific organizations; in others, as in astronomy, the value of amateur scientists in supplying observational data to professional researchers resulted in a more complex organizational structure—"an interlocking, coordinated network of astronomical researchers" in which amateur contributions were controlled and used by professionals.[11] Interwar anthropologists likewise sought to define their discipline's legitimate practices and practitioners more strictly in order to establish a firmly *scientific* identity for anthropology—an identity that was in many ways threatened by anthropology's reputation as a welcoming science for women and for people of color. When prominent anthropologist Alfred Kroeber wrote to Elsie Clews Parsons that, "if ever Anthropology gets to be prevailingly a feminine science I expect to switch into something else," he voiced a sentiment shared by many anthropologists who feared that a welcoming reputation imperiled the field's scientific status.[12]

Consequently, although white women, Native American, and African American anthropologists earned doctorates in increasing numbers, published prolifically, and won research grants from the new social science research foundations that emerged in the 1920s and 1930s, their intellectual contributions were also marginalized from their discipline's mainstream. Despite their adherence to new professional norms in earning credentials and receiving formal training, for instance, people of color and white women were largely excluded from the faculty positions where they could most readily influence the training of future professionals. As historian Margaret Rossiter points out, women faced substantial barriers in securing stable faculty positions; this generation of women anthropologists "built whole careers on little more than a series of temporary fellowships from the NRC and SSRC. In fact, there seems to have been a tendency . . . to give the fellowships to the women to 'tide them over' while the few jobs available went to the men."[13] Although a significant cohort of Native American and African American intellectuals studied anthropology during these decades, several, like Zora Neale Hurston and Ella Cara Deloria, did so without earning a PhD. Even among those who completed all degree requirements, barriers to full professional participation continued. African American anthropologist Louis Eugene King, for instance, was not awarded his doctorate until 1951 for a dissertation completed in 1932 because Columbia University, home of the department of anthropology most open to women and people of color, required publication of the dissertation before the degree would be conferred. This requirement particularly penalized scholars who lacked the personal wealth and social networks upon which publication depended during this era.[14] Although professionalization seemed to offer clearer paths into the discipline for white women and for people of color, it also masked ongoing discrimination based on gender and race that kept even many trained and credentialed scholars in positions of institutional marginality and insecurity.

Despite the marginalization that women and writers of color encountered in anthropology, this book demonstrates that many harnessed anthropological discourse to speak to public and professional audiences in a range of genres and fora. Studying the writing and rhetorical practices of these anthropologists, I investigate how their participation in an emergent scientific field gave writers such as Gladys Reichard, Ella Cara Deloria, and Zora Neale Hurston access to epistemic and rhetorical resources that they used for a host of rhetorical ends. Speaking as anthropologists, these writers were able to deploy anthropological concepts such as fieldwork and firsthand observation as rhetorical resources to ground their claims of expertise as well as their claims on their audiences' attention. At the same time, the inventive rhetorical practices these writers developed also undermined several foundational assumptions of emergent anthropological practice, such as the association between objectivity and distance. Because these writers spoke not only as anthropologists, but also from specific gendered and raced embodiments and identities, they created texts that simultaneously advanced and critiqued anthropological knowledge. In this way, the writers included in this study developed an alternative anthropological discourse that differed significantly from the deeply colonial practice that constituted nineteenth- and early-twentieth-century anthropology.

Contemporary anthropologists have increasingly recognized over the past thirty years that the discipline of anthropology emerged bearing deep entanglements with colonialism.[15] In the U.S. context that this book examines, institutions of colonial governance were particularly focused on the indigenous communities across the continent whose removal through genocide and forced relocation was viewed as crucial to the interests of nation building. Institutions such as the U.S. Department of the Interior and the Bureau of American Ethnology, along with allied epistemic techniques of surveillance and control, were important in creating the contexts of encounter where American anthropology took place.

The raced and gendered dimensions of this context of encounter appear vividly in the cover image, a 1916 photograph of Piegan leader Mountain Chief speaking into a recording device operated by ethnomusicologist Frances Densmore, one of the many researchers employed by the Bureau of American Ethnology. The staged setting of this photograph—a parlorlike studio in which two participants sit in straight-backed chairs around a phonographic cone—diverges from the scene of immersive participant observation that came to predominate in twentieth century anthropology. Yet the image foregrounds the *dependence* of anthropological knowledge production on human relationships marked by physical proximity and shaped by pervasive relations of power. The context of colonialism so clearly evoked in the cover image continued to characterize anthropological research, even as professional anthropologists developed writing and research practices that aimed to obscure or excise these contexts from their scientific publications. Such power-inflected relationships are precisely what this book sets out to investigate, through a study of anthropology's genres that treats this and other moments of encounter as rhetorical occasions, whether represented in or omitted from anthropological texts.

Scholars in Native American studies have critiqued the specific role anthropological knowledge-making practices have played in American settler colonialism, reminding us that American anthropology was founded upon the intellectual, governmental, and material domination and exploitation of indigenous communities throughout North America. Vine Deloria Jr. has critiqued the intrusion of anthropologists into the lives of Native Americans, satirizing anthropologists as an especially persistent and disruptive "tribe" and inverting the discourses of power that anthropologists have long levied to portray indigenous people as objects of knowledge rather than sovereign subjects. Anthropology's successful bid for scientific status in the early twentieth century depended upon identifying their own unique province of knowledge, distinct from the also-emerging disciplines of economics, sociology, psychology, and political science; consequently, claiming Native American communities for anthropology's intellectual jurisdiction helped to solidify the discipline's tenuous scientific status.

Despite institutional and intellectual variations across British, French, and

German traditions, similar practices linked colonialism with anthropology's emergence in these nation-states in the late nineteenth and early twentieth centuries as well.[16] French anthropologists, for instance, developed an emphasis on fieldwork much later in comparison to other anthropological traditions,[17] and German anthropologists appeared to their British counterparts to enjoy an enviable access to state resources, as German universities competed with one another and with other major European cities "to develop the largest institutions, the most extensive collections, and the leading publications" in anthropology.[18] No other tradition was as committed as American anthropologists were to a four-field approach that understood physical anthropology, archaeology, linguistics, and social/cultural anthropology as indispensably allied subdisciplines.[19]

Despite such distinctions, the era of colonial expansion that coincided with anthropology's establishment as a discipline provided substantial commonalities among these traditions. The practicalities of colonial administration served to underwrite anthropological research across several national contexts. For instance, the nineteenth-century British tradition of armchair anthropology depended heavily on access to the fieldworkers whom Sir James Frazer, Britain's foremost "anthropologist of the study," referred to as "men on the spot"—that is, the colonial administrators, missionaries, traders, and adventurers whose observations provided theoreticians with the material out of which they built their elaborate evolutionary schemes and syntheses.[20] Beginning in the early twentieth century, relations between colonial administration and British anthropology would become even more extensive and formalized; for instance, both Oxford and Cambridge began offering diplomas in anthropology that were specifically marketed toward "colonial civil servants,"[21] and Bronislaw Malinowski "insisted that colonial officials would be more effective rulers if they were trained by anthropologists to be sensitive to indigenous cultural patterns."[22] In France, although important figures such as Marcel Mauss had critiqued French colonial policy and argued for limiting ethnologists' involvement in colonial administration in the 1910s, administrative and intellectual shifts after World War I meant that "the practical need to rely on colonial figures [for ethnographic data] was less problematic to academics" than it had previously been, and France too developed extensive and intertwining lines of influence between colonial administration and academic anthropology.[23]

British, continental, and American anthropology also had in common an investment in mapping and collecting projects that shared both institutional and epistemic underpinnings with colonialism. Major efforts to map colonized territories, such as the Torres Straits Expedition of 1898, led by British anthropologists A. C. Haddon and W. H. R. Rivers, were sponsored by colonial states seeking to secure or extend their domination over subjugated populations, and helped simultaneously to build anthropological careers.[24] At the same time, widespread intellectual investment in the belief that modernity naturally and inevitably supplanted premodern societies and practices contributed urgency to the ambitious projects of collection that enabled anthropologists to fill museums and the pages of their journals. Many researchers in the British and American traditions in particular believed that the "most favorable moment for ethnographical work is from ten to thirty years after a people has been brought under the influence of official and missionary" institutions, a period that was, as Rivers explained, a sufficient length of time to render colonized people "more docile," yet not so long that their own social institutions would be completely eroded.[25]

Anthropological collection of both cultural knowledge and material artifacts resulted in the alienation of thousands of cultural objects, linguistic materials, and sacred stories from the communities to which they belonged.[26] Anthropological museums in continental Europe enjoyed strong state support in the late nineteenth century, housing in France significant collections of physical specimens used for anthropological instruction and public display; in Germany, where museums served as the primary institutional settings for anthropology, massive collections of material cultural artifacts were intended to foster cosmopolitanism and comparative ethnological studies, as "libraries of 'mankind.'"[27] In the early twentieth century, the nation-states in which anthropology developed viewed anthropology not only as a technique "to understand and help control people, but . . . [also] as a measure of imperialistic competition."[28] In many ways, anthropology both depended upon and cemented those "new forms of power, work, and knowledge" that characterized the spread of colonialism throughout the nineteenth and twentieth centuries,[29] resulting in a knowledge-making practice that would be characterized as a "science of other men in another time."[30] These historical entanglements with colonial domination continue to influence anthropology's contemporary practice; as a discipline, anthropology "descends from and is still struggling with techniques of observation and control" that constitute a long-lasting legacy of colonialism.[31]

The consequences of anthropological authority for indigenous communities' own sovereignty have been severe. Over time, Vine Deloria Jr. writes, "anthropologists have succeeded in burying Indian communities so completely beneath the mass of irrelevant information that the total impact of the scholarly community on Indian people has become one of simple authority."[32] Consequently,

Native American communities have had to contend repeatedly with anthropologist "experts" whose publications, testimonies, institutional positions, and authority as scientists have controlled public discourse, shaped legal decisions, and influenced popular images of what a Native American is and is not. The struggle among indigenous communities to wrest rhetorical sovereignty from anthropologists and other "Indian experts" is ongoing.[33]

This study suggests that anthropology's development as a discipline founded upon epistemic domination was not inevitable; instead, white women and scholars of color worked within American anthropological discourse to develop other grounds for anthropological knowledge in the early twentieth century. As anthropology emerged, women and anthropologists of color articulated an alternative scientific practice, which they promoted in publications targeting both professional and public audiences. While mainstream anthropologists were articulating their authority over indigenous peoples as a mechanism for generating scientific status, other epistemic practices—ways of making knowledge that did not depend upon domination—were also being articulated in anthropological texts. Offering a counterstory to the disciplining that accompanies professionalization, many anthropologists—including white women such as Gladys Reichard, Ruth Underhill, and Ann Axtell Morris, Native writers such as Ella Cara Deloria and D'Arcy McNickle, and African American writers such as Zora Neale Hurston and Louis Eugene King—created anthropological arguments that attempted to question the discourses of insularity, objectivity, and gender neutrality that scientific professionalization enforced, and that the racialized and gendered identities of these writers undermined.

Counterstories of Scientific Practice

The counterstory I tell in this book is not one I anticipated uncovering when I began investigating anthropological discourse in 2005. As a graduate student in a rhetoric and composition program, I was looking for insight into the relationship between personal experiences and forms of public expression that become knowledge; my advisor suggested I take a graduate seminar in the anthropology department to learn how contemporary anthropologists approached this issue in their own writing. The innovative texts I was introduced to by the professor of anthropology who continued to work with me on my dissertation project—texts such as Renato Rosaldo's *Culture and Truth,* Ruth Behar's *The Vulnerable Observer,* Orin Starn's *Nightwatch*—taught me that contemporary anthropologists were, indeed, undertaking the intricate work of theorizing the relationships between subjectivity and objectivity, between representation and self-representation, between experience and knowledge that animated my studies in rhetoric and composition.

Thus, in my first foray into the historical study of American anthropology, I was looking only for background, hoping to characterize the (objectivist, positivist, imperialist) tradition of anthropological writing in order to cast the ethnographic experiments of the 1980s, 1990s, and 2000s in high relief. I was not searching overtly for texts authored by women anthropologists or by people of color. Yet I kept coming across books—on the shelves in the library, or more typically stored off-campus but logged in the online catalog with intriguing titles such as *Autobiography of a Papago Woman* or *Dezba, Woman of the Desert*—that deviated significantly from the narrative of anthropology's professionalization that I had gleaned from late-twentieth-century anthropological texts. These odd books constructed knowledge in ways that looked very different from classic ethnographies like Malinowski's *Argonauts of the Western Pacific*. They were sometimes autobiographical, sometimes fictional, sometimes fragmented. They were self-reflexive in ways I had not anticipated. Like the experimental ethnographic texts of the 1990s, these books existed on the borders between other, more recognizable genres. And many were written by women and people of color, people who had training as anthropologists but who were missing from histories of the field, histories that often read as a litany of forefathers: John Wesley Powell and Lewis Henry Morgan, Franz Boas, Alfred Kroeber, Edward Sapir, Robert Lowie, Robert Redfield, and so on. The postmodern anthropologists who were crafting reflexive, multivocal, and public-oriented texts in their efforts to devise more humane forms of representation and knowledge production seemed to be echoing the strategies I saw in use among early-twentieth-century anthropologists whose deviant textual practices had been subjected to historical erasure. What explanations—intersections between gender, race, genre, and scientific professionalization—could make sense of this odd echo and could recover these earlier alternatives to the practice of anthropology as the exercise of domination?

These early-twentieth-century ethnographic experiments were compelling because my investigations into the role of the personal in academic writing had already introduced me to landmark ethnographic studies of teaching, learning, and literacy such as Shirley Brice Heath's *Ways with Words* (1983), Wendy Bishop's *Something Old, Something New* (1990), Ralph Cintron's *Angels' Town* (1997), Ira Shor's *When Students Have Power* (1996), Ellen Cushman's *The Struggle and the Tools* (1998), Julie Lindquist's *A Place to Stand* (2002), and David Seitz's *Who Can Afford Critical Consciousness?* (2004). These studies demonstrated the power of ethnographic research to illuminate in rich detail the tensions, struggles, and negotiations underlying the routine practices of central interest to our field: how people teach and learn and participate in public discourse, in classrooms, neighborhoods, workplaces and elsewhere. Rhetoric and composition researchers' vigorous interest in ethnography—not as the colonial practice of anthropological history, but as an interpretive, generative, and rhetorical research process—continues in the first decades of the twenty-first century as scholars use ethnographic methods to research classroom and extracurricular spaces of literacy; to investigate writing practices in professions, institutions, and across national and cultural contexts; and to examine subjects such as rural literacies, spoken word poetry, the authorship practices of online poker players, and the spatial and social practices of coffeehouse writers.[34] These varied projects underscore what Brown and Dobrin call the "resilience of ethnographic inquiry" and confirm its relevance to the study of communicative action central to our discipline.[35]

Although the innovative genres I recover in this book were short-lived, their authors marginalized and isolated from centers of institutional power, many of the ethnographic experiments I identify in the following chapters are likely to sound an echo for members of our discipline who engage with ethnography as a present research practice. The reflexive quality of contemporary ethnographies, for instance, finds echo in Ann Axtell Morris's field autobiographies. Morris deploys personal narrative to explain the intellectual motivations and personal attachments that propelled her into her archaeological field research, and in doing so opens up her research practice to readers' scrutiny. Julie Lindquist, in her powerful 2002 rhetorical ethnography of political discourse and class identification in a working-class bar, *A Place to Stand,* deploys a similar autobiographical maneuver, recounting her intellectual and personal history in order to foreground for her readers the role played by her attachments and identifications in her research practice. Multivocality—the creation within a text of distinct, sometimes contradictory voices, orchestrated rather than effaced by the ethnographer—is likewise a textual strategy that resonates across early and recent ethnographic experiments. The powerful multivocal quality of Zora Neale Hurston's *Mules and Men* resonates, for instance, with more recent ethnographies such as Ralph Cintron's *Angels' Town,* where Cintron interweaves his voice as ethnographer with the official discourse of documents of legality, with excerpts of dialogue from his conversations with research participants and friends, and with handwritten notes and others' retold stories.

These echoes should highlight the stakes of the institutional forces I trace over the course of this book that kept these innovative textual practices from significantly redirecting the positivist, imperialist ethnographic tradition. Although mainstream ethnography "often replicated the oppressive effects, if not the material conditions, of colonization,"[36] this book aims to demonstrate the presence within that tradition of other possibilities enacted by writers who, without the benefit of postmodern theories of knowledge or recent critical vocabularies, nevertheless voiced in their ethnographic texts an insistence that ethnographers should, in Bruce Horner's words, "acknowledge . . . their partiality, the effect of their work on the lives of those at the research site, and the rights of participants to have a say, and a hand, in the nature and direction of that work."[37]

Examining these forgotten discursive practices illuminates not only anthropology's history, but broader tensions between gender, race, and access to rhetorical resources of scientific discourse as well. The science of anthropology contains a fundamental tension related to the profound availability of its primary method of knowledge production—that is, ethnographic observation. Observation is a technique that is inherently democratic; no special technical equipment is required to conduct ethnographic observation, and the material of observation does not require complex measurements or statistical maneuvers for its interpretation.[38] The availability of anthropology's central knowledge-making operation was, in fact, emphasized in early efforts to recruit potential researchers; an early officer in the Anthropological Society of Washington, D.C., for instance, proclaimed that "any man, woman, or child" could be an anthropologist who had "sense and patience to observe and to honestly record the thing observed."[39] The mundane availability of observation as a research method highlights the rhetorical nature of anthropology's construction as a science; to establish their status as scientists in the early twentieth century context of professionalization, anthropologists had to build rigorous exclusions around a widely available method of knowledge production. This study analyzes the rhetorical work that was necessary to produce agreement around the notions of fieldwork and firsthand observation as elements of a rigorous scientific methodology. Constraining access to fieldwork as a rhetorical resource and access to the genre of the ethnographic monograph as a site for knowledge production shored up anthropology's scientific status early in the twentieth century. These constraints, which worked to limit the availability of fieldwork and firsthand observation as knowledge-making practices, were collective rhetorical accomplishments with wide-ranging implications for the practice and public importance of this new science. These collective efforts helped to generate what Levine, analyzing the relations among historians, archaeologists, and antiquarians, calls "the value-laden distinction[s]" that engendered professional standing for certain participants through the rigorously maintained exclusion of others.[40]

Studying this case also helps me to demonstrate for scholars in genre studies, rhetoric of science, and feminist histories of rhetoric the extent to which professionalization of this scientific community was both enacted and contested through revisions to ethnographic genres. If we looked only at the monograph, the most privileged institutional genre of the period, we would uncover a narrative that mirrors that of most other professionalized sciences and social sciences: disciplinary boundaries were articulated and enforced as they were built into the discipline's privileged textual forms. Earlier studies of genre change, such as Charles Bazerman's *Shaping Written Knowledge* and Alan Gross, Joseph Harmon, and Michael Reidy's *Communicating Science,* reveal how textual forms in scientific fields change over time in ways that reinforce scientific professionalization and strengthen boundaries between disciplinary insiders and outsiders. But by extending this investigation into the decades after the dominance of the monograph was established, we see that participants continued to redirect the aims and practices of their science, and they did so by adopting, adapting, and repurposing the rhetorical resources available in anthropological discourse. The short-lived genres I study in this project—field autobiographies, folklore collections, and ethnographic novels—might appear peripheral to the practice of anthropology, but the existence of these genres is revealing.

In particular, the emergence of these alternative anthropological genres in the 1920s and 1930s underscores the unfinished nature of scientific professionalization. The work that writers undertake in these alternative genres reveals the instability and unsettled quality of anthropological methods, aims, and audiences, despite the rigorous constraints embedded in ethnographic monographs during this period. I contend that these genres served as sites where the marginalized white women and people of color who wrote them continued to reshape and revise those methods, aims, and audiences that were ostensibly settled by the solidification of the monograph as the discipline's primary location for knowledge production. Writers of ethnographic novels, for instance, sought to create accurate knowledge about Native American education policies that would move public audiences to action; in this way writers countered the discourse of insularity that separated professional knowledge from public policy debates. Similarly, writers of color repurposed the resources of anthropological discourse to craft, in their folklore collections, accounts of African American and Dakota communities that contested the damaging abstractions that were typical of anthropological discourse, while white women anthropologists wrote field autobiographies that contested the discourse of gender neutrality and instead reinscribed gendered embodiment into their acts of knowledge production. In a range of anthropological genres, practitioners simultaneously deployed the professional discourse of anthropology and questioned whether that discourse could accommodate knowledge produced out of relations of reciprocity rather than relations of domination.

That the writers in this study deployed anthropological discourse for such divergent ends illustrates the high stakes that motivate a community seeking scientific status. Although writing in alternative genres such as folklore collections and ethnographic novels, these writers made use of specialized discursive and rhetorical resources to claim status for their arguments *as knowledge*. Rather than rejecting scientific discourse, the writers in this study deployed anthropological discourse to diverse ends in fictional, autobiographical, and other mixed-genre texts. Because science in the early twentieth century enjoyed enormous epistemic privilege and social prestige—benefits that arguably continue to characterize scientific communities and discourses—establishing their knowledge practices as *scientific* was something anthropologists approached with considerable urgency. For instance, Franz Boas worried publicly about the fate of any science in which "the lay members largely outnumber the scientific contributors. . . . The greater the public interest in a science, and the less technical knowledge it appears to require, the greater is the danger that meetings may assume the character of popular lectures. Anthropology is one of the sciences in which this danger is ever imminent."[41] As a science, anthropology could compete with other disciplines for resources being allocated by new philanthropic foundations, such as the Carnegie Institution of Washington and the Rockefeller Foundation, and by organizations such as the Social Science Research Council and the National Research Council.[42] Perhaps as important as access to these material resources was access to the epistemic status that a scientific discipline in the early twentieth century enjoyed. As participants in the broader community of scientists, anthropologists could argue for the objectivity and public usefulness of their intellectual program, as indeed Boas and other leaders in the field did repeatedly during the 1920s and 1930s.

Gaining status as a science enabled anthropologists to benefit from the ascriptions of disinterestedness, objectivity, and rationality that scientific communities enjoy. In fact, the apparent rationality and objectivity promised by scientific discourse have historically masked the gendered and racial assumptions that have frequently underpinned scientific practice. Many feminist science scholars have investigated the gendered culture of science, demonstrating that "gender inequalities have been built into the production and structure of [scientific] knowledge."[43] The fundamentally gendered and racialized culture of science worked against even the antiracist and protofeminist work of some early anthropologists. Indeed, Boas and many of his students explicitly pursued an antiracist agenda in their research, discounting the social evolutionist theories that held sway in the early twentieth century and seeking to lend scientific support to concepts such as cultural relativism and the greater importance of environmental factors (rather than "racial" or inherent factors) on qualities such as intelligence, creativity, and productivity.[44] Nevertheless, as feminist science scholars demonstrate, scientific discourse systematically constitutes its objects of knowledge *as objects,* subject to the scientist's superior control and understanding; consequently, scientific knowledge practices and institutions still perpetuate gendered and racist social formations and help to secure the material and epistemic privileges enjoyed by white, male, Euro-American elites.[45] Ultimately, this study underscores the enormous power of scientific discourse—its power for the communities trying to claim it, and its power over the communities that found themselves claimed as objects of scientific knowledge.

The implications of scientific authority in the case of anthropology extend particularly to the sovereignty of Native American communities, who continue to engage in the work of defining their own realities and futures against an expert discourse that has long wrested rhetorical and legal control from indigenous communities.[46] This study of anthropological discourse—its establishment as a professional science as well as the implicit critiques articulated by women and anthropologists of color throughout the 1920s and 1930s—underscores the link between knowledge production, professionalization, and the exercise of domination. In this case, gaining status as a professional science depended significantly upon gaining public authority over Native American artifacts, legal decisions, histories, and policies.[47] Study of the discourse of anthropology—a discourse overtly positioned in the early twentieth century as the authoritative discourse over Native American lives—reminds us that "despite the standard appeals to method and disinterestedness, professionalism is a *moral* matter inescapably, a matter of unequal relations and the anxieties they produce."[48]

In this way, this study of alternative anthropological writing produced by women and people of color in the early twentieth century also contributes to scholarly examinations of Native American rhetorical practices. The processes that authorized anthropological discourse to speak publicly about and for indigenous communities exercised domination in part through stripping those communities of what Scott Lyons calls "rhetorical sovereignty." Lyons identifies rhetorical sovereignty as "the inherent right and ability of *peoples* to determine their own communicative needs and desires . . . , to decide for themselves the goals, modes, styles, and languages of public discourse."[49] Rhetorical techniques of contestation and continuation exercised by indigenous communities—what Malea Powell, following Gerald Vizenor, calls "rhetorics of survivance"—pose a significant and still understudied response to practices of scientific racism and intellectual domination that so frequently characterized anthropological discourse. Survivance, according to Vizenor, "is an active sense of presence over absence, deracination, and oblivion; survivance is the continuance of stories, not a mere reaction."[50]

Studying writings by Native American anthropologists extends the study of "rhetorics of survivance" into the realm of professional discourse, examining how writers' gendered and raced identities reposition professional discourse. Through this framework, we can see the scholarly and popular writings of a figure like Ella Cara Deloria as not merely a reaction to the abstracted, isolated portrayals of her community that circulated in scientific and popular discourse, but also as a strategy of survivance, an active effort to respeak Dakota realities using the full range of discursive tools at her disposal. At the same time, in speaking scientifically from a deeply invested position, Deloria implicitly challenges the neutrality and objectivity that scientific discourse attaches to itself, repositioning scientific discourse and Dakota representations simultaneously.

Changing Genres, Changing Communities

This study uses the concept of genre to understand these discursive negotiations for several reasons. As scholars have thoroughly reformulated our field's understanding of genre over the past few decades, they have moved beyond classificatory schemes that label familiar categories such as mystery, comedy, drama, and so on, and instead have articulated genres as flexible, productive sites for achieving social and rhetorical actions.[51] In these formulations, genres are understood not as ossified forms but as flexible "constellations of regulated, improvisational strategies" that writers and speakers adapt to their varying rhetorical needs.[52] In contrast to prior formulations that portrayed genres as primarily formal conventions or sets of rules, scholars now emphasize the combination of constraints and creativity that genres embody for both writers and readers, viewing "both constraint and choice [as] necessary and therefore positive components of genre."[53] These reformulations position genre at the intersection between shared social norms and individual communicative actions, and consequently at the center of social life. As genres are taken up by the writers and readers who use them, they enable participants in groups as institutionalized as professional biologists and as dispersed as teenage authors of Harry Potter fan fiction to define community boundaries, reinforce shared values, coordinate collective activity, and accomplish all manner of social action.

Genres offer an especially useful mechanism for investigating discourse within a specific academic discipline because genres are often used by participants to regulate boundaries and to enact and enforce community norms. Because they lie at the intersection between shared social norms and individual, unique utterances, genres play a crucial role in the *disciplining* process that accompanies professionalization. This disciplining happens in multiple ways: by shaping the subject positions writers and readers may adopt, by shaping the rhetorical and epistemic practices writers may deploy, and by shaping the values writers and readers are assumed to share.[54] As genres "locate or position individuals within the power relations of institutional activity,"[55] they also serve to normalize and reproduce those relations and to stabilize the worldviews they imply—for instance, by constructing some people as knowers while positioning others as consumers or objects of knowledge and by authorizing certain versions of reality at the expense of other versions.[56] Because genres are ideological structures that both reflect and shape social relations through the actions they are used to accomplish, investigating the genres of a specific professional community offers scholars further insight into the connections between rhetorical activity and relations of power.[57]

The case of American anthropology underscores the normalizing function of genre. Across the first decades of the twentieth century, the anthropological community's methods for generating knowledge; practices for producing trained practitioners; and rhetorical strategies for garnering agreement, generating research problems, and allocating institutional resources were all in flux. During this period of fluctuation, the most privileged anthropological genre, the ethnographic monograph, served as a site where participants in this community articulated and reinforced those values, methods, and practices they wanted their fellow anthropologists to adopt. By cementing shared values such as objectivity and scientific rationality, writers of ethnographic monographs used this key genre to regulate and discipline the kind of knowledge their community created. Professional anthropologists made the monograph genre increasingly rigid, permitting a narrowing range of arguments and methods for knowledge production in order to differentiate between legitimate anthropologists and mere adventurers and amateurs. Genres constitute subjects as participants or nonparticipants of particular discourse communities; typically, "to do business within a specific community, we occupy the subject position offered by the genre or genres at hand."[58] Disciplinary communities thus use genres not only to produce knowledge or generate agreement, but also to determine—and to reinforce—distinctions between community insiders and outsiders. Appropriate production of a privileged genre, like the ethnographic monograph, can become a key criterion for admission, a device for admitting or denying entrance to potential practitioners. Indeed, the development of anthropology over the early twentieth century suggests that this function of genre can be a crucial component of a field's professionalization and establishment in the academy.

The epistemic component of genres makes this framework particularly useful for the study of scientific genres within a discipline undergoing such changes—changes that can be otherwise difficult to reconstruct in historical retrospect. Taking up a genre means taking up the forms of knowledge and the subject positions that genre organizes and makes available. The genres a discipline uses to generate appropriate, methodologically sound knowledge also function as mechanisms for *disciplining* the knowledge that members of the community create. For instance, by privileging the ethnographic monograph as the primary site for anthropological knowledge production, the professionalizing community of early American anthropology was able to categorize alternative knowledge-making practices—located in genres that differed from the monograph—as peripheral to the discipline, or outside its boundaries altogether. In this way, disciplinary communities can minimize the influence of alternative practices and critiques, which, if located in atypical genres, can be dismissed as unrelated to the discipline's central concerns. Consequently, examining the genres produced by anthropologists lets us see how epistemic practices were negotiated over these decades of institutional transformation.

Historical study of a community's genres creates an opportunity for scholars to engage in a practice I identify as rhetorical archaeology. In the knowledge-making practices they organize and make available to writers, genres "encode" epistemic traditions and "bear the imprints of scientific cultures"—imprints that genres concretize and thus make visible to historical researchers.[59] Carol Berkenkotter describes the genres a profession develops and discards as material traces of prior epistemic negotiations: "written genres, like pottery shards, bones, and rock strata, are material artifacts providing valuable information on how disciplines/professions that were initially undifferentiated established themselves as discrete knowledge-producing communities (specializations) with distinctive affiliations and forums."[60] Reconstructing these negotiations through historical genre study allows us to denaturalize the forms of knowledge production that, ultimately, won out in a particular professional community. By locating in discarded (or transmuted) genres the historical traces of alternative epistemic practices, we can uncover submerged disciplinary tensions and locate other grounds of knowledge.

These alternative visions of anthropological practice are possible because, even as genres reinforce shared norms, they serve also as locations for discursive and epistemic innovations. Because an individual text never *perfectly* enacts shared norms, shaped as each text is by the unique and unrepeatable rhetorical context in which it occurs, genres exist in a state of perpetual flux and revision as well.[61] Furthermore, the rhetorical and physical mobility of writers and readers, who shift across professional, personal, and public contexts, ensures that the genres used within a single community are repeatedly juxtaposed against those that circulate elsewhere. This prevents any particular genre from existing in isolation or exercising a totalizing effect on those who use it and opens up genres to continuous renegotiation.[62] Furthermore, as "constellations of regulated, improvisational strategies," genres permit writers to combine, overlay, evoke, adapt, and borrow rhetorical strategies *across* genres to achieve innovative effects.[63]

Genre analysis thus allows us to see both the enactment of community norms and the ways that writers negotiate and contest those norms. For instance, the women who wrote field autobiographies in the 1930s shared certain scientific values with their professional colleagues, such as the value of firsthand observation in ethnographic fieldwork, or the value of stratigraphy for dating archaeological specimens. Yet they also wrote about their gendered experiences in the field in ways that raised questions about the shared value of gender neutrality, and they drew from the genre of autobiography—reaching outside the boundaries of the monograph genre—in order to represent their gendered embodiment in relation to their fieldwork practice. This study recognizes the role of genre in reinforcing community norms, yet also demonstrates that genres can sometimes be taken up differently in ways that question or revise shared community values. Anthropological writings by white women and scholars of color reveal the extended, uneven accomplishment of professionalization in anthropology. These writers wrestled with the limitations of anthropological discourse for the range of rhetorical purposes they brought to their scientific work.

Such negotiations of genre, like the genres themselves, are deeply inflected by relations of power. Consequently, this study responds to the power-inflected questions Aviva Freedman and Peter Medway have posed for genre scholars: "How do some genres come to be valorized? In whose interest is such valorization? What kinds of social organization are put in place or kept in place by such valorization? . . . What opportunities do the relationships reflected in and structured by a genre afford for humane creative action or, alternatively, for the domination of others?"[64] To address these questions, this book examines the monographs, field autobiographies, folklore collections, and ethnographic novels anthropologists wrote in the early twentieth century, and finds that these genres—as configurations of rhetorical strategies and as sites for rhetorical action—substantially shaped relationships among anthropological rhetors, their audiences, their objects of knowledge, and the discipline of anthropology they enacted.

Portraying Space, Enacting Power

The centrality of spatial portrayals to the practice of anthropology offers insight for rhetorical scholars who seek to understand spatial dimensions of rhetorical practice. As a number of eminent anthropologists have noted, anthropological discourse is unique among scholarly fields in its reliance upon *being there*.[65] The phrase "being there" evokes the double sense in which spatial portrayals function epistemically in anthropology: both being *somewhere* in particular and being somewhere *not here* more specifically. Making knowledge in anthropology originates in *occupying space* within a particular community, recording firsthand observations and idiosyncratic experiences in the form of field notes, and translating these notes into textual products such as monographs and articles. Although this process culminates, as in other academic disciplines, by securing the agreement of other anthropologists through processes of peer review and publication, the fundamentally unrepeatable nature of ethnographic field research demands that anthropological writers perpetually confront what Clifford Geertz has called "the oddity of constructing texts ostensibly scientific out of experiences broadly biographical."[66]

Furthermore, the spatial distinction between "there" and "here" organizes the foundational difference between Other and Self, that privileged dichotomy upon which so much anthropological knowledge-making is premised.[67] Anthropologists write out of a tradition that "privileges direct observation and links it to a radical separation between 'home' and the 'field.'"[68] Anthropologist James Clifford, too, argues that travel *away* from one's home is a constitutive act that generates ethnographic authority.[69] Such spatial distinctions organize and generate the cultural difference that anthropology both enacts and seeks to explain. Although critical inquiry into these foundational logics has reshaped the conditions of knowledge production for contemporary anthropologists, nevertheless, "in many methodological, organizational, and professional aspects the discipline retains the shape it received when it emerged from—if partly in opposition to—early twentieth century colonial circumstances," including its reliance upon travel to sites both spatially distant and socially distinct in order to generate ethnographic knowledge.[70] Ruth Behar foregrounds the inversions and contradictions of ethnographic knowledge-making when she writes that anthropologists' "uncertainty and dependency on our subjects in the field is shifted into a position of authority back home when we stand at the podium, reading our ethnographic writing aloud to other stressed-out ethnographers at academic conferences held in Hiltons where the chandeliers dangle by a thread and the air-conditioning chills us to the bone."[71] Behar and many other contemporary anthropologists have attempted to work against the power differentials that enable anthropologists to go *there* to create knowledge that they speak about *here* almost exclusively to other anthropologists.

Recent scholarship in rhetoric has drawn attention to the subtlety with which space works rhetorically, shaping attitudes, influencing actions, and inducing identification, often without arousing audience awareness of its effects. Recognizing that "rhetorical practices create and maintain the space of their own operation," scholars have increasingly subjected such spaces to investigation.[72] Sites such as the Civil Rights Memorial or the Vietnam Veterans Memorial, for instance, locate, generate, and shape collective memories, collective identities, and persuasive accounts of a shared past, while other material environments, such as urban spaces, commercial buildings, and museums impact rhetorical performances and shape social practices in powerful ways.[73] Discursive portrayals of spaces also function rhetorically in powerful ways. For instance, portrayals of spaces such as classrooms and parlors circulate arguments about the bodies and practices that are and are not appropriate within these settings.[74] Chronotopes, or normative orientations to space and time, support implicit claims that are difficult to contest because they remain largely unspoken.[75] The concept of "rhetorical space" has emerged to foreground the interaction between the discursive and material dimensions of the spatial. Rhetorical spaces include the material environments where marginalized rhetors have endeavored to position their bodies to speak—parlors, classrooms, pulpits, stages, and so on—and, at the same time, the discursive realms that these rhetors have struggled to access and influence.[76]

In the case of anthropology, the field as a gendered site for research can offer insight into the power of spaces as simultaneously material and discursive resources in rhetorical practice. Fieldwork was viewed as particularly dangerous for women—an antidomestic arena in which anthropologists were expected to forego familiar comforts in order to more truly immerse themselves in the lives of those Others they studied.[77] Gaining physical access to the spaces of fieldwork was a crucial mechanism for garnering authority; both material resources (funding for travel, food, equipment, and payment to informants) and discursive performances (such as petitions for funds and follow-up reports) were required to support that access. And women's bodies, when women were present, often disrupted the ostensibly gender-free practice of field research. After the Laboratory of Anthropology, a Santa Fe-based field school for training in fieldwork techniques, was initiated in 1927, Elsie Clews Parsons was outraged to find that Alfred Kroeber, Alfred Kidder, and Edward Sapir had selected no women students for the field school in 1929. Parsons wrote angrily to ask Kroeber why he had "become so anti-feminist in regard to the Santa Fe Laboratory fellowships."[78] Sapir and Kidder felt equally attacked by this charge, and Sapir responded to Parsons to explain that "the share that women are taking in scientific work, particularly in field work, is just a bit more of a problem, it seems to me, than some are willing to admit."[79] In particular, including (unmarried, graduate-student) women in "mixed" groups during the extended excursions for field training organized by the Laboratory of Anthropology could lead to "highly disturbing and embarrassing problems," Sapir insisted. This language voices deep anxieties surrounding the intrusion of women's bodies, suggesting that the routine of fieldwork as a practice for initiating men into a professional community was significantly disrupted by women's extensive involvement in the discipline during the 1920s and 1930s.

Alongside these questions of embodied access to space, discursive portrayals of space in anthropological texts often function as resources for establishing who does and does not inhabit the same worlds, by distinguishing *then* and *there* from *here* and *now*. My study of anthropological discourse analyzes textual portrayals of space precisely because textual representations and material realities are mutually dependent. Through spatial representations, American anthropologists grounded knowledge claims and institutionalized their authority over the Native American communities they frequently studied.[80] These textual practices had material consequences, both within the discipline of anthropology and among the Native American communities upon whom that discipline depended.

My approach considers how material spaces are deployed discursively in arguments about who belongs to a community, who belongs in a particular space, and what practices are appropriate there. Tracing what I identify as "spatial-rhetorical practices" and examining how these practices are deployed across anthropological genres, I demonstrate that spatial portrayals served both to objectify indigenous peoples, serving the ends of professionalization, and to provide writers in this study with rhetorical tools for contestation and response. Because space is "not a thing but rather a set of relations between things," those relations are subject to revision.[81] Consequently, writers of field autobiographies, folklore collections, and ethnographic novels were able to revise relations between the subjects, objects, and ends of anthropological knowledge-making by revising anthropological genres. The writers in this study exploit the rhetorical resources available in alternative genres, including resources for spatial representations, in ways that challenge dominant discourses of objectivity, gender neutrality, and professional insularity. Furthermore, because embodiment shapes spatial experiences in significant ways, these writers use their embodied experiences as white women, as African American women, as Sioux women, as Salish men, and so on, to critique and revise dominant practices. These spatial strategies were enacted through genres, which organized differential access to rhetorical and epistemic resources for the anthropologists who adopted them.

In what follows, I investigate how anthropologists gained access to the powerful, privileged realm of science in the early twentieth century, and how—in response to this successful bid for scientific status—women and writers of color sought to renegotiate their own status within professional anthropology. As I examine these negotiations, the spatial concepts of access and position allow me to keep considerations of power firmly in view. Gaining access to privileged material and intellectual resources allows a writer to gain a position of power, and denying access—by using racialized and gendered identity markers to distinguish between those capable of observing truly and writing scientifically and those incapable, for instance—allows some members of a community to retain positions of privilege for themselves and not others. Although professional anthropologists denied rhetorical agency and power to the communities upon which they built their science, some writers located within alternative genres the epistemic and rhetorical resources that enabled them to articulate a different science, founded on relations of exchange and reciprocity rather than relations of domination.

Ultimately, this book examines how professionalization is both enacted through genre-based constraints and contested through genre-based rhetorical innovations. This investigation reveals the workings of power and discourse within a community making a bid for scientific status. My goal in this project is not merely to critique how anthropologists turned their field into a science in the early twentieth century; as Susan Wells argues in her investigation of nineteenth-century women physicians, it is generally unproductive to criticize people whose work is already done. Indeed, anthropology has produced copious criticism of its own historical practices as the discipline has struggled with its colonial legacy in the late twentieth and early twenty-first centuries. Instead, I examine the alternative forms of knowledge production invented by writers who tried, in their ethnographic novels, field autobiographies, and folklore collections, to enact a vision of anthropological science that rested on an alternative set of relationships. Examining genres that were ephemeral and emergent tells a story of ongoing negotiation of professional practice by participants in the discipline who sought other grounds for—and other uses for—scientific knowledge.

Ethnographic Monographs

Genre Change and Rhetorical Scarcity

Who may be an anthropologist? Every man, woman and child that has sense and patience to observe, and that can honestly record the thing observed.

—OTIS MASON, "WHAT IS ANTHROPOLOGY?"

The research which has been done on native races by men of academic training has proved beyond doubt and cavil that scientific, methodic inquiry can give us results far more abundant and of better quality than those of even the best amateur's work.

—Bronislaw Malinowski, *Argonauts of the Western Pacific*

ADDRESSING THE Anthropological Society of Washington (ASW) in 1882, Otis T. Mason outlined "the extent and boundaries" of the newly formed discipline of anthropology, boundaries that delimited potential practitioners in only the loosest terms. Anyone could be an anthropologist, Mason suggested, who had the capacity for patient observation and careful record keeping. While maintaining that "the anthropologist prosecute[s] his work . . . by the most vigorous and exacting methods," Mason also assured the all-male membership of the first anthropological society that theirs was "a science in which there is no priesthood and laity, no sacred language; but one in which you are all both the investigator and the investigated."[1] This insistence that anthropology was simultaneously "vigorous and exacting" yet maintained "no sacred language" was typical in the late nineteenth century, when anthropology emerged as a distinct discipline in the United States. Anthropology's project—to construct a full account of human history—seemed to expand each year as colonial enterprises and geographical exploration extended the territory under European and American scrutiny. With an ever-larger world of human variety to survey, Mason's emphasis on observation is not surprising, for it helped early anthropologists to negotiate between scientific rigor and pragmatic openness, demanding accurate firsthand accounts but accepting every "man, woman and child" willing to produce them.

Some nineteenth-century women took up Mason's welcome to position themselves among the members of this new scientific community. The Women's Anthropological Society (WAS), founded in Washington, D.C., in 1885 on the model of the ASW, argued that "the majority of the papers" presented at their meetings "represent the results of personal observation on the part of the authors. They are real contributions to knowledge."[2] As participants in a scientific field, these women could transform "personal observations" based on recreational travel into "real contributions to knowledge," could reframe travel and leisure as intellectual endeavors, and could present their observations as systematic research under titles such as "Hawaiians," "Customs and Manners of Scotch Highlanders," and "The Ancient Ruins of Mexico." Other papers presented at the society, with such titles as "How to Study Children," "Food in Its Relation to Child Growth," and "The Physical History of College Women," indicate another dimension of women's participation in this new science, namely, their privileged access to realms of activity marked as feminine. Because women were perceived as more capable than men at gaining access to domestic spaces, women's involvement was viewed as crucial to cataloging the complete range of human behavior. Thus, through firsthand observation in spaces both distant and domestic, even women who lacked formal scientific training were authorized to participate in what Mason referred to as the "vast territories" of scientific knowledge that the field of anthropology offered.[3]

After World War I, requirements for participating in anthropological research altered significantly, as the second epigraph shows. Bronislaw Malinowski's statement that research by "men of academic training" has shown itself superior to "even the best amateur's work" marks the presence of a more stringent criterion for determining "who may be an anthropologist" than that offered by Mason several decades earlier. In the foreword to his important 1922 monograph, *Argonauts of the Western Pacific,* Malinowski argues energetically for limiting the presence of amateurs in the discipline. He reframes the earlier involvement of amateur anthropologists as a symptom of anthropology's scientific immaturity and suggests that, in fact, anthropology is only now, in 1922, capable of attacking the problem of human history with properly scientific methods. He bemoans what he represents as anthropology's *late* development, writing that "Just now, when the methods and aims of scientific field ethnology have taken shape, when men fully trained for the work have begun to travel into savage countries and study their inhabitants—these die away under our very eyes."[4] By presenting "savage countries" and "their inhabitants" as anthropological material that, regrettably, "die[s] away" before anthropologists can complete their work, Malinowski participates in the long history of the racist practice scholars have referred to as "the anthropology of salvage," which portrays indigenous communities as inevitably disappearing and in need of anthropological recuperation.[5] He also inverts a line of argument previously used to justify including amateur participants in research. Whereas earlier anthropologists had argued that the disruptions of colonialism demanded urgent collection of ethnographic data by the missionaries, travelers, and colonial agents already in the field, in contrast, Malinowski here asserts that these changing conditions make "scientific, methodic inquiry" undertaken by "men of academic training" more essential than at any time in the past.[6] Thus, emerging out of anthropology's welcoming tradition, Malinowski's separation of genuinely scientific inquiry from the kind of knowledge produced by "even the best amateur" indicates the circulation of a new criterion that draws a tighter circle around a smaller community of legitimate practitioners.

This new criterion excluded as insufficiently scientific the amateur women who had previously presented their firsthand observations as "real contributions to knowledge" at Women's Anthropological Society meetings. When anthropological research demanded only honest observation, women without scientific training could access fieldwork as a crucial epistemological resource; once field research came to require scientific training to equip researchers with the "proper tools,"[7] attaining membership in this scientific community became far more difficult. Such arguments in *Argonauts of the Western Pacific*—alongside dozens of related, repeated arguments made by anthropologists throughout the 1920s and 1930s—built substantial rhetorical constraints into the monograph genre to create precise distinctions between legitimate and illegitimate practitioners, restricting acceptable research practice and arguing for anthropology's status as a rigorous science of culture.

Such arguments responded to exigencies created by a post–World War I context in which anthropology's scientific status was seriously undermined. As historian George W. Stocking Jr. argues, despite anthropologists' roots in diverse fields across the humanities, physical sciences, and social sciences, "in facing the public, they have in general insisted on their status as members of a larger scientific community, and on the whole, the world of science has given credence to that claim—though not without . . . serious questioning."[8] Such questioning was especially pointed during the interwar period, when social sciences such as sociology, psychology, and economics sought to distinguish themselves from one another to lay claim to the enormous funding opportunities newly available to rigorous sciences that promised to solve social problems.[9] The presence of women within many social sciences during this era unleashed fears of feminization that social scientists responded to with aggressively masculinized discursive practices and methodologies.[10] The "welcoming science" was not exempt from these fears, as Alfred Kroeber's threat to "switch into something else" if anthropology ever became "prevailingly a feminine science" underscores.[11] Consequently, many anthropologists during the interwar period felt that establishing more rigorous requirements for participation was key to shoring up their field's scientific status.[12]

Understanding how anthropologists accomplished their interwar transformation from "welcoming science" to "rigorous science of culture"—and attending to the exclusions enabled by such a transformation—requires the kind of contextualized, genre-based approach adopted in this chapter. Historians often point to Malinowski's 1922 monograph as instantiating a new scientific paradigm in anthropology—the paradigm of participant observation, a form of long-term and intensive fieldwork upon which a great deal of twentieth-century anthropological research was founded.[13] Certainly *Argonauts* is among the most widely read and taught anthropological texts of the last century, prompting Clifford Geertz to refer to Malinowski's Trobriand Islands research as "the most famous, and certainly the most mythicized, stretch of field work in the history of the discipline: the paradigm journey to the paradigm elsewhere."[14] Yet scholars in rhetoric have challenged the agency often ascribed to single, noteworthy scientific texts and instead have argued that discourses achieve effects not singly, but through networks of readers, writers, contexts, and exigencies that materialize what Jenny Edbauer calls "rhetorical ecologies."[15] In a rhetorical approach, Malinowski's arguments for limiting amateur involvement in the discipline must be contextualized against the backdrop of related intertexts as well as the material and institutional factors that prepared the way for persuasion.

Furthermore, scholars in rhetorical genre studies have demonstrated that individual texts take on cumulative effects in part through the mechanism of genre, which shapes the choices of later writers and influences the contexts in which those choices are made. Genres are crucial sites for understanding how power operates in a disciplinary community, not only because genres permit and invite certain actions, but also because, as Dorothy Winsor argues, members of a community "do not have equal rights to authorship of all genres nor are the texts different people produce equally likely to be regarded as [legitimate or appropriate] genres."[16] Thus, a contextualized, genre-based analysis argues that not *Argonauts* itself but more precisely the genre that *Argonauts* inhabited and altered can be seen as the locus of change, as a site where anthropologists enacted a narrower definition for determining who could participate in their discipline's activities during the early twentieth century.

To establish the monograph genre as a key site for enacting disciplinary transformation, I introduce the concept of rhetorical scarcity, which extends recent theories that treat genres as sites, spaces, and ecosystems. *Rhetorical scarcity* is a manufactured situation of intense and increasing constraint within a genre that significantly restricts rhetors' access to key rhetorical resources. Of course, all genres delimit possibilities for the writers and readers who use them, enabling certain rhetorical actions by circumscribing others. Constraints built into genres are the foundation of the creativity that genres enable, as Amy Devitt, Richard Coe, and others have shown. Nevertheless, writers experience some genres as more flexible than others, not merely because certain genres become so familiar that they feel comfortable to the writers who take them up, but also because genres vary in the intensity with which genre users *police* genre and community boundaries. Some genres accommodate enormous variety while others come to serve as "symbolically charged landmarks over which to mount a not-an-inch-further last-ditch defense of the status quo."[17] Although all genres enable action through the constraints and resources they organize, rhetorical scarcity helps us to examine the direction of genre change over time and treats genre constraints as both *manipulated* and *relative*. That is, relative to prior possibilities embedded within a genre, does the genre change in the direction of greater capaciousness and flexibility, extending the ways in which the genre can be taken up and inhabited? Or does it change in the direction of a kind of hardening of norms into absolute requirements, or a retrenchment into narrower limits and more severely delimited constraints? Whose interests are served by the direction of these changes?

In anthropological discourse, among the most crucial rhetorical and epistemic resources are representations of field spaces and fieldwork practices. These resources became far more constrained as anthropologists reconstructed the monograph genre as a site of rhetorical scarcity in the 1920s and 1930s. The increasing constraints built into the monograph genre allowed anthropologists to manage the value of rhetorical and epistemological statements; such constraints also enabled the monograph genre to perform what Charles Alan Taylor calls scientists' "rhetoric of demarcation," by which members of a community represent their practices as scientific in order to "exclude various non- or pseudo-sciences" from the epistemic authority that scientific status confers.[18] Using the concept of rhetorical scarcity enables me to link changes in this key genre to shifts in the needs and structure of anthropology's professional community, arguing that these genre changes mirrored and supported larger institutional changes taking place in anthropology across the early twentieth century.

In what follows, I first explain the theoretical underpinning of the concept of rhetorical scarcity, then demonstrate that the institutional structure of anthropology was significantly altered over the first half of the twentieth century. I then analyze dozens of ethnographic monographs across roughly six decades of anthropological activity, from 1885 to the end of World War II, to argue that related, repeated performances of this genre built a boundary between amateurs and trained scientists after World War I. This analysis traces a trajectory in which monographs shift from being flexible, variable, and capacious to becoming more rigorously bounded and policed. I argue that the constraints that marked the monograph after 1920 emerged because they allowed the genre to perform gatekeeping functions, limiting anthropological membership and delimiting anthropologists' relationships with their audiences and the subjects of their knowledge. Anthropologists in the interwar period worked to limit access to the monograph as a high-status genre, building into the form requirements that meant that not anyone with the capacity to observe could be an anthropologist, but only those with the proper training, deployed over an appropriate amount of time in a particular kind of environment, and described textually in routine ways. Investigating how these transformations were accomplished in a discipline that initially insisted its methods were "vigorous and exacting" even as the discipline maintained "no priesthood and laity, no sacred language,"[19] this chapter traces connections between textual and institutional changes in order to historicize and denaturalize the routine association in professionalized scientific discourse between rigor and exclusivity.

Genre Theory and Rhetorical Scarcity

Rhetorical scarcity extends scholarship that emphasizes the activity of genres in organizing rhetorical resources for social action, subject formation, and knowledge production. Many of these theories conceive of genres as sites, locations, and ecosystems, spatializing notions of genre in order to focus on the relationships that genres enable and the rhetorical resources that they organize. For instance, Catherine Schryer's influential formulation of genres as "stabilized-for-now or stabilized-enough sites of social and ideological action" asks us to picture genre as a ground that shifts, gradually, beneath one's feet: neither bedrock nor quicksand, but something in between, providing both firmness and flexibility so that rhetors can respond to perpetually shifting rhetorical circumstances. As "environments or habitats" that shape how rhetors perceive and act, genres powerfully shape relations among rhetors, audiences, and the world. The power of genres to constitute—to both enable and constrain—rhetorical possibilities has led Anis Bawarshi to theorize genres as "rhetorical ecosystems" in order to conceptualize genres as places "within which we recognize, enact, and consequently reproduce various situations, practices, relations, and identities." These spatialized theories of genre highlight the capacity of genres to change in response to the accumulated decisions of individual genre users. Furthermore, these theories help scholars to view genres not as static backdrops, but as ecosystems that shape, and adjust to, the practices of the rhetors who inhabit them.[20]

As rhetorical ecosystems, genres supply rhetors with resources as well as constraints, and many scholars recognize that constraints serve a significant role in genres' usefulness. We witness the productivity of genre constraints for individual writers, for instance, when a student, having identified his or her genre—"Blue Book essay exam," for instance, or "breezy news feature"—is better able to make subsequent decisions to shape a piece of writing. This productivity has led Richard Coe to argue that genres are "both constraining and generative—or, better said, generative because constraining." Because genre-based constraints usefully focus a writer's attention, some scholars have suggested that genres are not "restrictive curbs on creativity, [but instead offer] . . . invitations, as forms that give certain kinds of ideas or arguments expression." Constraints, then, are not inherently positive or negative, but instead fundamental components of the work—of arguing, identifying, communicating, and organizing social life—that genres enable.[21]

While recognizing the productivity of genre constraints for individual writers, it is still possible to critique the effects of the social and rhetorical activity that a genre privileges or permits. In their tendency to permit or invite only certain kinds of arguments, genres are "inherently ideological," embodying "the unexamined or tacit way of performing some social action."[22] As American anthropology professionalized, the monograph genre performed normalizing functions, stabilizing the status of anthropologists as knowledge-making authorities over the Native and worldwide indigenous populations they positioned as their objects of study. The monograph became an increasingly narrow space for locating anthropological arguments, circumscribing rhetorical possibilities even as the genre gained importance as a primary site for anthropological knowledge production. Examining these genre changes historically, we can ask what institutional functions such constraints served.

Such a question is particularly significant in scientific contexts, where genres and the textual practices they organize are crucial in the construction of "objectivity" and the privileged epistemic status that scientific and technical discourses enjoy.[23] As Berkenkotter and Huckin argue, not only is knowledge production "carried out and codified largely through generic forms of writing: lab reports, working papers, reviews, grant proposals, technical reports, conference papers, journal articles, monographs, and so on," but shared attitudes toward appropriate kinds of knowledge-making practices are produced as well. Genres "are intimately linked to a discipline's methodology" and typically "conform to a discipline's norms, values, and ideology."[24] Consequently, the genres a discipline uses to generate appropriate, methodologically sound knowledge also function as mechanisms for *disciplining* the knowledge that members of the community create. By privileging the ethnographic monograph as the primary site for anthropological knowledge production, for example, the professionalizing community of early American anthropology was able to construct a boundary between legitimate and delegitimized knowledge-making practices, affirming certain textual and material practices and discounting others.

The concept of rhetorical scarcity relies upon and develops this recent theoretical work. "Rhetorical scarcity" names a manufactured situation of intense and increasing constraint; a rhetorically scarce genre increasingly restricts rhetors' access to key rhetorical resources. Beginning from a perspective that understands genres as "a way in which power is constructed, organized, and put into effect,"[25] rhetorical scarcity complicates models that represent genres as evolving naturally toward greater efficiency or efficacy. Combining the ecological register of new genre theories with inflections from economics, the concept of rhetorical scarcity prompts scholars to ask how the direction of genre change can be manipulated to manufacture scarcity out of resources that are not inherently limited. In the ecological register, "scarcity" reminds us that rhetorical resources flow less easily into and out of a space with less permeable boundaries. In contrast, an environment that is loosely bounded or expansively defined is likely to make a greater variety of rhetorical resources available to practitioners.

At the same time, economic inflections of the term "scarcity" remind scholars that genre boundaries are not constructed naturally or inevitably, but through the actions of genre users who are always embedded in relations of power. Genre users can narrow the purposes, audiences, and available arguments of a genre by drawing firmer boundaries around a smaller center, *man-ufacturing* a situation of greater rhetorical scarcity, wherein access to some rhetorical resources becomes sharply limited. Furthermore, rhetorical resources, in an economic sense, can have greater or lesser value, and a situation of scarcity typically increases a resource's value. For instance, in a setting where few individuals have relevant experience, such as a newly formed community organization composed of people who have never participated in grassroots organizing, *any* such prior experience might become an invaluable rhetorical resource, in part because of the scarcity of that resource within that context. Furthermore, in the economic register, we recognize that both scarcity and value can be artificially manipulated by changes to a market. Access to resources can be limited by erecting firmer boundaries or by delimiting the market in a new way, such that participants who were previously inside find themselves outside newly drawn boundaries.

These inflections from economics also stress that rhetorical resources are not inherently limited; rather, they are constructed within genres as available or unavailable, appropriate or inappropriate. Consequently, *access* to certain resources is what a genre constrains. For example, in anthropological monographs, there are surely as many opportunities for firsthand observation available to writers after 1920 as there were before. What becomes constrained is access to a particular rhetorical resource—in this instance, by the repeated rhetorical act of defining the resource of fieldwork in far more limited ways. Genre users can work to instantiate increasingly sharp boundaries between their favored genres and those affiliated with neighboring communities, or can work to control access to genre-based resources in order to limit or expand community membership. Thus, the economic register can help us see scarcity as a manufactured phenomenon, rather than any limitation inherent in the rhetorical environment. Ultimately, these economic inflections remind rhetoricians that access to resources is mediated by relations of power.

In the monographs I examine in this chapter, the crucial rhetorical resource organized by this genre is that concept known as "fieldwork." The twin practices of (1) being in the field and (2) representing field experience textually serve as vital assets in anthropological arguments, as their role in the claims to legitimacy made by the Women's Anthropological Society make clear. The significance of these practices across pre-1920 as well as post-1920 monographs remains stable; what changes significantly between the earlier and later period is access to fieldwork as a rhetorical resource.

Anthropology's Changing Context

Enormous changes in the discursive practices and institutional situation of anthropologists took place during the roughly sixty-year period under investigation in this book, between 1885 (when the Women's Anthropological Society was founded, shortly before the *American Anthropologist* began publication) and 1945 (when post–World War II restructuring altered the aims and institutions of many academic disciplines). Over these decades, anthropology emerged first as a protoprofessional community, characterized by diverse research methods, practitioners, and publication outlets, then became after 1920 a thoroughly professionalized academic discipline with standardized avenues for entry into the profession and a large and complex institutional apparatus for credentialing new members.[26] This process of professionalization depended upon several related factors, including the "setting of disciplinary boundaries . . . ; establishment of institutions for scientific research, such that a scientist could expect to earn a living by his inquiries; emergence of a community of scholars in contact with one another; [and] standards for membership in that community, through formal training or research results."[27] During the late nineteenth century, only some of these requirements were met; instead, nineteenth-century anthropology in the United States was an extremely heterogeneous and loosely organized field in which the topics that were considered to be anthropological, the manner and the institutions in which these topics were discussed and researched, and the practitioners who constituted the anthropological community were all exceedingly varied.[28]

Anthropology emerged in the nineteenth-century United States out of a cluster of precursor disciplines, both humanistic and scientific in nature. The members of the first anthropological society in the United States, the Anthropological Society of Washington (ASW), came together from an array of occupations and from prior training in diverse fields. Those in attendance at the initial meeting of the ASW in 1879 included, for instance, "a banker, a naval officer, a civil engineer, an antiquarian, several physicians," and staff members of several government offices, including the Geological Survey, the Pension Office, the Smithsonian, the Surgeon General's Office, and the newly formed Bureau of Ethnology, which would soon be renamed the Bureau of American Ethnology (BAE).[29] The constitution of the ASW, adopted at the next meeting, proclaimed that the society "shall [aim] to encourage the study of the Natural History of Man, especially with reference to America, and shall include

Archaeology, Somatology, Ethnology, and Philology."[30] The earliest leaders of the new science reflected this variety of disciplinary backgrounds as well. Lewis Henry Morgan, whose 1851 *The League of Iroquois* was called by later anthropologists "the first scientific account of an Indian tribe ever given to the world," was a New York attorney who studied Native American institutions and material culture in his spare time.[31] John Wesley Powell, first president of the ASW and founding director of the Bureau of American Ethnology, was a Civil War hero who had first become famous for his 1869 and 1871 explorations of the Colorado River.[32] Franz Boas, frequently cited as the father of American anthropology for his long career at Columbia training several generations of graduate students in anthropology, received his doctorate in physics in Germany and studied botany, geography, and mathematics. These early researchers and dozens of others brought the diverse methods, practices, and predilections of their prior training to the heterogeneous discipline of anthropology they constructed in the final decades of the nineteenth century.

Such diverse studies, undertaken by amateurs, by government employees, and by trained physicians, philologists, and historians were not easy to coordinate. As rhetorical scholar Brent Henze has argued in relation to British ethnology, it was sometimes difficult for participants in this nineteenth-century science to articulate how practitioners' exceedingly heterogeneous rhetorical performances constituted examples of "the same ethnological discourse."[33] As early anthropologists drew on their prior experience across assorted precursor disciplines, they produced dramatically varied discourses. This variation is evident in the range of venues where anthropological material presented at early meetings of the ASW was ultimately published: governmental venues, including the Smithsonian and the Bureau of American Ethnology publication series; scientific journals such as *Science, American Antiquarian,* and *American Naturalist;* and popular periodicals, including the *Century Magazine* and *Lippincotts.*[34] The variability of anthropological discourse continued even after the ASW began publishing its own journal, the *American Anthropologist,* in 1888. The first volume of the *American Anthropologist* includes studies of material culture, religious rituals, human physical development, language variation, historical migration, and theories of evolution. Specific articles range from "Discontinuities in Nature's Methods," a philosophical argument that human brains evolved through processes different from the evolutionary processes shaping animal intelligence, to "Games of Washington Children," which lists, as exhaustively as possible, the games played by white European-American children in Washington, D.C.

Throughout the late nineteenth century, the diverse intellectual backgrounds of the field's earliest researchers strongly shaped the wide range of discursive practices and research methods used within the nascent discipline.

The studies initiated by nineteenth-century anthropologists were shaped further by the post–Civil War context of American expansion. The political desire to assert a national identity, to rationalize treaty-breaking and westward expansion, and to control, intellectually and militarily, an ever-larger national landscape provided a strong incentive to undertake the exploration, collection, and surveying projects that many of the earliest anthropologists pursued. Consequently, a great deal of early anthropological research in the United States was carried out under the auspices of government-sponsored expeditions and military campaigns. After the Civil War, a series of geological, topographical, and, eventually, ethnological surveys of new territorial acquisitions in the West resulted in the creation, in 1879, of the Bureau of American Ethnology, directed by Powell.[35] Powell's development of a large-scale and well-staffed program of field research over the next two decades, and his success at winning congressional appropriations for the BAE by arguing for the strategic importance of anthropological studies of Native Americans, laid the groundwork for the academic discipline of anthropology that was to develop over the first two decades of the twentieth century. The institutional apparatus Powell generated through the bureau—for instance, by hiring field researchers and by providing early publication venues for their anthropological studies, in the form of BAE annual reports, bulletins, and the *Contributions to North American Ethnology* series—provided the impetus, the personnel, and the institutional resources that helped to initiate anthropology's later transformation into a professionalized, academic discipline.

After World War I, several features of this protoprofessional community altered in significant ways. First, the discipline's primary institutional location shifted toward universities and away from government agencies and museums. After Powell's death in 1902, congressional appropriations to the Bureau of American Ethnology were cut significantly, and the new director, W. H. Holmes, was less successful than Powell had been at arguing for the strategic importance of the BAE's field research programs.[36] Consequently, the new profession's "center of gravity" had by 1910 shifted decidedly away from government appropriations for funding and directing professional activity.[37] Over the same period, museums, which had previously been crucial to the business and gradual professionalization of anthropology, became less influential as university instruction grew more important. Around the turn of the century, a significant percentage of anthropological training and instruction had taken place in museums, and "museum curators formed the core of university teaching staffs" that were beginning to develop.[38] For instance, when the first department of anthropology was founded at Harvard University in 1890, that department was a direct outgrowth of the vigorous research program undertaken at Harvard's Peabody Museum, and instruction in anthropology at Harvard took place in the museum itself.[39] The museum as an institutional location for anthropology was especially crucial between 1890 and 1920, when government funding was dropping off; early historians Collier and Tschopik argue that "before the period of the great philanthropic foundations, [museums] marshaled the financial support that made possible the steady growth of anthropology."[40]

Anthropology's transition into a university-based academic discipline is evident in the growing importance of the PhD as a credential and the steep rise in the number of doctorates awarded across the first decades of the twentieth century. In part because nineteenth-century anthropology was located institutionally in museums and government agencies, only a very few PhDs in anthropology were granted before 1900; by 1912, only 20 doctorates in anthropology had ever been awarded, all to men.[41] After World War I, this number began to rise quickly; between 1921 and 1930, 42 new PhDs in anthropology were granted. The proportion of women earning these degrees rose even more steeply, as increasing numbers of women across fields in the United States pursued higher education. For instance, between 1921 and 1938, the number of men earning doctorates in anthropology doubled (from 54 to 100), while doctorates awarded to women in anthropology increased ten-fold (from 2 to 20) over the same period.[42] In the decade leading up to World War II, between 1929 and 1941, 149 men and 30 women earned PhDs in anthropology from U.S. universities.[43] Although a prior generation of men and women had converted their colonial, missionary, and governmental work into claims for legitimacy as anthropologists, the accelerating numbers of PhDs awarded after World War I indicate a growing consensus that anthropology required specifically *university* training.

As the number of PhDs awarded grew, the number of departments offering both undergraduate and graduate instruction in anthropology grew as well. Franz Boas established at Columbia University in 1899 the first graduate department of anthropology; his first PhD student there, Alfred Kroeber, received his degree in 1901 and then became head of a new graduate department of anthropology at the University of California, which in turn trained and granted doctorates to many more graduate students.[44] As this pattern continued—newly credentialed anthropologists left from major centers of instruction at Columbia, California, and Harvard to establish new graduate programs—universities became increasingly the centers for disciplinary practice, and the flexible standards of participation that had welcomed bankers, engineers, physicians, travelers, and other varied practitioners in earlier decades became less flexible as well.

Changes in the structure of social sciences in general altered after World War I, and these changes were clearly felt in anthropology. Several major research-oriented philanthropic foundations emerged, particularly the National Research Council, the Carnegie-funded American Council of Learned Societies, and several Rockefeller philanthropies, including the Social Science Research Council and the Laura Spelman Rockefeller Memorial, all of which became major sources of funding for social science research after 1918. The Rockefeller philanthropies alone "injected more than fifty million dollars into the advancement of the social sciences in the United States during the 1920s and early 1930s," pursuing the goals of "making the social sciences more scientific in order to promote social and economic stability, to eliminate subjective studies of social phenomena, and to develop more effective methods of social control."[45] The pronounced "scientism" of this period, which insisted that proper study of social phenomena should mirror the methods and language of natural sciences as closely as possible, was evident across many disciplines, including economics, political science, sociology, linguistics, psychology, and education.[46] In this context, divisions among social science disciplines became more pronounced, as sociologists, economists, psychologists, and political scientists sought to distinguish their methods and practices more precisely in order to argue for the importance of their particular program of research. Anthropologists, likewise, pursued the status and funding available to rigorous, academic, highly specialized professionals undertaking scientific research into an array of emerging social problems and concerns.[47] Thus, the post–World War I context of research funding through philanthropic foundations repositioned anthropology as one social science among many—competing, in some ways, in a sibling rivalry with neighboring disciplines over resources.[48]

The post–World War I emergence of research councils and philanthropic foundations clearly influenced the institutional business of anthropologists. The records of the American Anthropological Association (AAA) underscore this shift. Before 1920, correspondence among the officers of the AAA primarily managed internal affairs such as getting and keeping members, communicating to members about debts and membership dues, and informing other officers when payments were received or owed to ensure that membership rosters and journal mailing lists were kept accurate. As late as 1917, Pliny Earle Goddard, editor of the *American Anthropologist,* wrote to Alfred Tozzer, secretary of the AAA, to voice his feeling that the list of association members published in the journal should retain even those members in arrears, so as not to alienate anyone who might want to participate in the association.[49]

This emphasis on internal business shifted in the immediate post–World War I context as anthropology's position relative to other social sciences became increasingly important. In 1919, for instance, a flurry of letters between Goddard, Tozzer, and Clark Wissler, president of the AAA, discussed the necessity of nominating and electing six delegates from the association to convene with the National Research Council (NRC) in June of the same year—a feat the officers had difficulty accomplishing in their dispersed institutional locations and without an institutional precedent, as subsequent letters of complaint from anthropologists not included in the process make clear.[50] This pattern continued as the business of the AAA increasingly demanded coordination with other social sciences. For example, dozens of letters between AAA officers discuss a proposed encyclopedia of the social sciences, an enormous undertaking requiring collaboration with representatives from the American Economic Association, the American Sociological Society, the American Statistical Association, the American Association of Social Workers, the American Political Science Association, and the American Historical Association. Although work on this ambitious interdisciplinary collaboration proceeded slowly and involved substantial costs of time and finances from the organizations involved, anthropologists repeatedly voiced their desire to ensure that the field was well represented and positioned advantageously relative to other social science fields in the encyclopedia and in similar interdisciplinary endeavors.[51]

Within this context, anthropologists also had to contend with the antagonism and skepticism generated by the relative prominence of women, Jews, and other minority practitioners in their field. At Columbia, which awarded the great majority of the PhDs earned by women before the mid-twentieth century, Franz Boas and Ruth Benedict actively recruited women and Jewish students.[52] In addition, Boas in particular pursued an antiracist research agenda, especially in his anthropometrical studies of immigrants, aiming to dismantle social evolutionary arguments and to counter beliefs about inherent and natural intellectual differences between races.[53] These practices contributed to a perception of anthropology as leftist, pro-immigrant, pro-Jewish, and feminized—a perception that was damaging, if not damning, during a post–World War I context marked by heightened anti-Semitism and anti-immigrant sentiment in the United States, well-funded eugenic research, and general suspicion of leftist intellectual and political activity. While undertaking their transformation into a fully formed scientific discipline, "practiced by those properly credentialed through postgraduate training," anthropologists' reputation as activists undermined their claims to produce legitimate science.[54] Thus, interwar anthropologists undertook the task of defining their discipline's legitimate practices and practitioners more strictly in order to establish their scientific identity more firmly.

Ethnographic Monographs before 1920

In light of these profound institutional changes, no single text, even a text as widely read and taught as *Argonauts of the Western Pacific*, could enable anthropologists to respond to the shifting exigencies facing this social science during the interwar decades. How, then, was anthropology's increasing professionalization marked in the ethnographic monograph, its most privileged site for the production and circulation of knowledge? In anthropological arguments, firsthand observation and its textual representation constitute the most valuable means for establishing the legitimacy of anthropological knowledge claims; how did anthropologists manage fieldwork as the crucial rhetorical resource organized by this genre? How was access to fieldwork shaped by access to other institutional resources across these transformative decades?

Following the practice of other historians of anthropology, my analysis of monographs is organized into two periods.[55] The first period spans anthropology's protoprofessional period from roughly 1885, shortly before the Anthropological Society of Washington began publishing the *American Anthropologist*, to roughly 1920. The second spans the interwar period, from 1920 to 1945, when shifts in institutional location, historical context, and funding sources prompted anthropological boundary work to clarify the discipline's legitimate practitioners and practices.[56]

In analyzing these monographs, I have taken up Carolyn Miller's suggestion that we define genres not by what they *look like*, but by what they *do*. That is, genres should be identified in relation to their function within a discourse community, by the purposes they serve among the rhetors and audiences who use them rather than by formal characteristics such as length or the presence or absence of any particular trait.[57] Focusing on how genres are used and on the resources they make available to writers, one resists identifying any single characteristic that would identify a given text as participating in a particular genre, making this approach particularly appropriate for analyzing texts produced during a period of transition, when a community pursuing shared goals might develop shared uses for texts that exhibit otherwise dissimilar textual features.

Indeed, potential for variation—in length, method, audience, form, and other measures—is one of the characteristics of the early ethnographic monograph genre that is most crucial for its function within anthropologists' developing discourse community. The primary actions undertaken by most early anthropological monographs include creating new anthropological knowledge and distributing that knowledge among a community of diverse practitioners still only loosely defined. The term "monograph"—as it emerges from my analyses and as it appears in reviews, notes, and bibliographic articles published in the early twentieth century in anthropologists' professional journals—denotes an extensive treatment of subject matter connected, in some fashion, to the range of interests anthropologists maintained. "Extensive" is relative, ranging from the 1,500-page treatment Albert Gatschet devoted to Klamath ethnology and language in his 1890 "Klamath Indians of Southwestern Oregon" to the article produced by Alfred Kroeber out of his dissertation, the first PhD that Franz Boas directed at Columbia, in 1901. Relative to what anthropologists knew about Kroeber's topic, "Decorative Symbolism of the Arapaho," Kroeber's 28-page article in the *American Anthropologist* constituted an appropriately exhaustive treatment to merit its identification as a monograph by Kroeber's colleagues.

In addition to variation in length, early monographs also accommodated significant variation in the disciplinary training of the writer, revealing the ongoing presence of pre-professional members in the field's protoprofessional development. Between 1885 and 1920, the field of anthropology was populated simultaneously by men who had completed advanced training in another discipline, such as medicine or natural science, as well as by the first generation of writers to earn their PhDs in anthropology. For example, Aleš Hrdlička, foremost physical anthropologist in the United States, studied medicine at the New York Homeopathic Medical College before publishing his monograph, *Physiological and Medical Observations among the Indians of Southwestern United States and Northern New Mexico,* in 1908. The same year, the monograph *The Pima Indians* was published by another physical anthropologist, Frank Russell, whose 1898 PhD from Harvard was the first doctorate awarded for physical anthropology in the United States.[58] Similarly, Franz Boas—with his graduate and postgraduate training in physics and geography—published numerous ethnographic monographs around the turn of the century, alongside the work of the graduate students who were beginning to earn their PhDs at Columbia under his direction. The monograph genre these writers enacted was thus capable of accommodating shifting and overlapping research careers, as researchers who had been trained in diverse pre-professional disciplines—or scarcely trained at all—continued to work alongside those earning degrees in anthropology.

Monographs written by women during the pre–World War I period show similar variation in the status and background of the writer, though the expense of publication meant that women were unlikely to publish their research without some form of financial support. Although women did not begin earning PhDs in anthropology until roughly 1920, women conducted anthropological research during this early period both from paid institutional positions, for instance, as museum researchers, and from unpaid and unofficial positions. Alice Fletcher was the most eminent woman in the former category; her paid anthropological research for the Peabody Museum and the Bureau of American Ethnology resulted in numerous monographs and made her the only woman invited to the founding meeting of the American Anthropological Association.[59] More typically, women who published monographs initially conducted unpaid research and only afterwards achieved the (even marginal) institutional connections that would enable publication. This pattern framed the career of Frances Densmore, who trained as a musicologist, conducted extensive unpaid research between 1893 and roughly 1907, and then afterward became affiliated with the BAE, which paid Densmore and published many of her subsequent studies. Likewise, Matilda Coxe Stevenson worked initially as an unpaid researcher, completing field research while accompanying her husband, who was a paid employee first of the Hayden Geological Survey and later of the BAE. Stevenson eventually became a paid researcher with an institutional affiliation when she became in 1890 the first woman hired on a permanent basis by the BAE.[60] Although not all of the women who participated in anthropological research published monographs, women who attained a degree of institutional affiliation found the monograph genre flexible in accommodating variation in kind as well as degree of research training.

The degree of analysis to which the data contained in a monograph was subjected varied substantially as well. For instance, Alice Fletcher's 1904 monograph, *The Hako: A Pawnee Ceremony,* follows each description of a ceremonial event with the interpretive explanations of Fletcher's translators and the leader of the ceremony being observed; Fletcher's monograph also concludes with an extensive (nearly ninety-page) "Analytical Recapitulation" that returns to the ceremonial descriptions and offers Fletcher's own interpretations of the significance of each element in the ceremony. In contrast, George Dorsey's 1905 monograph, *The Cheyenne,* published through the Field Columbian Museum's Anthropological Series, deploys an organization similar to that used in Fletcher's text, descriptively tracing a sequence of ceremonial events, but Dorsey's text omits interpretive remarks made by participants in the ceremony and concludes with a much less extensive (roughly six-page) discussion of the ceremonial data, primarily pointing out potential questions for further comparative investigation. Many other monographs, including Pliny Earle Goddard's *Jicarilla Apache Texts,* published in 1911 by the American Museum of Natural History, and Boas's 1901 *Kathlamet Texts* and 1910 *Kwakiutl Tales,* contain still less analysis, consisting entirely of myths collected and recorded by the anthropologist for future analysis as linguistic and cultural data.

Finally, the degree of technical language deployed in early monographs varies as well. Fletcher's monograph *The Hako* includes exceedingly complex musical and linguistic notations; Albert Gatschet's 1884 monograph *A Migration Legend of the Creek Indians,* published in Daniel Brinton's Library of Aboriginal American Literature, uses several specialized registers for discussing Creek kinship structures, tribal divisions, and linguistic characteristics. In contrast, texts such as Frank Hamilton Cushing's *Outlines of Zuni Creation Myths,* published by the Bureau of American Ethnology in 1896, is presented in a highly accessible, narrative form. As might be expected from a writer who also published his Zuni research in *The Century* and other literary periodicals, Cushing traces in his BAE monograph the history of Zuni encounters with Spanish priests and missionaries in lightly ironic language, noting, for instance, that around 1598 "the Franciscan Friars, although sometimes baptizing scores of the Zuni . . . had not antagonized their ancient observances or beliefs; and the warriors who had accompanied [the priests] had never again raised their fearful batons of thunder and fire. . . . But all this was soon to change."[61] A typical mixture of technical and narrative language is evident in James Mooney's 1896 monograph, *The Ghost Dance Religion and the Sioux Outbreak of 1890,* also published by the BAE. In this work Mooney shifts between registers, at times using a scientizing third-person narrator to create distance from the data, as when he notes that "the author . . . carried a kodak and a tripod camera, with which he made photographs of the dance."[62] At other times, Mooney uses a historical and philosophical register more aligned with earlier nineteenth-century humanistic studies, as when he notes that across cultures and times a community's "hope becomes a faith and the faith becomes the creed of priests and prophets, until the hero is a god and the dream a religion, looking to some great miracle of nature for its culmination and accomplishment."[63]

Thus, the monograph genre across the late nineteenth and early twentieth century accommodated significant variation, allowing monograph writers to analyze and interpret *or* to primarily collect and transcribe data; to deploy technical and scientific *or* humanistic and historical registers; and to write authoritatively whether their research was paid or unpaid, accomplished as their occupation or their avocation. Early anthropological monographs constituted a site for knowledge production that, crucially, was flexible and capacious enough to accommodate the variety of forms of anthropological knowledge that marked the earliest decades of the discipline's emergence. Among these diverse textual features, two common strategies helped the monograph genre to coordinate the profound heterogeneity of early anthropological activity. First, writers consistently used a practice I identify as *spatial synecdoche* to link ethnographic data to an imagined map, and second, they used *fieldwork* in a flexible way as a knowledge-making practice and readily available rhetorical resource.

Spatial Synecdoche

Spatial synecdoche, a rhetorical resource often used in pre-1920 monographs, functions to coordinate the anthropological community's extremely diverse knowledge-making practices, helping early anthropologists perceive their (often dramatically) different projects as organized by and related to a shared institutional goal. In synecdoche, a part stands in for a whole; this conversion, according to Kenneth Burke, "stresses a *relationship* or *connectedness* . . . that, like a road, extends in either direction," allowing the user of synecdoche to emphasize relationships from one scale to another (such as from species to genus).[64] Spatial synecdoche in ethnographic monographs likewise works to represent spaces in their relations and connections to one another. During a period characterized by anthropologists' feverish collecting, early ethnographic monographs often situated the community being studied *in space,* in relation to an emerging cultural, archaeological, and linguistic map. Many monographs from this period begin with a spatial orientation that positions the community being studied in relation to other tribes and often within regional or national frames as well. For example, in his *Migration Legend of the Creek Indians,* Gatschet organizes his ethnographic material spatially to connect the Creeks, the primary object of his study, with "the tribes and nations living around them."[65] In an extended spatial orientation that is typical for pre-1920 monographs, Gatschet writes: "Beginning at the southeast, we first meet the historic Timucua family . . . and after describing the Indians of the Floridian Peninsula, southern extremity, we pass over to the Yuchi, on the Savannah river, to the Naktche, Taensa and the other stocks once settled along and beyond the mighty Uk'hina, or 'water road' of the Mississippi river."[66] Mapping the territory that surrounds the focus of his study, Gatschet provides other anthropologists with a mechanism for placing his individual study alongside others; that is, he articulates where his contribution fits within the larger map of knowledge that is under construction by the whole community of anthropologists.

Franz Boas creates a similar spatial rationale in his 1897 monograph, *The Social Organization and the Secret Societies of the Kwakiutl Indians*. This monograph begins with a section that defines cultural boundaries *through* spatial boundaries that separate "The Indian Tribes of the North Pacific Coast": "The region inhabited by these people is a mountainous coast intersected by innumerable sounds and fiords. . . . Thus intercourse along the coast by means of canoes is very easy, while access to the inland is difficult on account of the rugged hills and the density of the woods. A few fiords cut deep into the mainland, . . . forming an effectual barrier between the people of the interior and those of the coast."[67] The geography of this region, in Boas's account, *explains* the cultural distinctions he investigates in the study; cultural exchange has been limited, he argues, by the very nature of the environment inhabited by the people he studies. Here, Boas's detailed geographical description makes the physical landscape into a rationale for the selection of an object of study; mountains and fjords trace natural rather than artificial boundaries that position the specific community in Boas's study within the larger cultural region where that study is framed.

In such instances, the goal of collecting is cumulative: to fit enough pieces of data into the field's anthropological map to eventually enable anthropologists to recognize spatial and temporal patterns that would reveal the workings of human history. Whether tracing the historical range of adjacent tribes, as Gatschet does, or describing geographical features that have separated cultures on the North Pacific Coast from one another, such careful spatial descriptions simultaneously construct boundaries around a particular community and link that community to a larger project of anthropological mapping. Such repeated spatial descriptions enable anthropologists to link their circumscribed studies to the vast project of creating a detailed, complete, coherent map of human cultures. For instance, Boas nests the specific tribe of his study within the regional frame of the North Pacific Coast, which he in turn inscribes within national (Canadian, American) and continental (North American) boundaries. Through such detailed spatial descriptions, the knowledge produced and circulated by a monograph is meaningfully *bounded* and simultaneously *articulated*—linked—within an encompassing anthropological map. This persistent portrayal of data in relation to an imagined map functions institutionally, allowing early anthropologists to coordinate the collection activities of diverse, dispersed practitioners. Spatial synecdoche in early monographs suggests that anthropologists need only continue their urgent collecting activities to fill out their map of human variation; although the world is large, each piece of collected data could be fitted into this geographic framework and thus contribute to the anthropological project.[68]

Flexible Fieldwork

Although fieldwork was a particular emphasis of Boas in training generations of anthropologists during his four decades at Columbia,[69] fieldwork was by no means universal in its meaning or its application in producing monographs during the formative pre-1920 period. Anthropological fieldwork could take a number of forms, most of which depended less on the linguistic competence and long-term participation that later models of fieldwork demanded.[70] In much of Boas's published research, his model of fieldwork involved touring through a region to find bilingual informants who would discuss customs, beliefs, and rituals for Boas to transcribe. Boas worked closely with one collaborator, George Hunt (Tlingit), who served simultaneously as informant, interpreter, and collector of linguistic and ethnographic material in Boas's fieldwork among the native peoples of the North Pacific Coast. Many others relied on a similar though less intensive form of fieldwork, remaining in one village for a few weeks at a time collecting firsthand reports from a number of informants. This model was used, for instance, in Leo Frachtenberg's *Lower Umpqua Texts,* in which Frachtenberg describes fieldwork as the tedious process of eliciting myths and tales from informants whose knowledge and memories are not always reliable.[71]

Many early monographs follow a model of fieldwork as text collection; this model is evident in Pliny Earle Goddard's 1904 monograph, *Hupa Texts,* in which Goddard records chants, songs, and stories in an indigenous language and then achieves translation through the paid services of a bilingual interpreter. These less intensive forms of fieldwork allowed a researcher to collect data even without linguistic competence by relying on multilingual informants and interpreters, and allowed even short stays in the field to yield copious data collected in such a manner. Thus, these flexible forms of fieldwork served early anthropologists' urgent desire for collection insofar as it permitted researchers to gather data even amid haphazard, truncated, and disrupted itineraries.[72] When contrasted with the rigidity that the term "fieldwork" would attain during the

1920s, the variety of methods of firsthand observation deployed by writers of early anthropological monographs is striking.

In the context of the discursive variability that characterized early anthropology, these shared characteristics of monographs can be understood as meeting crucial institutional needs, especially the need for the diverse activities of heterogeneous practitioners to be (and to be perceived as) coordinated. While the monograph remained a highly flexible site for the rhetorical actions of knowledge production and distribution, the resource of fieldwork remained readily available—to trained as well as untrained practitioners, to amateurs as well as professional researchers, and to those undertaking only short-term and unfunded trips into the field. The flexibility and availability of fieldwork as a rhetorical and epistemological resource, as well as practices of spatial synecdoche that positioned each study within an overall anthropological map, enabled the diverse participants in this emergent science to generate and authorize new knowledge even in the midst of significant institutional and epistemic transformations.

Ethnographic Monographs after 1920

Amid the myriad institutional and historical changes that characterized the interwar period, the monograph genre was substantially altered through the practice of writers who constructed fieldwork in more constrained ways. Anthropologists throughout the 1920s and 1930s report on their field methods more specifically and extensively than earlier monograph writers, and what they construct through such statements is a version of fieldwork as intensive, long-term participation in the ongoing everyday life of a community. Malinowski articulates the cluster of values connected to a more constrained form of fieldwork in the introduction to *Argonauts,* where he writes, "I have lived in that one archipelago for about two years, in the course of three expeditions to New Guinea, during which time I naturally acquired a thorough knowledge of the language. I did my work entirely alone, living for the greater part of the time right in the villages. I therefore had constantly the daily life of the natives before my eyes, while accidental, dramatic occurrences . . . could not escape my notice."[73] The key points of divergence from earlier, flexible forms of fieldwork are highlighted here: two years rather than a few months of habitation; a "thorough knowledge of the language" gained by working "right in the villages" rather than through interpreters and informants; remaining "entirely alone" rather than conducting fieldwork alongside work with colonial offices or missionary organizations.[74] These elements identify new requirements for firsthand observations, requirements that anthropologists identified repeatedly in monographs from the interwar period. As many anthropologists repeatedly articulated these constraints, they collectively reshaped the monograph as a high-status institutional genre and redefined the crucial resource of fieldwork as less readily available, limiting the flexibility that marked the genre in earlier decades and manufacturing a situation of rhetorical scarcity for subsequent writers.

One major component of the more limited version of fieldwork articulated in many later monographs, not just in *Argonauts,* is an expectation that researchers spend longer periods of time in the field. Writers after 1920 generally indicate some period from eight to twelve months as devoted to field research exclusively: Robert Redfield cites eight months of fieldwork for his 1930 book on Tepoztlán, though he laments that time as "too short . . . for such a monograph." Margaret Mead draws on nine months of fieldwork for her 1928 *Coming of Age in Samoa;* Hortense Powdermaker spent "ten and a half months" conducting participant observation on Malinowski's model for her 1933 book, *Life in Lesu.* Marian Smith's statement that her monograph is based on "work . . . done in the field from October, 1935, to May of the next year" is a typical formulation; Horace Miner's study of folklife in a Canadian village, for instance, is based on "continuous residence in the parish from July 1, 1936, to June 1, 1937." Wendell Bennett and Robert Zingg explain similarly that they "began our residence here in October, 1930" and spent "the next nine months" intensively investigating highland Tarahumara life. The growing importance of the fall-to-spring academic calendar is evident in these timelines, which argue for the greater epistemic value of a period of fieldwork research at least as long as an academic year.[75]

In addition to such attestations, later monographs frequently include detailed itineraries that craft an explicitly scientific rationale for research travel. Ralph Linton's 1933 book, *The Tanala: A Hill Tribe of Madagascar* traces his movements through Madagascar with elaborate specificity, charting progress month-by-month with specific place-names and dates such as "during July and August of that year, the northern part of the island was crossed from the head of Antongil Bay to Ampanihy, on the northwest coast," and "in November, 1926, I sailed from Tamatave to Farafangana, on the southeast coast, and after two months there, devoted to study of the Antaifasina and Antaimorona tribes, continued overland to Fort Dauphin. After a month's stay at Fort Dauphin I crossed the southern end of the island to Tulear." Malinowski includes both a list of subexpeditions with their dates and a detailed narrative account of how each month was occupied during the two years he spent in the Trobriand Islands. An even more exaggeratedly detailed itinerary is provided in John Alden Mason's *Archaeology of Santa Marta Colombia,* in which Mason outlines in over ten pages his progress toward and movement through Colombia, including even such mundane research activities as "seventeen days spent in packing the large collection, boxes and packing materials being difficult to secure." Such itineraries provide a scientific specificity to the vagaries of "fieldwork" and represent research as the all-encompassing activity of the anthropologist. As these texts portray anthropological travel as *properly* determined by research interests and scientific problems, they introduce rhetorical constraints around the activities in which a professional anthropologist can engage. In this way, including itineraries helps to constrain the value of fieldwork experiences that had previously taken place alongside governmental, educational, or mission-related work.[76]

Longer terms of field research demand funding; indeed, most of these texts also specify an organization supplying funds for the author's research during the academic year. These sources include national and international organizations such as the Social Science Research Council, cited by Redfield, Miner, and many others, and the National Research Council, which funded Mead's research in Samoa. Local and university-based sources are also identified, such as the Acculturation Fund, cited by Reo Fortune for his 1932 monograph *Omaha Secret Societies,* or Columbia University's Council for Research in the Social Sciences, which supported Marian Smith's and Reo Fortune's work as well. Designating an academic funding source in these texts implicitly carries proscriptions against other forms of nonanthropological employment; in this way, institutional changes and textual changes operate together to heighten the material and rhetorical value of an academic affiliation.

The longer periods of fieldwork prescribed in later monographs are also constructed as intensive—that is, devoted entirely to the observation of community life and collection of data—to distinguish proper fieldwork from the kind of research that could take place alongside other duties, such as education, mission work, and colonial administration. None of the writers of post-1920 monographs portrays himself or herself as conducting fieldwork alongside other work, and many writers take pains to demonstrate the degree to which they lived among their research subjects, in a state of constant observation. Mead, for instance, writes: "I spent the greater part of my time with them [the girls of the community]. . . . Speaking their language, eating their food, sitting barefoot and cross-legged upon the pebbly floor, I did my best to minimize the differences between us and to learn to know and understand all the girls of three little villages on the coast of the little island."[77] Such a statement contrasts strongly with those of pre-1920 monographs, where earlier writers frequently provided only the names of informants and interpreters who visited the writer's residence to produce and translate oral texts.

The emphasis on intensive firsthand observation of ongoing daily life is heightened in the discussions of method that increasingly appear in monographs after 1920. Miner, in his 1939 monograph on French-Canadian folk culture in a rural parish, assures his reader that throughout his months of "continuous residence," his "own language and creed were no bar to social contact and full participation in the life of the community." Similarly, Bennett and Zingg begin their long methodological discussion by asserting the intensive nature of their fieldwork: "First and foremost of the methods used was the observation of native life in an isolated, non-Spanish speaking, Tarahumara region. We lived with the Tarahumaras, went to their homes, observed them in their daily activities, and attended their *fiestas.*" The implicit message of such statements—that other anthropologists should adopt similarly intensive field methods—is made explicit later, when they write that "field work should be carried on while living with the people to be studied, participating as fully as possible in their daily round of activities." Such assertions, repeated across the monograph genre after 1920, indicate many writers' awareness that intensive "social contact and full participation" were emerging requirements, shaping the epistemic value of their fieldwork experiences.[78]

The demand for more long-term and intensive periods of fieldwork generates a related demand for fieldwork to take place in a state of isolation from other white people—further distinguishing legitimate fieldwork from the activities of missionaries, traders, and other "nonscientific" amateur anthropologists. Describing "proper conditions for ethnographic work" in *Argonauts,* for instance, Malinowski writes that these requirements "consist mainly in cutting oneself off from the company of other white men, and remaining in as close contact with the natives as possible, which really can only be achieved by camping right in their villages."[79] Other monograph writers after 1920 likewise assert their isolation by refraining from textual indications that might suggest otherwise. Professional anthropologists' correspondence from the field amply documents their interactions with a network of white colonial agents: the traders who ran stores on reservations, the Bureau of Indian Affairs agents who enforced federal policy in local communities, the vast structures of colonial administration that supported and enabled anthropologists' presence "in the villages" they studied.[80] Across post-1920 monographs, however, anthropologists obscure such interactions to support their self-portrayals as distant from other European or American people and immersed in isolation in the daily lives of members of a different culture.

The argument that all time in the field was occupied by research and that fieldwork decisions were directed solely by considerations of scientific merit is now known to be a significant fiction. For instance, Malinowski's fieldwork in the Trobriand Islands was so extended in part because the outbreak of World War I prevented his return to his native Poland; he punctuated his stay in the Trobriands with lengthy intervals in Australia, and the publication of his field diaries in 1967 revealed long periods of time spent reading novels, socializing with other white Europeans, and isolating himself in his tent rather than pursuing the observation of everyday life as he claimed in *Argonauts*.[81] The historical circumstances, colonial governments, and institutional structures that enabled long-term field expeditions like those undertaken by Malinowski, Linton, Mason, and many others are eliminated from monographs, which instead represent research travel as motivated exclusively by scientific rationales rather than being shaped by historical accident, personal relationships, and global imbalances of power.

In post-1920 monographs, *spatial synecdoche* still functions to link the small part studied with a cultural whole, but this spatial strategy is altered to accomplish the more overtly scientific aim of generalizability: that is, by suggesting that the part has been studied so fully that it reliably represents a larger whole. In this way, spatial portrayals in later monographs construct the microcosm/macrocosm dynamic that Burke claims is a hallmark of synecdochal reasoning. This "relationship of convertibility" between two terms is posited by ethnographic writers who assert that the small scale of their studies mirrors and recapitulates the relations that would be observed on a larger scale.[82] Malinowski, for instance, writes that the "geographical area of which the book treats is limited to the Archipelagoes lying off the eastern end of New Guinea. Even within this, the main field of research was in one district, that of the Trobriand Islands. This, however, has been studied minutely." Consequently, he asserts that his "ethnographic material" covers "the whole extent of the tribal culture of one district" and represents "the totality of all social, cultural and psychological aspects of the community."[83] As in the examples from Boas and Gatschet above, Malinowski carefully positions his site of study in relation to a broader map.

Yet Malinowski's claims to completeness depend less upon the work of other researchers in nearby districts—others' contributions to fill out the map—than they depend on his assertion that the life in this one district has been studied so "minutely" that his findings can be extended to cover a larger cultural area than the one he observed directly. Mead, likewise, asserts generalizability from part to whole in her study of Samoa, claiming that "because one girl's life was so much like another's, in an uncomplex, uniform culture like Samoa, I feel justified in generalising although I studied only fifty girls in three small neighboring villages."[84] Similarly, Robert Redfield asserts that because the village of Tepoztlán lies within the most populous state of Mexico's crucial central plateau, that village can stand in synecdochally for villages in general, which in turn mirror the spatial and cultural relations that characterize all of Mexico.[85] Thus, in post-1920 monographs, one village in one district stands in for an entire archipelago; one group of individual adolescent girls can substitute for an entire population; one small community, treated as "typical," can appear to mirror in microcosm the social relations at play across a vast and complex nation-state. By such synecdochal maneuvers, the intensive study of one small population can achieve the aims of generalizability that are so important in scientific knowledge production.

This scientific aim of generalizability is also illustrated in later monographs by photographs that abstract the anthropologist's field experiences, presenting specific people and occasions as typical. For example, Horace Miner's 1939 *St. Denis: A French-Canadian Parish* creates visual abstractions through captions that portray individual people and places in typified terms; in photographs such as "An Old *Canadien,*" "A Quebec Farmhouse," and "A Saturday Haircut for Sunday," Miner converts the specific observations made in his field research into representative people and places and routine, even ritual, behaviors. Many photographs in Robert Redfield's 1941 *Folk Culture of the Yucatan* accomplish a similar act of abstraction. Redfield includes numerous hyperrealistic close-up photographs of the faces of indigenous Yucatecans, often depicted in front of an out-of-focus background and presented without captions of any kind. Such close-up images of unidentified people convert specific individuals into typified instances, their characteristics generalized and essential rather than unique. These visual texts counteract the radical lack of repeatability that characterizes anthropological field research.

These mechanisms for creating generalizable, method-bound knowledge helped anthropological field research more closely mirror the research practices of other scientists. At the same time, the more constrained form of fieldwork repeatedly constructed in post-1920 texts helped to reconstitute the monograph as a rhetorically scarce genre, one in which sharply delimited values and constraints helped anthropologists to distinguish real scientists from nonscientists. Malinowski asserts in *Argonauts* that only those with scientific training merit the title "ethnographer." It is such training, completed *before* embarking on fieldwork, that provides a crucial measure of reliability for an anthropologist's results: "the Ethnographer has to be inspired by the knowledge of the most modern results of scientific study, by its principles and aims. . . . Foreshadowed problems are the main endowment of a scientific thinker, and these problems are first revealed to the observer by his theoretical studies."[86] In advocating for "foreshadowed problems" that are tested against observations from the field, Malinowski attempts to shift the *kind* of science that anthropology pursues. In contrast to the inductive method of data-gathering for later analysis that was adopted by anthropologists in the protoprofessional period, Malinowski restricts the "most modern" scientific methods to the deductive process of formulating theories and hypotheses that must be tested against the anthropologist's fieldwork data.

Collective revisions to the monograph genre, rather than Malinowski's specific arguments, were key to the effort to constrain what fieldwork required and who was capable of producing it. As anthropologists revised this genre after 1920 to demand longer periods of intensive, problem-focused fieldwork, they reshaped who could be considered an anthropologist. The routine of fieldwork advocated by monograph writers during the interwar period—a routine that begins with scientific training in a university setting, where extensive reading of anthropological theory identifies a problem that can be solved by fieldwork, followed by at least nine months of intensive firsthand observation, and several subsequent months devoted to "working up" the material for publication—limited the community of anthropologists in material ways. By revising this genre, by enacting a situation of rhetorical scarcity in the discipline's most privileged site of knowledge production, anthropologists collectively countered the once-pervasive belief that anyone capable of observation was fundamentally qualified to participate in the field.

Historicizing Genre Change

The ethnographic monograph underwent significant revision between the emergence of anthropology as a "welcoming science" in the late nineteenth century and anthropology's consolidation as a rigorous science of culture in the early twentieth century. The transformation of the monograph from a loosely bounded, flexible site for knowledge production into a more stringently constrained professional genre both responded to and reinforced broader institutional transformations taking place across these decades. Rhetorical scarcity offered anthropologists a crucial mechanism for enacting more restrictive requirements for participation in their professional community. Responding to a changing institutional context, Malinowski, Mead, Miner, Powdermaker, Redfield, Linton, Mason, and many other writers collectively remade what a monograph could look like and could *do* during the 1920s and 1930s. Because fieldwork was a rhetorical and epistemic resource of particular importance to anthropologists, the constraints placed on access to this resource can be seen as maneuvers to redefine the boundaries of the anthropological community.

An investigation of how this genre was collectively revised over several decades suggests that a more rigidly constrained genre was able to meet new institutional needs for anthropologists—in particular, the need to shore up scientific legitimacy and to define more stringent criteria for membership in order to participate as a *scientific* social science in the years following World War I. Limiting the availability of rhetorical resources, especially the key resource of fieldwork, provided several important benefits to the professional anthropological community, including fewer practitioners, less variable methods, clearer distinctions between insiders and outsiders, and consequently greater access to the material resources that became available in the interwar period for rigorously scientific social research. Certainly these benefits helped anthropologists respond to post–World War I transformations in institutional structure that privileged rigorously professionalized communities.

Yet the connection between rigor and exclusivity that anthropological writing during this period enacted is historical, not inevitable. Scholars can denaturalize this link through historical investigations into the role of power in the operation of genre change. For instance, this particular tactic—limiting access to a privileged institutional genre—is not the only way a professional community can respond to concerns about legitimacy or authority. Historian Jan Golinski demonstrates how early chemists responded to a crisis in their institutional legitimacy by involving the public in more fundamental ways in their research process; limiting amateur participation or outsider involvement is not the only avenue available to scientists when their legitimacy appears to be in question. Indeed, even using such terms as "specialization" and "professionalization" to describe changes in scientific communities implies a teleology of scientific progress that historical studies should aim to disrupt rather than reify.[87] Historical investigations into a community's privileged forms of knowledge production can help scholars in rhetoric underscore genre change as the cumulative effect of human choices, choices that can be used to restrict other writers' access to the rhetorical resources a genre makes available.

Historical genre study can further reveal the relations between institutional power and specific, privileged textual forms, insisting that the privilege afford-ed to certain textual portrayals of fieldwork, for instance, is not inevitable but a historical and rhetorical achievement. When monograph writers repeatedly insisted that their research travel was governed entirely by their scientific aims, for instance, and routinely circumscribed any textual portrayals of the econom-ic negotiations that undergirded their ability to access sites of field research, they helped to mask the ongoing dependence of anthropological research on systems of colonial surveillance and management. Historical genre study can remind us that the textual practices that won out in a community existed in relation to other rhetorical possibilities.

Attending to how a genre becomes more or less flexible, capacious, and rich with possibilities for writers can also generate insights about who is permitted to use a genre and to what ends. As scholars such as Sidonie Smith and Cristina Kirklighter show, writers can repurpose a genre through uses that expand the resources for rhetorical and political action that can be located there.[88] Detailed studies can reveal the long-term, accumulated effects of individual writers whose decisions can ultimately narrow or expand a genre's possibilities. Link-ing genre change with institutional priorities, as this chapter has done, also underscores the power of a disciplinary community to circumscribe writers' efforts to repurpose or repoliticize a privileged institutional genre. Alternative textual practices can be minimized when the writers who adopt them are de-nied access to forms of institutional power—including access to networks of colleagues, resources to enable publication, and opportunities for their research to be taken up in routines of citation, review, and circulation.

The textual and material practices I examine in later chapters are among those excised from or prohibited within the monograph genre. Posing a coun-terpoint to the rhetorical scarcity that marked monographs in the interwar period, alternative and experimental ethnographic genres proliferated in an-thropological discourse during these decades. Elsie Clews Parsons, introduc-ing *American Indian Life,* the collection of ethnographic fiction by prominent anthropologists that Parsons edited in 1922, lamented that the "forbidding monographs" so prized by her fellow anthropologists were so little suited to such tasks as communicating with a broader public.[89] Parsons was not alone in this lament. A number of Native, African American, and white women practitioners of anthropology found the narrowed bounds of the monograph inhospitable for their rhetorical purposes, which often included resisting their discipline's practices and intervening in broader public debates. Thus, Parsons was among the dozens of anthropologists during the interwar period who not only wrote standard academic genres such as monographs and journal articles, but produced mixed-genre, experimental textual forms as well. The emergence of experimental genres in these decades—including not only the ethnographic novels, folklore collections, and field autobiographies examined in this book, but also radio scripts, dialogues, short stories, educational brochures, and other ephemeral forms—suggests that anthropologists' rhetorical purposes exceeded what professionalized academic genres were capable of accommodating. Although rhetorical scarcity in the monograph genre helped anthropologists to define their community's boundaries more clearly, writers both within those boundaries and along their margins created new genres in the 1920s and 1930s that influenced disciplinary practice and shaped public perceptions. As subsequent chapters demonstrate, rhetorical scarcity can thus prompt unanticipated innovation, as writers create new rhetorical spaces to accommodate their diverse rhetorical and intellectual needs.

Field Autobiographies

Rhetorical Recruitment and Embodied Ethnography

At the time of my advent into the sacred circle I was already familiar with their names, for I had pored over books and reports which they had written. . . . For an assorted gang of thoroughbred good sports, witty conversationalists, and loyal friends, I whole-heartedly recommend American archaeologists.

—Ann Axtell Morris, *Digging in the Southwest*

It was nice of you to root for me, but I shall believe something comes of it only when it does. Nothing has yet. But it will come about as follows: Kidder will speak of it to Sapir. The latter will answer if not the words at least the spirit, why bother with such a moron as that? Now I, *I* have lots of students who could do the work and do it *well* why don't you take this one, and that one, etc. And then he will.

—Gladys Reichard, letter to Ann Axtell Morris, 1932

A S ANTHROPOLOGY professionalized during the early decades of the twentieth century, the women who pursued careers in "the welcoming science" entered into an arena of contradiction. Against the backdrop of the significant changes in anthropologists' rhetorical practices discussed in chapter 1, many women practitioners found themselves renegotiating their status relative to new disciplinary hierarchies. Whereas the amateur members of the Women's Anthropological Society had been able, in the 1880s, to justify their papers as "real contributions to knowledge" simply by recording firsthand observations gained from their leisure and travel experiences, the professional anthropological community of the 1920s and 1930s demanded long-term, intensive fieldwork, undertaken with institutional support and completed apart from commercial or directly colonial activities. These material and epistemological demands heightened distinctions between professional and amateur researchers, clarifying opportunities but also creating challenges for women anthropologists during these decades.

On one hand, public statements like that offered by Ann Axtell Morris, above, continued to announce anthropology as a science in which women were welcomed, integrated, and invited to participate actively. Indeed, avenues for advancement should become both clearer and more rationalized within a professionalized social science; one of the promises of professionalization was that admission into the professional community would be meritocratic, based on credentials and performance rather than informal networks—networks from which women were so often excluded during the protoprofessional period. Discussing her entrée into archaeology in her popular field autobiography, *Digging in the Southwest,* Ann Axtell Morris recounts that her interest in the ancient past led her first to college where she "absorbed a diploma-ful of history" before a professor finally explained that the discipline she was looking for was called archaeology. Morris explains that "if there was an 'ology' that told the story, and if there were 'ologists' who knew anything about it, my course lay clear. And so the spring I graduated from college I set sail for France to join the American School of Prehistoric Archaeology in Europe." Having a clear path to pursue—in this case, a college degree followed by postgraduate professional field training—allowed Morris and other potential archaeologists to gain entry into a community of "good sports, witty conversationalists, and loyal friends" who, in her account, readily welcomed her as a member.[1]

On the other hand, private correspondence between women anthropologists—such as the letter quoted above from Gladys Reichard to Morris—registers discontent among women who found that professionalization did not alleviate but merely masked ongoing discrimination. Reichard's fabricated dialogue between two eminent anthropologists—A. V. Kidder, who had received financial support from the Carnegie Foundation for several projects in the same geographical area where Reichard worked, and Edward Sapir, the most prominent linguist of the period who held faculty positions at Yale and the University of Chicago—underscores important realities faced by a woman seeking full professional membership. By portraying men affiliated with powerful institutions as privately passing judgment on the work of a woman ("such a moron as that") and colluding to share professional rewards among themselves, Reichard registers her awareness that informal networks of influence continued to keep qualified women from receiving the rewards that their work might merit. Predicting that the student of one of her colleagues will receive funding, rather than Reichard herself as an established and widely published scholar, she acknowledges that informal relationships, unreasonable dislike, and selfish guarding of resources all continue to exert power within professional communities, despite the apparent rationality of professionalization. Reichard also grimly recognizes that her own network of informal relationships carries less weight than others' networks; Morris's support, though kindly extended, exerts less influence than Kidder's or Sapir's would. Women in less powerful institutional positions were less able to exert their influence to benefit others in their network, thus sharing their marginality as much as they shared their support.[2]

These divergent portrayals of the congeniality of anthropology as a professional home for women mirror what historians of science have argued about the professionalization of sciences in general: that women have historically found varying degrees of access and exclusion among professional scientific fields. In some cases, where professionalization was slow to solidify disciplinary boundaries, as in the field of pharmacy at the turn of the twentieth century, women were able to exploit the rising value of university credentials to establish themselves as members in significant numbers.[3] In other cases, as in the well-documented case of midwifery and obstetric medicine, the establishment of professionalized medicine constructed medical authority as masculine and separated that authority from women's embodied experience.[4] Across many scientific disciplines, the discourses of gender neutrality, objectivity, and meritocracy that pervade professionalized science often "uphold meritocratic ideals while eliding structural inequalities in scientific institutions."[5] As feminist scholars have demonstrated, the marginality that people of color and white women have historically experienced across scientific disciplines has not been idiosyncratic, but instead has been pervasive and institutionalized, despite the promise of meritocratic advancement in professionalized disciplines.[6]

In anthropology, increasing professionalization held contradictory implications for women. Certainly many women benefited from the changes that altered anthropology during the interwar decades. As graduate training became increasingly important, the percentage of women earning PhDs in anthropology rose substantially, especially at Columbia, where Franz Boas's well-known support for women and Ruth Benedict's presence on the faculty attracted a higher proportion of women graduate students than the national average.[7] As anthropology became more established in both undergraduate and graduate curricula, some women attained stable faculty positions, primarily at women's colleges and private undergraduate institutions. For instance, Dorothy Keur began teaching at Hunter College in 1928, the year she received her MA from Columbia; she attained the rank of assistant professor in 1940 and earned her PhD in 1941; she remained teaching at Hunter until her retirement as full professor in 1965. Frederica de Laguna began her long career at Bryn Mawr in 1938, and Gladys Reichard taught anthropology at Barnard College from 1923 until her death in 1955. These women built undergraduate anthropology programs at private institutions that funneled a significant number of women into graduate programs in anthropology.

Furthermore, teaching positions afforded these few women a degree of institutional stability that many more women anthropologists lacked. As increasing numbers of women pursued advanced degrees in anthropology, significant barriers continued to curtail their professional advancement and to limit their ability to influence future disciplinary practice. For instance, graduate institutions hired women as faculty only very rarely, a practice that significantly curbed women's opportunities to influence their discipline's development. With the exception of two high profile women—Ruth Benedict at Columbia and Erna Gunther at the University of Washington—almost no women anthropologists taught in graduate anthropology programs until the mid-1950s, effectively preventing women from participating directly in the training of future anthropologists. Some male anthropologists intervened actively to prevent women from gaining faculty positions, as Edward Sapir did in 1928 when one of his own graduate students at the University of Chicago, Charlotte Gower, applied for a new faculty position at the University of Michigan. Sapir wrote to his former student Leslie White to alert him to the position, explaining to White that Carl Guthe at Michigan was "trying to get a man to do some teaching and also museum work in anthropology" and suggesting that Guthe "may be able to make you a better offer than he is prepared to make Charlotte."[8]

A belief that women needed faculty jobs less urgently than men was frequently used to justify their exclusion from stable employment. Ruth Bunzel described, for instance, a discussion of her job prospects with fellow anthropologist Alfred Tozzer, who told Bunzel that "he knew I was not destitute, he knew I had a family and that they lived in a certain way, quite decently, and served good meals (sic!), and presumably they could take care of me. He felt no responsibility; if Boas thought I needed a job he would have to find it for me."[9] Bunzel replied to Tozzer that he was "misinformed if he thought that my family could or would 'take care' of me; and anyway that it was not for that that I had fitted myself for a career in anthropology."[10] The perception that women could be excluded from faculty positions because they would be "taken care of" by their families or their (eventual) husbands was pervasive. Although Boas worked to place his female graduates in faculty positions, he was almost alone in this endeavor. During the 1920s and 1930s, when new male PhDs were filling faculty positions and starting new departments of anthropology, "discrimination against women (and Jews and nonwhites) for faculty positions was not merely present but open and explicit."[11]

Women's lack of faculty positions had several consequences. In addition to limiting their opportunities to train future anthropologists, this exclusion also caused many women to pursue their anthropological research from marginal institutional locations, often with only unstable, temporary, or limited funding, as Rossiter and other historians have shown. As the academic calendar came to shape patterns of anthropological research more strongly—with a summer and sometimes winter field season followed by time during the academic year when anthropological faculty "wrote up" their findings for publication—women in temporary positions found themselves able to earn funding only for data collection; they were rarely afforded the institutional space and time required to write up results for publication. Anthropological archives hold the unpublished field research of dozens of women who could secure funding only while they were actively gathering material in the field. Ruth Underhill, for instance, tried repeatedly and without success to secure an academic position in the decade after she completed her PhD at Columbia in 1934. She continued to conduct field research and to prepare manuscripts for publication, explaining to Boas that in her "efforts—so far futile—to get a job for the future, a publication would be of the greatest help."[12] Yet publication of a book generally required a financial subsidy from a university or an organization such as the Southwest Society. When her worsening financial situation compelled her to take a job in the Soil Conservation Service, which kept her in the Southwest where she had been conducting field research, Underhill wrote apologetically to Boas that taking the job "does not mean, of course, that I want to remain in soil conservation any longer than I have to. I needn't even mention to you the drawbacks of government service: you probably know them all. However, at the time I took the job I couldn't get on any longer without any money so it was a necessity and I plan to keep it until I can get some sort of academic position."[13] Underhill's struggles to earn a living and maintain her research without the security of a faculty position underscore the extent to which institutional marginality diminished women researchers' opportunities to secure additional professional rewards through publication. Even after taking the job, Underhill worriedly asked Boas whether "this kind of employment, which offers nothing but a salary, is a good way to spend a year" and asked him again to help her arrange for the publication of her research, "since these publications are considerably more important to me than any government work."[14] Thus, despite the promise of rationality that accompanied professionalization, women who earned advanced credentials still found themselves pursuing research and seeking professional advancement from institutional locations that were marginal, unstable, and underfunded.

The ostensible rationality of professionalized science sometimes masked persistent forms of discrimination by insisting that disciplinary hierarchies were meritocratic. Gender discrimination, when cloaked by professional discourses of gender neutrality, became even harder to combat, as Ruth Bunzel's career makes clear. After earning her PhD and writing an award-winning dissertation at Columbia, Bunzel, whom Boas called "one of the best among the younger people,"[15] spent years setting up an ambitious, interdisciplinary Carnegie-funded research project in Guatemala that would coordinate research efforts among geographers, archaeologists, linguists, historians, and other experts, only to find herself replaced as project director in 1933 by Sol Tax, a new male PhD who lacked her experience and qualifications. To justify her replacement, the anthropologists responsible for the decision, including A. V. Kidder and Alfred Tozzer, circulated rumors about "improprieties" leading to her replacement—rumors that Bunzel said were "made up by someone out of whole cloth."[16] In private correspondence, Bunzel and other female professionals identified Bunzel's removal from the project as gender discrimination; Reichard, for instance, referred to Bunzel's situation to justify her pessimistic attitude to Morris, explaining that "things like that hurt one's faith."[17] Yet Bunzel felt powerless to contest such discrimination in public, asserting that although Kidder and Tozzer "give evidence of having bad conscience about this whole matter," nevertheless "you know how men feel towards those whom they have treated unfairly. They will not feel any better or more kindly if it is pointed out to them that I am better than Sol Tax."[18] Although women anthropologists successfully advanced their careers by harnessing many of the tools of professional science— by earning credentials, pursuing technical and theoretical research, winning fellowships, and publishing in scholarly venues—situations like Bunzel faced in Guatemala underscored the extent to which many women were still prevented by gender-based discrimination from reaping the full rewards that professionalization of the "welcoming science" seemed to promise.

The field autobiography genre constitutes a response to the contradictory exigencies of professionalization and gender-based marginality. Field autobiographies construct autobiographical narratives that focus on a period of field research rather than on traditional considerations such as family and personal history; they recount much less than a life story, but much more than research results. As the titles of Ann Axtell Morris's two field autobiographies suggest—*Digging in Yucatan* and *Digging in the Southwest*—these texts differ from traditional autobiographies in that they provide personal narratives focused entirely on the practice of undertaking field research: setting up a dig site, selecting a new area for excavation, piecing together the significance of archaeological objects as they are unearthed, and so on. But they differ from typical research reports insofar as they are structured as narratives of the experience of conducting research. For instance, Morris narrates both the trials and the glamours of field research, such as when Charles and Anne Morrow Lindbergh visited the Morrises' Canyon del Muerto excavation and helped the research team explore their archaeological site from the air. Both Morris's and Reichard's field autobiographies include humorous accounts of research projects that failed to develop as anticipated, of trips to field sites that ended in floods or flat tires, of long waits for informants whose business took them miles away. In these ways, field autobiographies combine the rhetorical resources of genres that are, typically, strongly divergent: the technical genre of the monograph or research report and the narrative genre of autobiography. As Wendy Sharer argues, inserting personal information or advocacy statements into texts typically governed by strictly technical concerns generates a rhetorical practice Sharer calls "genre work," a genre-based form of rhetorical innovation that permits writers to meet and to contest community-based discursive norms simultaneously.[19] In the case of the field autobiography genre, the narrative and personalized nature of autobiographical texts, combined with the orientation toward knowledge-production typical of research-based technical writing, are merged in a new genre, making alternative rhetorical resources available to the writers who adopted it.

In this chapter I argue that by writing and publishing field autobiographies in the 1930s, Ann Axtell Morris and Gladys Reichard gained access to an array of rhetorical resources to respond to their professional marginality. In particular, they accessed resources for enacting the spatial-rhetorical strategy of *inscription* into the powerful research spaces of their field. Field autobiographies—by rendering the practice of field research personal and by gendering the embodied self in the field—provided these women scientists with an array of rhetorical strategies for counteracting their disciplinary marginality and foregrounded the identity of the researcher in ways that ran counter to the depersonalizing tendencies of other professional research genres.

Such rhetorical strategies exploit the constitutive capacity of genres to articulate new possibilities for the writers and readers who produce them. If, as a number of scholars have argued, taking up disciplinary genres helps to transform "individual participants into particular kinds of subjects that conform to the community's existing forms and goals," then employing different genres— or using routine genres *differently*—can position participants as different kinds of subjects enacting an alternative set of forms and goals.[20] In their field autobiographies, Reichard and Morris combined technical research with first-person narrative in lively, accessible language; by doing so, these writers simultaneously secured their identities as professional anthropologists and gendered the bodies undertaking field research in their discipline. By *personalizing* research, these writers challenged, however inadvertently, the presumptive professional discourse of gender neutrality, instead inscribing their embodied selves into the spaces and the processes of anthropological work.

Rhetorical Resources of Field Autobiographies

Because this genre combines technical information derived from field research with the narrative structure of autobiography, the field autobiography made unique spatial-rhetorical resources available to Morris and Reichard. The genre work enabled through the specific conjunction of forms not usually combined—namely, technical research, typically presented impersonally, here incorporated into a personal autobiographical narrative—meant that this genre provided Morris and Reichard with a space from which to generate implicit arguments about professional practices in anthropology that could not have been located in more mainstream professional genres like the monograph. Drawing from my analyses of Morris's *Digging in Yucatan* (1931) and *Digging in the Southwest* (1933) and Reichard's *Spider Woman* (1934), I identify field autobiographies as a distinct genre wherein writers narrate the story of the self in relation to a particular field site or disciplinary community. Because field autobiographies focus specifically on a period of field research but use self-representation and embodied experience to describe that research in autobiographical terms, this genre yields distinct rhetorical resources for inscribing the self in relation to a field site and a professional community.

As autobiographies, the texts I examine below authorize the self to speak personally by grounding knowledge in the lived experience of a single individual. As scholars such as Caren Kaplan, Sidonie Smith, and Julia Watson show, autobiographical writing offers substantial resources to writers whose racialized, gendered, or otherwise "marked" identities might undermine their authority to create knowledge in official public contexts.[21] Autobiographical writing permits the writer to speak from the position of the body and to use her embodied authority to ground a range of claims. In this way field autobiographies generate knowledge very differently from genres such as technical reports and monographs, genres in which the identity of the researcher is minimized as irrelevant to the production of knowledge. Those texts are authorized by their writer's expertise, which reports and monographs simultaneously establish, through networks of review, circulation, and citation that confirm the text's status as knowledge.

Field autobiographies constitute a small subset of a larger autobiographical genre, the vocational autobiography, which emerged in the 1920s and 1930s as women's increasing access to higher education and professional forms of employment generated enormous public interest in women's working lives.[22] Vocational autobiographies provided first-person narratives focused on women's vocational training, career choices, educational experiences, relationships with colleagues, and excitement about and commitment to their work. These texts were published by women surgeons, chemists, nurses, actors, journalists, political leaders, literary agents, and other public figures, and attained broad readerships during these decades.[23] Although Morris and Reichard's three texts are the only book-length autobiographies by anthropologists I have located, the broader context of vocational texts targeting women readers provides a significant backdrop to Morris and Reichard's decision to publish autobiographical accounts of their fieldwork experiences.

Although field autobiographies draw resources for narration and self-representation from traditional autobiographical genres, this genre focuses narrowly on a specific period of field research. Consequently, the field autobiography presents the writer as a researcher, establishing her identity primarily in relation to a research community rather than in relation to a personal or familial history. Reichard, for instance, merely opens her field autobiography at the moment her field research begins, omitting entirely any account of her parents, her childhood, or her education, except the education she received in spinning and weaving at the hands of her Navajo teachers. She finishes her autobiography, likewise, in a chapter titled "Degree in Weaving," by recounting a day that informally becomes "the day for [her] comprehensive examination in rug-making," ending the book with the conclusion of her field research.[24] Morris only includes information about her early life that explains her path into archaeology. She relates a story, for instance, that demonstrates that she was "possessed of the archaeological urge long before I would have known what the word meant." She responds as a six year old to the question, "what do you want to do when you grow up," posed by "a Sunday visitor, who probably was having some difficulty in making conversation with my mother's prim little daughter," with this plan: "I want to dig for buried treasure, and explore among the Indians, and paint pictures, and wear a gun, and go to college." This prompts the visitor to "[look] from my starched white collar to her own neat shiny shoes, [and murmur] 'And so would I.'"[25] Morris passes over grammar school and college in a paragraph, in search of the profession that would permit her to pursue this plan laid out when she was six; after finding archaeology at last, the rest of her autobiography narrates a sequence of digs throughout the U.S. Southwest, rich with personal anecdote but also constrained entirely to the business of excavation and interpretation of artifacts. Such a focus in field autobiographies does not indicate that the self is not important, but in this genre the self is framed in relation to the work of archaeological and anthropological research.

Furthermore, field autobiographies narrate the writer's identity in relation to a particular research *site*—a location in the field, such as the Chichen Itza ruins in the Yucatan, Canyon del Muerto in Arizona, or on the Navajo reservation near Gallup, New Mexico. Although both writers narrate their passages across these areas in the process of their research, both limit their scope spatially in ways that emphasize the significance of fieldwork to their identities as researchers. For instance, Reichard's field autobiography primarily narrates her daily activities with the Navajo family that has agreed to teach her to weave, but she includes in the narrative her excursions with this family to sings, council meetings, and other events across an expansive region. She does *not* recount what occupies her, however, during her months spent every year *away* from this field site, back at her home in New York. The first section of *Spider Woman* ends with Reichard packing her car, saying good-bye to Red-Point's family, and driving away from Ganado, Arizona; the next chapter begins as she arrives back at Ganado the following summer and catches up with the family once again.[26] The spatial scope of these books is further clarified by the maps and photos that form their frontispieces. The front and back inside covers of *Spider Woman* present a pencil-drawn map of the Four Corners region of the southwest United States, spanning east and west from Flagstaff, Arizona, to Taos, New Mexico, and north and south from Socorro, New Mexico, to the San Juan River in southern Utah, while the interior covers of Morris's *Digging in the Southwest* consist of a wide-angle photograph of an immense canyon and rock wall, in which two massive caves—one clearly the site of an archaeological excavation—are highlighted. Field autobiographies, then, offer writers a means for forging a relationship between a narrated self, a specific material location, and a broader academic community: in this case, the professionalizing disciplines of archaeology and anthropology.

The rhetorical resources available in the field autobiography genre can be understood through the concepts of "presence" that rhetorical scholars Nathan Atkinson, David Kaufer, and Suguru Ishizaki have developed to identify how texts call upon and make salient to their readers features drawn from distinct genres.[27] Any genre makes certain elements present and salient to readers, who interpret the inclusion or omission of particular textual features against the backdrop provided by the genre frameworks that both writers and readers call upon. For instance, against the backdrop of the genre of autobiography, Morris and Reichard's field autobiographies omit much that their readers would expect them to include, such as accounts of their family history and revelations from their private, nonwork life. Reichard, for instance, says nothing at all about her life in New York, her marital status, or her family background; Morris refers to her marriage only briefly, in her second book, referring to Earl Halstead Morris as "a very excellent archaeologist and a most excellent husband—a combination which, to my mind, cannot be beaten."[28] Yet both writers include many personal details that readers would not typically expect from a genre in which research is reported, such as the writer's feelings about and reactions to the research she is undertaking, as when Reichard—confronted both with the conclusion of her first stay with Red-Point's family and with the failings of her still-inadequate weaving—writes, "I am glad to be alone as I endeavor to keep my disappointment from dissolving in tears."[29]

The field autobiography genre differs meaningfully from traditional autobiography and traditional monographs or technical reports by placing different emphases against the backdrop of expectation those genres create. Like technical reports, for instance, field autobiographies emphasize research, but they present the embodied acts of research processes rather than the final, eventual research product.[30] At the same time, omission of many of the elements readers expect in traditional autobiographies reinforces researchers' work-related identities. Through such omissions and inclusions, field autobiographies project Morris and Reichard as members of a professional community.

These features of the field autobiography genre yield significant rhetorical gains for Reichard and Morris. The first and most obvious benefit is that the genre enables these anthropologists to legitimate their identities as professionals. Both writers were significantly marginalized within their professional networks; their field autobiographies can be seen as a productive response to such marginality in ways I discuss more fully below—in particular, by establishing their professional identities textually in popular publications that garnered recognition of those identities among broader audiences. For instance, although Morris never held a faculty post, her widely circulated field autobiographies lent support to her status as an archaeologist, not merely an archaeologist's wife.[31] By describing her participation in ongoing archaeological debates and discussions, these texts do much of the rhetorical work of confirming her identity as a participant in an intellectual community. The rhetorical resources of this genre allow Morris to construct a position for herself within the field of archaeology in two senses: within the material site where archaeological research happens, and within the social, intellectual, and discursive milieu of the academic community which provide "the field" and "fieldwork" with their meaning and value. Because field autobiographies focus on the self in relation to the field—the discipline as well as the spaces where disciplinary work takes place—this genre offered particular benefits to women such as Morris and Reichard, who had to write themselves into their discipline.

However, it would be a mistake to read Morris's and Reichard's field autobiographies exclusively as vehicles for authorizing and legitimating themselves as individual researchers. Regardless of their intentions, which are largely inaccessible at this historical remove, the combination of personal narrative and research report enacted in their field autobiographies bear implications not only for Reichard and Morris's careers, but for the practice of anthropology as well.[32] As genre scholars have shown, innovative textual combinations and new genre uses can exert influence as innovations are taken up by subsequent rhetors in response to related rhetorical situations, and by pressuring assumptions surrounding the appropriate uses of the genres a writer has drawn from.[33] By wedding the authority of professional research with the personality of the writer, field autobiographies not only attach the researcher's authority to the writer's person but also exert influence on antecedent genres, the monographs and autobiographies from which the rhetorical resources of field autobiographies are drawn. They may influence how readers understand research by personalizing its creation, placing pressure on other researchers' claims to impersonality and objectivity as privileged modes of knowledge production. This reciprocal influence results in a genre in which the individual writer gains authority, while the practice of scientific research itself is opened up to scrutiny.

Consequently, in the sections that follow, I demonstrate that in their field autobiographies, Morris and Reichard not only lay claim to professional membership but also ground implicit arguments about their professional community. That is, by combining the impersonal knowledge-producing capacity of the technical report or monograph with the autobiography's resources for self-representation, Morris and Reichard produce texts with the power to shape their community, its current practices and potential futures. Capitalizing on the field autobiography's resources for self-inscription into professional spaces, Morris and Reichard create texts that describe for other women the specifically gendered pleasures of fieldwork and that locate ethnographic practice in embodied, situated experience. Even as this genre helps these writers garner broad public recognition for their identities as researchers, I suggest that their practices of self-inscription constitute a challenge to the discourses of gender neutrality and objectivity that were so pervasive in the privileged genre of the monograph, and ultimately constitute a rhetorical opportunity for converting their expertise into influence over the membership and practices of their profession.

Ann Axtell Morris and the Gendered Pleasures of Fieldwork

Ann Axtell Morris published two popular field autobiographies in the early 1930s that established her identity as a professional archaeologist. In fact, the phenomenal success of her two books, *Digging in Yucatan* and *Digging in the Southwest,* made Morris one of the most famous archaeologists of her day. *Digging in Yucatan* dramatically exceeded her editors' expectations, going into multiple printings and producing boxes of fan mail for Morris. Helen Ferris, editor-in-chief of the Junior Literary Guild, the Doubleday division that published the book, wrote to Morris to announce that everyone at Doubleday was "delighted with the reception" her first book received. Ferris called the early reviews "perfectly grand" and encouraged Morris to proceed immediately with writing whatever book she planned to undertake next.[34] Reviewers of both books praised Morris's "zest and knowledge and humor" as well as her skillful ability to "enable any one new to archaeology to understand what it is all about . . . and why archaeology is interesting and important."[35] That *Digging in the Southwest* was a selection not only of the Junior Literary Guild but of the Scientific Book Club as well suggests Morris's appeal for adults as well as for the high-school-aged readers targeted by her publishers. Her books elicited praise from prominent academics such as Ruth Benedict, who predicted in her review of *Digging in Yucatan* for the New York *Herald Tribune* that after reading Morris's first book, "young archaeologists will be storming every academic door."[36] Both books went into multiple printings and sold briskly through the 1940s.

Morris's popular texts were widely read, reviewed, and admired, and her identity as an archaeologist—not merely an archaeologist's *wife*—was unquestioned by her many reviewers, indicating the substantial rhetorical resources field autobiographies offered to writers seeking to establish a professional identity. During a period when a career in archaeology increasingly required advanced credentials, specifically a PhD, Morris successfully portrayed her single year of postgraduate field training in France as sufficient grounds for her readers to see her as a "full fledged archaeologist"; although such discipline-specific training distinguished her from an amateur, nevertheless that year formed the whole of her formal postbaccalaureate education.[37] Morris's field autobiographies argue for her identity as an independent researcher, even though her archaeological career took place entirely in conjunction with the research of her husband, Earl Halstead Morris. Earl Morris, who also lacked a PhD, was already an established archaeologist when Morris met and married him in 1923, after she returned from her field training in France. Shortly after their marriage, Ann and Earl began a massive Carnegie-funded dig at Chichen Itza in the Yucatan Peninsula of Mexico, which Earl directed for roughly four years. Despite her archaeological training, Morris did not initially have a formal role in Earl's Chichen Itza project.[38] After 1928, Ann collaborated with Earl in excavating a series of sites throughout the U.S. Southwest, especially in Canyon del Muerto and Canyon de Chelly in Arizona, again supported by Carnegie funds.

Throughout these years of research, Ann never held a faculty position and was officially employed by the Carnegie Institution only briefly during the Chichen Itza dig; usually she was listed in yearly reports to the Carnegie Institution as a "staff artist," assisting painter Jean Charlot in his reproductions of murals. Apart from her field autobiographies, her academic publications primarily consisted of brief reports of ongoing excavations included in Carnegie Yearbooks; in the final report of the Chichen Itza dig, published by the Carnegie Institution in 1931, Morris appears only as third author, and the disembodied, impersonal language of this technical monograph subsumes Morris's contributions into a collective identity voiced primarily by Earl Morris, who is lead author of the text.[39] The professional opportunities Ann Morris experienced as a researcher with postgraduate training but no Ph.D. contrast with those enjoyed by her husband, whose only training was informal, yet who was appointed director of these long-term, Carnegie-funded archaeological digs. Occupying a more marginal institutional location than her husband, Ann Morris was not sought as an authority to review others' works, nor was she typically paid for her research.[40]

Lacking an institutional location otherwise, Morris negotiates her status as an archaeologist through her publications. Morris's autobiographical writing demonstrates the claim of rhetorical scholar Nedra Reynolds that rhetors often "inscribe *who* they are by showing *where* they are."[41] Morris's field autobiographies accomplish precisely this kind of rhetorical identity construction, establishing her presence in the field to construct an identity for herself as a legitimate archaeologist. In contrast to her limited visibility in her few academic publications, Morris's self-inscriptions in her field autobiographies emphasize her presence in field excavations and her independent initiation into the discipline. Though both her autobiographies describe digs directed by her husband—first his excavation of Mayan ruins at Chichen Itza in the Yucatan, and then the series of excavations Earl and Ann pursued in Canyon del Muerto in Arizona—Morris takes care to show that her interest in archaeology preceded, rather than followed, her marriage. Her texts highlight her work digging, painting, interpreting data, and collaborating in all aspects of the projects, not merely observing the archaeological activities of others, and she emphasizes her skill and care as a researcher in both autobiographies. For instance, in a chapter in *Digging in Yucatan* titled, "I Excavate a Temple Myself," Morris relates how she located a small temple buried near the larger Chichen Itza excavation, deduced its ceremonial significance, and quickly secured permission to excavate it herself. Morris convinces Sylvanus Morley, director of Middle American Archaeological Research for the Carnegie Institution, to put her in charge of the temple by arguing to Morley—and to her audiences—that she could direct the excavation quickly and competently. Because she is willing to "throw in the wages of a competent director free"—that is, direct this side project herself without pay, a strategy commonly deployed by women seeking opportunity in the face of discrimination—Morris convinces Morley that "the whole thing seemed such a bargain we couldn't afford not to do it."[42] Through this exchange Morris bolsters her authority and positions herself at the head of her own project, "bossing my own gang of workers on my very own mound."[43] Minimizing her secondary role in the Yucatan excavation, and highlighting in both books the significance of those finds she can claim as her own, Morris inscribes herself into the field of archaeology as an active, independent researcher, working her "own mound."[44] Here and elsewhere in her field autobiographies, Morris uses strategies of spatial inscription to generate recognition for her identity as an archaeologist.

Yet the rhetorical effects of Morris's field autobiographies exceed these individual benefits. One major effect centers on what I call *rhetorical recruitment*. Morris's depictions of field research invite other would-be participants into anthropology, potentially shaping her discipline's boundaries through such recruitment. For instance, both Morris's field autobiographies share access to technical knowledge rather than withholding insider information by treating it as too complex for nonspecialists. Morris identifies the substantial specialized knowledge an archaeologist must attain—including knowledge of geology, botany, zoology, chemistry, as well as "the processes of preserving fragile specimens"—yet she does not make acquiring such knowledge seem daunting.[45] Morris, in fact, summarizes a great deal of complex information in both books, asserting that the "immediate result" will be to make "you, my gentle reader, quite as learned in the essentials as myself."[46] Morris's field autobiographies educate audiences about the methods and practices of archaeology, not just the dramatic unearthing of buried treasures, and thus actively invite readers into her discipline.

Morris's rhetorical recruitment efforts hinge upon the strategies of inscription she uses to position herself among a community of welcoming professionals. An emblematic instance of such positioning takes place when Morris translates insider chatter at the annual archaeological gathering at Gallup, New Mexico. Acknowledging that, for outsiders, "archaeologists' conversation sounds as mad as that of so many March Hares," she proposes "a transcription of some of this chat" to demonstrate that "once their code is learned it is not difficult to see why people who engage themselves in such fascinating work spend all of their associated time together talking 'shop.'" To provide evidence that their "code" can be decoded, Morris translates archaeological discourse for her readers on several occasions. "For instance," Morris writes, "say that one enters the perfectly civilized dining room of El Navajo hotel," whereupon Dr. Morley immediately shares "all the main facts of the last season—'There's another cheese box under the Caracol, and Karl found a jade necklace, and I've just located a new Ahau, and there are more *garapatas* than ever.'" To help readers make sense of these "facts," Morris explains: "Now none of this is true. The Caracol hasn't a cheese box under it—it's just the long-lost original foundation; Karl didn't find a jade necklace, because there is no true jade in America; no one could call the glyph Ahau new, since it was carved a good thousand years ago; and there couldn't possibly be any more *garapatas* (wood ticks) because we well knew that their population quota was full the previous season."[47] Such translations display Morris's own familiarity with the discursive norms of this community, underscoring the work these texts do to position her as a legitimate participant inside professional boundaries; yet Morris also counters the insularity of professional anthropology as she makes insider discourse legible to prospective archaeologists.

Morris further invites her readers into her community by modeling the questions and responses likely to excite or to irritate professionals. For instance, she dismisses with a sigh the perpetual rumor of "a man who knows a man who knows where there's a pictograph of a man fighting a dinosaur," but she registers the seriousness of Frank Robert's announcement that "he has found the burial ground of a village of round-skulled people who had with them the kind of pottery very definitely supposed to belong with the long-skulled people." Morris explains that insiders find such a report "awfully upsetting, because Frank knows what he sees when he sees it, so there's no possibility of error. But it spoils some of our best theories dreadfully." In these descriptions and throughout her texts, Morris introduces readers to the relative believability of various claims, the major and minor disagreements over issues such as "the Southwestern time sequence" that animate the community, and the foundational beliefs—such as the "fixed law of stratigraphy"—upon which archaeological practice is based.[48]

Reviewers of Morris's works repeatedly highlight the procedural and educational value of her field autobiographies, suggesting that Morris's efforts at rhetorical recruitment met with some success. One *New York Times* review of *Digging in the Southwest* notes that Morris explains "how the archaeologist goes about his work, the fundamental ideas which are always observed and the specific techniques that automatically come into play," including both the "aims" and the "general rules" that guide archaeological research.[49] Reviews aimed at high-school-aged readers also emphasize the procedural knowledge to be gained from Morris's books. One review notes that *Digging in the Southwest* will be especially appealing to high-school-aged readers with a latent interest in archaeology, for whom the book will not only "stir their enthusiasm" but will also "give them a realization of what it means to follow archaeology as a calling."[50] For both adult and young adult readers, Morris's popular books educated audiences about her field's methods and practices, not just the adventure of camping and excavating. By writing field autobiographies that functioned as primers on archaeological practice, Morris invited her readers to participate in her discipline, giving shape to disciplinary boundaries even from her marginal institutional position.

The genre's resources for self-inscription enabled Morris to articulate her invitation to readers in specifically gendered ways. Discussing her fieldwork not only in technical but also in personal terms, Morris represents herself after her marriage as not saddled with domestic duties, but instead "definitely homeless," likely to use the word "home" to refer to "hotel, house, or apartment, to my birthplace or where my luggage is stored, to a straw-thatched tropical hut, to a Spanish hacienda, to a flapping khaki tent in the desert, or even to a tentless bedroll spread beneath the stars."[51] Positioning herself in this variety of spaces— and in particular, spaces that evoke distance, mobility, and adventure—Morris presents her readers with a portrait of fieldwork as an antidote to domestic confinement. She quips in *Digging in the Southwest* that if her respectable parents had handed out marriage announcements, they would have had to acknowledge that the newly married couple could be found "at home (in a tent) [in] Canyon of the Dead, Arizona."[52] Thus, Morris contrasts the norms and practices of the archaeological field with those norms that govern other spaces—such as the norm among married white women of Morris's class that demanded they be home to callers at specified times.

If the field autobiography genre locates Morris in the field, Morris then uses that location to narrate the gendered pleasures of fieldwork, which include adventure, intellectual stimulation, and greater freedom of movement and activity. For instance, in many cases Morris portrays fieldwork as offering escape from confinement. She positively delights in the dangers of archaeological fieldwork. On her first professional trip to the Southwest, Morris writes that she was "almost immediately . . . nearly starved and drowned, not once but several times." Yet these experiences served to convince Morris that she had found her proper profession, causing her to decide that her "whole previous existence had been but a grey little soft shadow of the perfectly grand possibilities that life could offer to a person who would take the trouble to investigate."[53] In a discipline where women's presumed inability to cope with the discomforts of fieldwork helped to keep many women cataloguing in museums rather than participating in digs, Morris's portrayal of these discomforts as "perfectly grand possibilities" retains a strongly gendered resonance.[54] Through her identity as a researcher, Morris suggests, she is able to access physical spaces coded in opposition to the norms of middle-class womanhood, including the expectation that domestic stability was of primary importance or the belief that women were incapable of withstanding the bodily discomfort that accompanied field research. Instead, Morris casts her professional identity as offering her an excuse for engaging in otherwise unacceptable gender performances, presenting archaeology as a profession that "furnishes all the excitement of treasure-seeking decently concealed under the respectable cloak of science."[55] Morris's field autobiographies suggest to readers that she dons the "respectable cloak" of her professional identity in order to access certain gendered pleasures related to intellectual and physical activity in material spaces that were coded as dangerous, remote, and unsuitable for women.

Visual texts in both autobiographies reinforce Morris's professional identity and highlight the gendered appeal of fieldwork. Photographs of Morris digging, organizing specimens, and handling archaeological material in field sites provide visual support to her assertions of technical skill. In photographs, Morris grins at the camera while poised above a Basket Maker grave she has just uncovered, or she stands alongside a trench dug to determine stratigraphy during excavation.[56] In another photograph she displays the results of her small Yucatan excavation, above the caption "I proudly exhibit the beautiful and fragmentary sculptured panel from my temple to Dr. Morley."[57] Morris's accomplishments and independence as a researcher are manifested in these photographs, reinforcing her identity claims.

Other photographs support the project of rhetorical recruitment, highlighting the gendered pleasures of fieldwork that Morris shares with her readers. Several photographs, for instance, visually reinforce the argument that women can find adventure and intellectual pleasure in the spaces of archaeological field research; these images show Morris happily engaged in work while surrounded by vast desert expanses, dramatic ruins, and excavated mummies. In other images Morris hangs from a rope against the sheer face of a cliff wall and perches atop the domed roof of a temporary house, still under construction, which will serve as a shelter for researchers during their season in the field.[58] Including such visual texts extends this genre's capacity for spatial inscription, insofar as such photographs normalize and legitimate the presence of a woman's body in spaces often perceived as too dangerous for women.

Some photographs recruit women in particular by emphasizing the field as a space of escape from middle-class gender norms. For instance, Morris captions an image of herself in front of a canvas tent surrounded by rocks and rubble with the exuberantly ironic statement, "Woman's place is in the home!" Another photograph, captioned "Mr. and Mrs. Earl Morris at Home," shows their small tent, dwarfed by the imposing landscape, with a thin plume of smoke indicating that they are "home" to receive callers.[59] Such photographs assert that the trappings of middle-class female domesticity—including confinement indoors and the routine of receiving social calls—lose their claim upon an archaeologist engaged in professional pursuits. The spatial-rhetorical strategy of inscription is crucial to the individual as well as the public effects of Morris's field autobiographies. In emphasizing her field activities, both verbally and visually, Morris resists physical and rhetorical confinement to domestic spaces and lays claim to a research identity that legitimates her presence in the deserts and jungles where her archaeological work takes place.

Donning what Morris calls the "respectable cloak of science" is a crucial step in gaining access to these field spaces and to the pleasures they afford to women as researchers. Morris's invitation to her readers to participate in archaeology is decidedly anti-amateur. For instance, Morris strongly discourages untrained archaeologists, arguing that "once [anyone] breaks ground in the study of a particular location, that site is ruined beyond all help for anyone else. If he misses a single observation, that fact, and it might be an invaluable one, is lost for all time. Hence, you see, the responsibility is tremendous."[60] Justifying her anti-amateur position by appealing to a researcher's responsibility toward "facts" themselves, Morris reflects the prevailing faith in empiricism and technical expertise. But her position can also be seen as a pragmatic recognition of changing institutional realities. Nancy Parezo and Margaret Hardin point out that some interwar publications encouraged women who lacked specialized training to volunteer in museums as a way to gain entry into more demanding archaeological work—a contention that was mostly misleading, for in the newly professionalized context, such amateurs were almost never advanced to positions of authority or integrated into professional hierarchies.[61] In contrast, Morris highlights higher education and formal training as necessary precursors for fieldwork. Morris's field autobiographies do not challenge the movement toward professionalization already powerfully underway in the early 1930s— and, indeed, someone in Morris's contingent institutional location could hardly be expected to undertake such a challenge. Instead, these field autobiographies guide readers toward avenues for legitimate participation. That is, Morris's texts reflect ongoing shifts in the discipline at large, acknowledging the necessity of formal training and directing potential women practitioners toward opportunities to attain that training.

Rhetorical recruitment in field autobiographies can be seen as an effort to enact a more welcoming professional community, one that fully achieved its meritocratic goals. Morris consistently portrays professional archaeologists as ready to welcome knowledgeable and trained women as colleagues. Morris asserts that for both women and men who are "hard-boiled about facts" but who never "object to ants in the porridge, nor think of Indians as low-down dirty savages," archaeology offers clear avenues for entry into a warm community of "thoroughbred good sports, witty conversationalists, and loyal friends." Again, Morris's insertion of herself into this community offers her readers an example of archaeologists' willingness to share their knowledge with newcomers. She writes that although her first year among the archaeologists at Gallup left her "fairly lost beneath the torrent of unfamiliar words and strange ideas," she was quickly welcomed into "the sacred circle"; now, having "acquired a magnificent technical vocabulary," Morris finds that her "initial and generalized ignorance of ten years ago has since given way to a large number of highly specialized and acutely detailed ignorances." For those seeking scientific opportunity, Morris repeatedly asserts that the archaeological community is marked by its members' "untiring efforts to learn and their willingness to teach."[62]

That this portrayal does not quite align with the reality of Morris's and other women's marginalized status in the discipline does not negate its rhetorical significance. Indeed, this not-yet-realized quality of the welcoming community that Morris describes recalls Carolyn Miller's characterization of a rhetorical community as a "virtual entity, a discursive projection, a rhetorical construct. It is the community as invoked, represented, presupposed, or developed in rhetorical discourse."[63] Certainly the inclusive group of "good sports and loyal friends" whom Morris portrays as her professional community represents an ideal that was unevenly realized in practice, and in Morris's own experience. For instance, despite Morris's bachelor's degree and formal postgraduate training in fieldwork, Sylvanus Morley's 1924 report, following Ann's first season on the Chichen Itza project, merely mentions that in addition to a paid staff of six, "Mrs. E. H. Morris was of invaluable aid in copying the mural paintings from the Temple of the Warriors and in assisting Mr. Morris in connection with the excavations and repair work."[64] In subsequent yearly reports, Ann is listed among the staff as "Mrs. E. H. Morris, artist" when she begins to be paid a very small monthly stipend for her work copying murals.[65] Even when Morley's reports to the Carnegie include Ann's account of her own excavations in relation to the larger Chichen Itza project, she is identified with designations—assistant and artist—that contest her identifications as a "full fledged archaeologist."[66] The discrepancy between the welcoming community Morris represents in her field autobiographies and the gendered inequalities she encountered in her professional life does not suggest that Morris's portrayals were *inaccurate;* instead, the inclusive disciplinary community Morris depicts, one willing to respect and reward all trained, hard-working members, represents the meritocratic ideal that professional women like Morris and Reichard hoped to achieve. Morris's field autobiographies simultaneously project and actively recruit members into the kind of welcoming professional community her works portray.

Gladys Reichard and Embodied Ethnography

Gladys Reichard also draws upon the rhetorical resources of field autobiography to influence her disciplinary community by using the genre's resources for spatial self-inscription to reimagine ethnographic research. In her 1934 field autobiography, *Spider Woman,* Reichard presents ethnographic research as a situated, embodied, and potentially disruptive practice, demonstrating how the combination of technical and personal writing that characterizes this genre puts pressure on routine research practices. As she inscribes her embodied presence into the ethnographic frame, Reichard challenges the fiction of detached observation adopted by many of the major ethnographic works of her contemporaries, contests the spatial modes of knowledge-making that the monograph genre had solidified, and offers instead an alternative way of inhabiting space as an ethnographer.

Reichard's position within the emerging hierarchies of professional anthropology was both more stable and more central than that occupied by Morris. Reichard, born in Pennsylvania in 1893, was raised in an intellectual, Quaker household; after high school, she taught elementary school for six years before entering Swarthmore College, where she graduated with a degree in classics in 1919. Like Morris, she discovered anthropology at the end of her time as an undergraduate. Once she learned of this field as a potential career, she wrote to Franz Boas, seeking information about academic and professional opportunities.[67] After inquiring whether she intended to study anthropology merely as a hobby or to prepare for an occupation, Boas advised Reichard that certainly a master's degree would not be sufficient for professional advancement and directed her to pursue the PhD.[68] In 1919 Reichard entered Boas's graduate program at Columbia University on a Lucretia Mott Fellowship from Swarthmore. She earned her PhD in 1925 following the successful publication of her dissertation on Wiyot grammar and began working in 1923 as an instructor in anthropology at Barnard College, where she eventually attained the rank of full professor and continued teaching until her death in 1955.[69]

Her position at Barnard was particularly notable for providing Reichard with a stable income and institutional affiliation during a period when many women with similar credentials and publications were excluded from faculty positions. Although Reichard did not train graduate students at a PhD-granting institution, she still directed many of her women undergraduates into anthropology; her students at Barnard who became anthropologists include Nathalie Woodbury, Alice Kehoe, Kate Peck Kent, Eleanor Leacock, and Frederica de Laguna. Her incorporation into professional hierarchies was further accomplished through her prodigious publication record, which included a dozen books with university and popular presses as well as dozens of articles in journals such as the *American Anthropologist,* the *Journal of American Folklore,* and the

International Journal of American Linguistics. She was awarded several research fellowships, including the John Simon Guggenheim Memorial Fellowship, which funded a year of study in Germany that resulted in her award-winning book, *Melanesian Design.*[70] She held positions within anthropology's professional organizations, serving as secretary of the American Folklore Society from 1924 to 1935, for instance, and as program director for Section H (Anthropology) for the American Association for the Advancement of Science in 1945. All of these measures indicate Reichard's access to material resources to support her career and her integration into the emerging professional apparatus of her discipline.

Though more fully enmeshed than Morris in anthropology's institutions, Reichard still had cause for dissatisfaction with professionalized anthropology. Despite her professional successes, Reichard still felt frustrated at her lack of influence within her profession, writing to Morris in 1932, "do *I* ever get asked to teach the Southwest Laboratory or to talk at the symposium of the A. A. A. or to write for the Social Science Encyclopedia, or any of the things that get advertising?"[71] These opportunities were increasingly important in the professional context of interwar anthropology, and though her stable teaching position at an undergraduate college was extremely valuable, it did not provide such high-profile opportunities for shaping the direction of the field. Another concern was that her close affiliation with Franz Boas, her powerful mentor, had been the source of many of the opportunities she had had; she chafed at her recognition that her research prospects were "all on account of Papa Franz and I am sure I would not get a cent were it not for him."[72]

Reichard experienced firsthand the significant ways in which her professional community failed to welcome equally all talented, qualified practitioners, and attempted, like Morris, to shape that community through her writing. While Morris used the resources of the field autobiography genre to influence her discipline by recruiting outsiders, writing popular books that garnered interest among young women readers, Reichard used the genre's resources—especially resources for narrating the self in relation to a particular community and material context—to generate alternate forms of ethnographic representation. By narrating her research process in *Spider Woman,* Reichard crafts an alternative vision of how anthropologists can be (and should be) positioned within the communities they study.

Reichard's portrayal of field research in *Spider Woman* differs most markedly from classic ethnographic representations in consistently inscribing her embodied presence within the space of field research. The opening scene of the field autobiography registers Reichard's physical presence as she moves into a space rich with sounds, smells, and other sensory perceptions: "White-Sands lay silent and motionless in the dead light of mid-afternoon. Here and there a soft, capricious wind stirred up a tiny whirl of dust. A muffled lazy cluck came from a contented huddle of feathers where a hen leisurely gave herself a dust bath."[73] Reichard arrives to seek instruction in weaving from a family of expert weavers who have been recommended to her as possible teachers. As she searches through a small family settlement to introduce herself, Reichard establishes that the perspective from which she observes and moves through this space is resolutely human, not omniscient, and tied to her embodied point of view. For instance, after not finding the family in their shade (a term for a Navajo house), Reichard walks to another house within the settlement, where she finds that "the door was closed but the lock hung loose in the hasp. A cursory glance through the crack above the door showed that it, like the shade, was empty." After looking and listening further, she and the trader who accompanies her visit another home, the door of which "is open, and from its interior comes a dull *thump thump,* the sound of the comb pounding firmly, regularly, and rapidly the yarn which is becoming a Navajo rug."[74] Here and throughout this field autobiography, Reichard's activities remain visible to her readers, included within the frame of her analysis. She walks, sits, cooks, asks questions, drives herself and other members of the community from place to place, relaxes, reads, engages in community disputes, and, above all else, weaves. Learning to weave, as the student of Maria Antonia and her daughter Atlnaba, takes place for Reichard in relation to a wide-ranging and ongoing participation in the life of this family and community.

Because Reichard's field autobiography continues in this narrative mode throughout the length of the book, it differs significantly even from those ethnographic monographs, like Malinowski's, that begin with a narrative "arrival scene" before turning to the distanced, objective mode of presentation characteristic of professional anthropological discourse in the early twentieth century. For instance, Malinowski's mythic arrival scene in the opening chapter of *Argonauts* asks his readers to "imagine [themselves] suddenly set down . . . alone on a tropical beach close to a native village, while the launch or dinghy which has brought you sails away out of sight"; this opening scene provides his readers with a human vantage point, though only momentarily.[75] As critical anthropologists since the 1980s have noted, this "subgenre of ethnography" known as the "tale of entry" typically serves to establish the ethnographer's presence and authority in order to set aside methodological questions raised by the radically unrepeatable nature of fieldwork experiences.[76] After a brief arrival narrative, the ethnographer's position in the text customarily becomes unfixed, generalized, and distant from firsthand experience, seen in language such as Malinowski's subsequent assertion that "it is important as a characteristic of the kinship conditions of this people, that a man receives sorcery gratis from his father, who according to the traditional kinship system is no blood-relation, whereas he has to pay for it to his maternal uncle, whose natural heir he is."[77] Such a discursive stance, one that Vincent Crapanzano calls "a roving perspective [adopted to enable the] 'totalistic' presentation" of ethnographic claims, removes the ethnographer from association with specific speakers sharing information during specific moments of encounter.[78] Counteracting this tendency, Reichard renders the *whole* of her fieldwork—not merely her moment of arrival—from an embodied narrative perspective.

Reichard's participation in this community life is often registered in the text spatially, as she inhabits and moves through specific social and material spaces. For instance, her increased comfort within the extended family that hosts her is marked by her integration into the family's space at ceremonial events; after traveling to a sing, a curative and ceremonial community event, Reichard writes that although Marie and Atlnaba "sit down at the back of the shade, the hostess brings me a kitchen chair. Marie and Atlnaba smile at the thought that I need it, but I sit on it for a while to be polite. As we wait and watch the extensive cooking operations, various Navajo filter in. The young men shake hands somewhat bashfully, then stand about outside the shade. Women enter quietly and sit in the semicircle with us."[79] The precise way in which Reichard inhabits this social space indicates the degree of her integration in this community, as a white woman and ongoing participant in Red-Point's family. Reichard's whiteness marks her as visibly different from her teachers, who know that Reichard would be comfortable sitting on the floor as is Navajo custom, yet her racial identity prompts a polite hostess to bring her a chair to sit in. At the same time, her gendered identity becomes something she shares with the other women who sit together in a semicircle, while men stand separately outside the shade. Reichard's habitation with Red-Point's family renders her comfortable with, but not identical with, other community members with whom she shares space over the course of *Spider Woman*.

Additionally, Reichard's movement over the vast distances of the Navajo reservation solidifies her embeddedness within this community and provides her with further opportunities for observation and knowledge production. For instance, when several men are discussing their plans to retrieve a Douglas fir needed for use in a medicinal ceremony, she and two of the men in Red-Point's family arrange to travel all night in Reichard's car to retrieve the fir; on many other occasions, Reichard records conversations in which she and members of Red-Point's family negotiate their arrangements for traveling to sings and other community events.[80] For instance, as Reichard discusses the effectiveness of sings with several women, that discussion is interrupted by a momentary opportunity to pursue other kinds of ethnographic research: "Dan rides up as we talk. The men are going to brand cattle. Do we want to watch them? In no time we have a full auto."[81] In the course of this impromptu trip, Reichard talks with several women about a family member who has converted to Christianity and now makes fun of the sings the rest of her family participate in. On these and other occasions, travel not only provides opportunities to gain further insight into community practices, but also repeatedly shifts Reichard's relations with the people who provide her with access to ethnographic knowledge.

Unlike most ethnographic texts, *Spider Woman* does not relegate Reichard's spatial movement and participation in community life to a field diary or a brief statement of method, but incorporates these things thoroughly into the knowledge-making frame of the book. That is, Reichard's observations—as she sits with other women inside a shade while a meal is prepared, or watches one of her teachers negotiate prices with a trader—contribute to the account she is constructing in *Spider Woman* of the role of gender within the realms of activity that help Navajo community life cohere. Ultimately, Reichard's text traces a network of spatial lines over the territory she must cover in order to accompany Red-Point's family and the broader White Sands community in their activities. Reichard's embodied presence and her interactions with an extensive community of individuals ground the anthropological knowledge her book constructs. Although Reichard moves beyond the small community of White Sands over the course of the book—driving her car into neighboring communities, sometimes over long distances as her movements follow the movements of the family with whom she lives—her progression through these spaces always happens at the scale and from the perspective of her own body.

As she ties the perspective in this field autobiography to her body, she also registers sensory experiences and emotional responses to her work and to the landscape, presenting rather than omitting bodily sensations from the frame of ethnographic research. Positioning herself in space precisely, for instance, she describes her evening routine in which she takes her "bed roll outside . . . [and lays] it on the gentle smooth slope of my housetop, a vantage point from which the whole settlement may be observed." From this vantage point, Reichard writes, "leaning against my bed roll, I have leisure to enjoy the panorama. . . .

My eye roves from the rose-colored sand still covered with gray-green grass because of late rains, to the hoar-green sagebrush and over the somewhat lumpy plain abundantly dotted with pine and juniper." Reichard also includes in *Spider Woman* her emotional responses to her fieldwork, characterizing herself at different moments as envious, eager, tired, frustrated, and exhilarated.[82] She vividly portrays her restlessness on a hot day in the hours before a sandstorm:

> My weaving does not hold me, and I tire quickly of learning my Navajo language, a pursuit that usually interests me for hours, more hours than there ever are. With a conscience guilty at reading in the daytime I open a book. It is not interesting, nor are the magazines I have. I must be tired; I will try to sleep, even if the Navajo women never do [in the daytime]. But there is a fly on my nose—its buzzing sounds like a saw in the tense silence. I will go outside. But there is no wind and the flies are worse than they are inside. Besides, ants crawl vigorously over tarpaulin and over me. I go back in. I think I am hungry and eat some crackers. I repeat my list of entertainments. Those hours which usually flit so fast I cannot see them, now drag interminably.[83]

Including the body of the researcher in this way, by registering the sensory experiences, exhaustions, and frustrations that accompany field research, Reichard counteracts the tendency of professionalized anthropological discourse to eliminate such traces in order to shore up the researcher's authority. Against the implicit argument of monographs that anybody *there* would have observed the same thing, Reichard's text reminds her readers that anthropological research is undertaken by a specific individual—one whose moods shift from exhilaration to exhaustion, and who hears, smells, and reacts to her sensory experiences—not by a disembodied recording device or a universal eye that transcends the limitations of embodiment.

This spatial strategy of inscription, used throughout the field autobiography, permits Reichard to position herself in precise relation to the specific individuals with whom she interacts. For instance, when she is first introduced to Atlnaba, Reichard neither removes herself from view nor assumes a disembodied stance: "Now Old-Mexican's-Son, the trader, who is introducing me, directs a witty greeting to the woman at the loom. She, for the first time, shows awareness of our presence. . . . The woman interrupts her weaving long enough to turn on me a gleaming smile and to indicate a strong low box on which I, being a stranger, may sit. As we talk and smoke, the woman weaves, her swiftly moving fingers causing the blanket to grow visibly." Here, as she is introduced to the woman weaving, Reichard allows the reader to witness her specific (social and spatial) position at the onset of her research: she is greeted, but a stranger; as a stranger, she is invited to inhabit the space of this home in certain ways because she is not yet as "at home in this Indian family" as the trader who brought her there, who "finds himself a place on a soft sheepskin where he half reclines."[84] The social relations that inhere in this scene are registered in the field autobiography through precisely modulated embodied behaviors—sitting rather than standing, reclining to indicate familiarity, and so on.

Reichard's practices of self-inscription also enable her to counteract the tendency of ethnographic discourse to maintain the fiction, as Crapanzano argues, that the ethnographer's "presence does not alter the way things happen or, for that matter, the way they are observed or interpreted."[85] In her introduction to Atlnaba, for instance, Reichard's influence upon the scene is noted when Atlnaba interrupts her weaving to welcome and acknowledge a stranger in her presence. Although the interruption is momentary, inscribing it within the text affirms that Reichard is present, herself an element in the scene, not merely a disembodied eye whose observations have no effect. As another reader of *Spider Woman* notes, the difference between Reichard's textual technique and that of standard ethnographic writing is striking in this passage, where Reichard keeps "herself fully within the frame of reference though not the center of attention."[86] Self-inscription enables Reichard to mark her presence in this social scene while still turning our attention toward the practices taking place there.

The embodied perspective Reichard adopts for her ethnographic observer keeps her in contact with, rather than separated from, the other people in whose community she participates. Placing herself in the ethnographic frame gives her the opportunity to position her coinhabitants in specific spatial and social relations as well. For instance, as Reichard sits on top of her house one evening, she notes the activities of family life surrounding her: a granddaughter, Ninaba, brings a herd of sheep into their corral for the evening; Ninaba's grandmother Maria Antonia chops wood; others begin preparations for their evening meal. From her vantage point atop the small mound from which her cellarlike home has been dug, Reichard observes that "fire gleams through the cracks of the shade made of odds and ends fitted about the piñon tree where Maria Antonia does her summer work. She is out at the woodpile making the chips fly. Her beehive of activity is within calling, but not within talking, distance of me. The smoke of her cedar fire, mingled with the pungent odor of the sage stirred up by the chewing goats, and with the dust of their pawing, is wafted to me on the gentlest and coolest of breezes."[87] By sounds, sights, and smells, Reichard notes carefully the degree to which these two women share the same space, and she articulates their distance precisely: Maria Antonia is "within calling, but not within talking, distance." The embodied position from which Reichard narrates allows her to include the sensory details that index these careful degrees of distance and connection: flames glimpsed through slats of wood, smells of smoke, sage, and dust.

Moreover, Reichard uses her body for her research, which concerns the weaving practices of Navajo women and the design principles that guide their artistry. With the help of the accomplished weavers who agree to teach her, Reichard trains her body to adopt the postures and complete the activities that enable these Navajo women to make their works of art. For instance, Reichard watches a weaver, Marie, closely in order to mimic her actions: "She throws her yarn through, pounds it down, withdraws the batten. Now she presses the heald rod against the loops of the heald and she has a different shed, the alternate warps are forward. A casual flip of the fingers across the warp, and the weft throwing and pounding are repeated."[88] But taking up these bodily postures herself shows them to be far more complex than her initial observation, however close, revealed: "I at first think this flipping an unnecessary, possibly an aesthetic, gesture like the elaborate motions of a bootblack's flannel. But when I take up the weaving position myself I find it serves a very useful purpose. . . . The swift light flip of the fingers separates such of these fibers on the forward warps as adhere to those behind."[89] As she tries to train her body to mirror the movements that accomplished weavers conduct easily, Reichard repeatedly registers both her awkwardness and her concentration, noting that "all those things which are done so easily, so casually by the Navajo women begin to take on unsuspected difficulties when I try them."[90] Reichard's discursive practices of inscription allow her to emphasize the embodied component of field research, as Reichard not only *observes* the embodied behaviors of weaving but also *practices* those behaviors herself. This practice provides Reichard with insight into aspects of weaving and design she did not previously have, insight that no amount of close observation could have provided.

As Reichard inscribes herself in research spaces, she portrays research as something that takes place *over time* as well. Positioning herself as a student learning to weave, for instance, Reichard begins her text from the position of not knowing; she approaches those who will teach her, negotiates with them for the terms of her instruction, proceeds through time and shared space to make inroads into a practice so complex that she recognizes that after several summers she has only mastered its most basic elements. Reichard also registers within the frame of the field autobiography her multiple arrivals and departures, permitting the reader to view the truncated, seasonal progression of her research. She writes, for instance, of Red-Point's family helping her pack her car and embracing before she drives away at the end of her first summer of weaving, and follows this with her return the next summer, where she finds the family arrangements somewhat altered—Marie and Tom have moved to Los Angeles—and portrays herself eager to resume her learning and start a new blanket. Such an account contrasts sharply with the typical practice in monographs of masking fieldwork disruptions and obscuring the material circumstances that enable the anthropologist's presence in the field. Including or omitting such temporal markers has epistemic consequences. For instance, in addition to marking truncated spans of field research, Reichard also narrates time spent in the field that does not seem immediately fruitful; this allows her to represent the knowledge-making process in anthropology more realistically than accounts that condense or minimize the time required to forge relationships and learn language skills. This practice contrasts strongly with most presentations of anthropological research at the time, which often speak after the fact from a position of authority, rather than from the position of yet-to-know that characterizes the onset of research.

Indeed, spatio-temporal portrayals are always attended by epistemic implications, as scholars such as Catherine Schryer and Jordynn Jack argue.[91] The most significant implication of Reichard's spatial portrayals in *Spider Woman* is her implicit argument, through these spatial inscriptions, that the ethnographic researcher is enmeshed in social relations and that she participates in those relations as an active presence. For instance, at the end of a long and successful sing, Reichard and Red-Point, the singer who is husband to Reichard's teacher, Maria Antonia, sit together sharing a cigarette and take up a litany that confirms their shared participation in a community:

As he lights the proffered cigarette, he looks through the smoke and says, "White-Sands is beautiful."

Before either of us realizes it, we are intoning a litany:

"The fields are beautiful," I respond.

"The vegetation is beautiful," he encourages.

"The trees are beautiful."

"The houses are beautiful."

"The women are beautiful."

"The men are beautiful."

And together we say, "The children are beautiful."

Then I, "The Chant is beautiful."

"The offerings are beautiful."

"The prayers are beautiful."

"The paintings are beautiful. All has been restored in beauty," concludes the old Chanter, as he once again strides off to attend to the details of the final night.[92]

In this passage, Reichard and Red-Point exchange lines in a litany that confirms their shared vision of the landscape before them and their shared estimation of the community they both have been participating in during the nine nights of the ceremonial sing that has just concluded. Their exchange of this routine generic form, the litany, becomes charged with meaning *because of* the specific context in which they speak these lines. Including this moment in her research narrative enables Reichard to show how she and Red-Point are taken up into a community together, both by the discourse that provides each of them with lines to speak and by the shared experience of the sing in which each has participated. Reichard shows, furthermore, that their participation differs: she remains seated as an observer while Red-Point bears responsibility to "attend to the details" required to bring this community event to its conclusion.

In this passage and throughout *Spider Woman,* Reichard's presence alters the community and family life she intrudes upon, at times positively and at other times negatively. For instance, the members of Maria Antonia's family, although they agree to teach her, must take time from other tasks in order to establish a place for her to live and to instruct her; these costs for the family that accommodates her are included in rather than omitted from Reichard's narrative. At times, when Reichard registers the work they undertake on her behalf, she sheepishly acknowledges moments when she should be more helpful a participant than she is. At other times, the resources she brings with her to Red-Point's family—especially her car—allow her to contribute meaningfully to the projects that occupy the family, as when a flock of sheep are struck by lightning one night and Reichard works with members of the family to bring the remaining sheep to safety.[93] Reichard's participation in Red-Point's family allows her access to the forms of knowledge she desires as an anthropologist—but such participation also embeds Reichard in relations of responsibility that bear their own entailments.

Furthermore, by keeping her ethnographic perspective tied to the body, rather than looming above the social and material environment in a perspective that suggests omniscience, Reichard recalls her readers to the intimacy of observation as a research practice. As she lives in and moves through this social and material landscape, her observational powers extend as far as a human eye can see, and no further—and only into spaces where her body is permitted, as when her relationship with Red-Point's family grants her access to sit inside the tent during a sing she would not otherwise be allowed to attend.[94] Ethnographic knowledge is formed from an embodied position, and Reichard's rhetorical choices remind her reader that such a position implies limitations on knowledge and entails relations of human intimacy that demand recognition and recompense in turn.

By representing the ethnographer as a disruptive, embodied presence, enmeshed in human relations rather than apart from them, Reichard constructs a version of ethnographic practice that bears methodological implications. One particularly rich spatial concept that Reichard exploits is the concept of the threshold. Early in her entry into the community where she will study, Reichard positions herself on the threshold of Atlnaba's home: "We stand respectfully at the doorway for a time, looking in and allowing our eyes to become accustomed to the dimness of the light, a contrast to the harsh glare from which we came."[95] By embedding this moment within an ongoing narrative, Reichard refers here to a specific threshold: that dividing this private space from the surrounding community. The home on the other side of this threshold is a specific one, filled with the material markers of habitation; this particular house "bulges with life. Bursting sacks of wool hang from its sides. Long, clean, brightly colored skeins of spun yarn hang from the beams and loom posts. The box on the floor at the woman's side has strands of pink and red, orange and green. . . . A cat rubs our legs."[96] The specificity of Reichard's description makes it clear that she stands at the threshold of a particular home, the home of the teacher Atlnaba whom Reichard is momentarily to meet, observing local customs such as the politeness of standing at a threshold before entering a home. But this lingering portrayal of her first entrance in a new field site can also be read as emblematic of her ethnographic method, indicative of a particular attitude toward what she will encounter as an ethnographer. For instance, by "allowing [her] eyes to become accustomed," Reichard indicates an expectation of adjustment on the part of the ethnographer in coming to inhabit a new space. Becoming accustomed requires time, patience, and a willing expectation. The passage also indicates Reichard's attitude toward the processes by which an ethnographer comes to know; poised on this threshold, Reichard is not passing from a state of all-knowing into utter confusion; nor from a state of utter confusion to one of total knowledge. Although the ethnographer-at-the-threshold recognizes that the circumstances inside are different—dimness, rather than glare—Reichard portrays these as differences of degree rather than absolutes.

In deploying these spatial strategies in her ethnographic novel, Reichard opens up possibilities for ethnographic knowledge-making that exceed the epistemic opportunities available in the monograph. She positions the ethnographer within specific spatial configurations relative to the community she studies. That position is embodied; the body, occupying space, moves and acts and interacts within an ongoing situation. This situation, crucially, involves other specific bodies, families, and personalities as well, not simply a series of interchangeable informants. The position Reichard adopts places her neither as an objective outsider whose distance confers knowledge, nor as an immediate and automatic participant, empowered by what Malinowski calls "the ethnographer's magic," the capacity of the fieldworker to plumb "the real spirit of the natives" and thus achieve a degree of knowledge denied even to cultural insiders themselves.[97] Instead, the ethnographer is emblematized at the threshold of a specific home, in a specific moment, inhabiting a particular body, and adopting a disposition to learn. Reichard's alternative practice also encompasses *representation* of the ethnographic process; she inscribes her presence into her text because how that observing, learning self is positioned bears a crucial relationship to the nature of the knowledge being produced. Including herself within the frame, Reichard both treats the ethnographer as a subject for scrutiny and portrays the ethnographer as embedded within ethical relations, human and familial contexts that demand a degree of accountability and acknowledgment that the forms of representation crystalized in the monograph deny.

Countering Strategies of Distance

The power of Morris's and Reichard's spatial inscriptions to generate alternative accounts of research practice becomes especially evident in contrast to more typical research texts. In their field autobiographies, these two writers configure knowledge, embodiment, and power in ways that contrast strongly with those relationships enacted in ethnographic monographs during the same period. Through the spatial and temporal requirements of scientific fieldwork during these decades, monographs in the 1920s and 1930s positioned writers, readers, and objects of knowledge into relations of power that mimicked and reinforced colonial structures. That Reichard's and Morris's spatial strategies portray their knowledge-making practices *differently* will be perhaps most evident through comparison with a counterexample: in this case, with Robert Redfield's 1930 monograph, *Tepoztlán, a Mexican Village,* an exemplary text in its time that epitomizes the configurations of distance, knowledge, and power that Reichard's and Morris's texts contradict.

Redfield positions himself, the ethnographic observer, at a great distance from the object of his study, while also portraying the observer as already an expert whose authority is in place from the outset of his text. Redfield introduces the reader to Tepoztlán, the village where he locates his study, initially at a scale that can only be described as atmospheric: he positions his observer at a point high enough above the North American continent to take in at a glance the entire geophysical space of Mexico, viewing its central plateau "bounded on the north by a tableland which dips down northward into a region where the rainfall is too slight for agriculture" and "on the other three sides . . . by steep escarpments which rise three thousand feet above the plateau before falling sharply away to the sea."[98] From this scale he provides a series of frames that focus the viewer closer and closer in to the village, constructing in the process a series of synecdochal spatial relations between the sites he glimpses: the continent, the country, the central plateau, the state of Morelos, the ring of mountains that surrounds the village, and finally, Tepoztlán itself. Through this series of frames, and especially through a center/periphery organizational device that he uses repeatedly to situate each frame relative to the next, Redfield constructs his study site as a microcosm, with generalizable relations at each scale exactly copied onto the scales above and below. The relations of center and periphery Redfield observes at the scale of the continent also inhere at the scale of the state and, finally, in the cultural processes he observes in the village: "The village, like Mexico itself, has a center and a periphery."[99] Redfield's spatial depictions result in a portrayal of Tepoztlán as maintaining a synecdochal relation to a series of larger-scale environments within which the village is nested. Furthermore, the repeated device of center and periphery creates an impression of necessity surrounding Redfield's ethnographic data; he initially implies, then later states outright, that he observes identical center/periphery relations in each successive frame because the environment itself shapes the cultural dynamics that play out within it.

Redfield also constructs a vantage point for his observer relative to the landscape he has mapped out, a vantage point characterized by domination and distance. Zooming in from the continent to the scale of the state, Redfield pauses at the highest point at the northern edge of the state and from that great height looks down toward the mountains to locate the village below. This practice contrasts strongly with, for instance, Reichard's observations from her position on the top of her house, which places her "within calling, but not within talking, distance" of Maria Antonia.[100] One important rhetorical consequence of Redfield's spatial choices is that they allow him to portray the ethnographer as occupying a position of extreme distance and yet possessing, even at the very beginning of the monograph, knowledge so expansive that it borders on omniscience. His vision encompasses a country; it is powerful enough to scan a state and pick out one village for ethnographic attention from amid a "maze of slighter mountains that from this eminence are no more than hills."[101] The ethnographer, positioned so powerfully, shares his vision with his readers, who likewise possess a vision powerful enough to identify and isolate their object of knowledge from such a distance.

In contrast, the researcher inscribed into Reichard's and Morris's texts is not positioned as *already knowing* from the start. Instead, these writers use the narrative resources of an autobiographical genre to recount a process of creating knowledge, a process that "takes place," as contemporary writing scholars remind us, in the richest sense of the phrase: that is, in specific material sites, through embodied activity, and by way of forming social relations that embed the ethnographer with others in a shared space. Observation from a distance— particularly from the remote locations of atmosphere and mountaintop that Redfield adopts—would be not only impossible, but, according to the method Reichard and Morris demonstrate, also unenlightening. Instead, through their innovative use of genre-based rhetorical resources, these writers portray a researcher who inhabits a particular local environment and whose embodied self lies within the frame of ethnographic study, changing and interacting with the social processes she observes. *This* observer, unlike the omniscient ethnographer who views Tepoztlán from afar, is herself subject to scrutiny and embedded within the ongoing human relations that, in fact, make *knowing* possible.

Inscribing Embodiment in Professional Practice

The spatial-rhetorical strategies Morris and Reichard adopt in their field autobiographies provide evidence of women anthropologists' inventive responses to the contradictions that their participation in professionalized science revealed. Even as anthropology's professionalization seemed to offer women clearer paths to career advancement, many women practitioners found themselves contending with gender discrimination in forms that were obscured and thus especially difficult to combat. The rhetorical resources Morris and Reichard accessed through their field autobiographies provided these writers with a textual space in which to counter the pervasive discourse of gender neutrality that professionalization promoted, instead personalizing the production of anthropological knowledge.

Differences between the institutional locations of these two writers shaped their use of the field autobiography genre. Morris, whose professional writing was almost entirely contained within collective publications that rendered her intellectual contributions invisible, directed her field autobiographies toward popular audiences, a strategy that enabled her to garner public recognition for her identity as a researcher. At the same time, her texts pressured professional practice by recruiting women into fieldwork as an embodied activity that was capable of providing women with specifically gendered pleasures, such as escape from domestic confinement and household responsibilities. Thus, self-inscription in Morris's field autobiographies countered widespread beliefs about women's lack of suitability for archaeological fieldwork, as Morris positioned her body within the field sites and professional boundaries of anthropology and indicated to her young readers how they, too, might undertake to include themselves in anthropology's disciplinary practice.

Some evidence remains to suggest that Morris's books did indeed guide young women (and men) toward avenues for professional preparation. In response to a request from Doubleday editor Dorothy Bryan, who asked Morris for fan mail that could be quoted to promote a reprinting of *Digging in Yucatan,* Morris returns "a couple of letters from young female archaeologist fans" who "wanted to know where to go to college and what to take after they got there that would make them into full fledged archaeologists."[102] One of Morris's young female fans, Alice Ruth Bruce, wrote in 1937 for the *Washington Post*'s series "I Aim to Be—" that she found Morris's autobiographies to be "the most useful books" for a potential archaeologist. Though only fifteen, Bruce had been a member of the New Jersey Archaeological Society for seven years; her essay in the *Washington Post* reveals that she had already requested college application materials from Columbia, "which has fine archaeological courses," and demonstrates a remarkable degree of familiarity with the professional practice of anthropology, including its apparatus of professional organizations, its assumed background knowledge in geology and history, and the importance of credentials and higher education for membership.[103] As Morris emphasized technical expertise, careful research, and specialized training as requirements for entry into a discipline that offered women mobility and excitement under a "respectable" scientific cloak, she alerted many such "young female archaeologist fans" to the training they would need to participate within a changing professional context. Whether such training would ensure *full* professional participation is a matter Morris largely elides in her field autobiographies. Indeed, the experiences of institutional marginality that Morris and Reichard shared suggest that coursework, field training, credentials, and publications still did not ensure women's equitable access to professional rewards.

Reichard's more secure institutional position shaped the audience she targeted in her own field autobiography, which was primarily directed toward readers already inside her discipline. Reichard's rhetorical efforts to inscribe her embodied fieldwork experiences into the textual forms of anthropological knowledge can consequently be seen as offering her colleagues an alternative to discursive practices that minimized, omitted, or rendered invisible the embodied encounters out of which ethnographic knowledge was produced. Though Reichard's book was widely reviewed in scholarly and some popular publications, evidence of its efficacy in revising disciplinary practices is harder to come by. As Anne Freadman argues, no rhetorical performance can thoroughly secure its desired uptake; instead, it exerts ongoing influence only by having its meanings repeatedly taken up and renegotiated.[104] There is little evidence that *Spider Woman* provoked such negotiations during Reichard's lifetime, as mainstream anthropological practice continued to reinforce the knowledge-making practices found in monographs. This absence of uptake can be considered in relation to material limitations that kept writers like Reichard from positions of disciplinary influence, as well as in relation to the myriad ways in which a writer's marginality becomes compounded over time: for instance, through ritual recitals of disciplinary history that fail to consider women's textual innovations, and through traditional historiographic practices that foster the "deeply entrenched habit of standing in one place . . . [and] shaping inquiries with a particular set of interests in mind."[105]

Nevertheless, the embodied, situated ethnographic practice Reichard describes in *Spider Woman* provocatively prefigures the forms of reflexive ethnography developed by anthropologists in the 1980s and 1990s. Crapanzano's landmark 1980 ethnography, *Tuhami: Portrait of a Moroccan,* for instance, narrates Crapanzano's research practice alongside his portrayal of Tuhami; through this narration, Crapanzano generates a form of knowledge that deliberately articulates the limitations of disembodied traditional ethnographies. *Tuhami,* like Reichard's much earlier experimental text, uses narrated, embodied experience to emphasize the profound contingency of anthropological knowledge, which depends upon human relations and embodied encounters between specific individuals. The presence of such arguments in early twentieth-century anthropological texts like *Spider Woman* suggests an alternate history for American anthropology if the inventive rhetorical practices located in field autobiographies and other alternate genres had been permitted to influence professional practice, rather than isolated from the disciplinary mainstream.

Collectively, Morris's and Reichard's rhetorical practices underscore for scholars in rhetoric the power of experimental genres to comment on or to reimagine insider practices. Despite their institutional marginality, these writers promote research practices that make use of rather than deny their own gendered bodies; in doing so, they underscore more recent scholarly insights into the capacity of personal writing to "dramatize the limitations of masculinist practices and assumptions."[106] Morris's and Reichard's strategies of inscription contest the ostensible rationality and gender neutrality of professional discourse, supporting emergent scholarly perspectives that understand academic fields as fundamentally "gender-marked bod[ies] of knowledge, social practice[s], and form[s] of cultural commentary."[107] At the same time, the knowledge-making these writers undertake in their field autobiographies can help scholars to untie professional discourse from some of its values; by *using* that discourse differently, Morris and Reichard open discursive fissures among otherwise tightly associated terms, including neutrality, objectivity, and accurate and rigorous knowledge.

Folklore Collections

Professional Positions and Situated Representations

I cannot tell you how essential it is for me to take beef or some food each time I go to an informant—the moment I don't, I take myself right out of the Dakota side and class myself with outsiders. If I go, bearing a gift, and gladden the hearts of my informants, with food, at which perhaps I arrange to have two or three informants, and eat with them, and call them by the correct social kinship terms, then later I can go back, and ask them all sorts of questions, and get my information, as one would get favors from a relative. It is hard to explain, but it is the only way I can work. To go at it like a white man, for me, an Indian, is to throw up an immediate barrier between myself and the people.

—Ella Cara Deloria, letter to Franz Boas, 1932

I was glad when somebody told me, "You may go and collect Negro folklore." . . . From the earliest rocking of my cradle, I had known about the capers Brer Rabbit is apt to cut and what the Squinch Owl says from the house top. But it was fitting me like a tight chemise. I couldn't see it for wearing it. It was only when I was off in college, away from my native surroundings, that I could see myself like somebody else and stand off and look at my garment. Then I had to have the spy-glass of Anthropology to look through at that.

—Zora Neale Hurston, introduction to *Mules and Men*

THESE REFLECTIONS on folklore from Ella Cara Deloria, the Yankton Nakota writer and anthropologist, and Zora Neale Hurston, the African-American novelist, playwright, and folklorist, highlight the contradictions inherent in the position of being a "native ethnographer," one who studies as an anthropologist the practices of her home community. As Deloria insists in her letter to her mentor, Columbia Professor of Anthropology Franz Boas, her

relation to her informants as an insider—more specifically, as someone embedded within a kinship system that draws all the members of her community into
relation—provides her with ready access to cultural information. But eliciting
that information from informants also requires Deloria to follow kinship practices that Boas expressed impatience with, in letters to Deloria that request
her to conduct her research more quickly and at less expense.[1] These kinship
requirements include investments of time and material resources that Deloria
tries to explain as she describes her research process: by bringing "beef or some
food each time . . . [to] gladden the hearts of [her] informants," and showing
patience by first establishing social relations and only returning "later . . . [to]
ask them all sorts of questions," Deloria ensures that she *remains* a community
insider even as she takes up the role of anthropologist. In these ways Deloria
initiates the relationships that she values both as a community member and as
an ethnographer by carefully positioning herself in the social space of this community. By following protocol for social visits and calling her informants "by
the correct social kinship terms," Deloria establishes a recognizable relationship
with informants as grounds for ethnographic research. To neglect to establish
these relations would be "to go at it like a white man"—something that would
obstruct rather than facilitate Deloria's access to the linguistic, religious, and
cultural information she seeks and that Boas greatly desires as well.[2] Deloria
articulates to her mentor what he seems to have failed to grasp from her previous letters: that being a *native* ethnographer, an insider who brings stores of
prior local knowledge to bear upon her research, generates benefits as well as
demands that shape Deloria's ethnographic practice.

In contrast to the intimacy that Deloria emphasizes, Zora Neale Hurston,
in her innovative folklore collection, *Mules and Men,* reflects on the value of
distance as a technique for generating knowledge. According to Hurston, the
native ethnographer must take up at least to some extent the "spy-glass of anthropology," inserting distance between herself and the practices of her community in order to understand those practices in new and more thoroughly articulated ways. Hurston's passage speaks to the capacity of anthropological study
to authorize—or perhaps reauthorize—a writer's serious investigation into the
stories, tales, legends, and other cultural productions of a specific community.
As Hurston explains, such investigation is not wholly new to her, for she has
been immersed in the practices of African-American folklore "from the earliest
rocking of [her] cradle." Nevertheless, as an anthropologist Hurston adopts a
new stance toward these familiar stories and practices—a stance premised on
distance rather than the familiarity of knowledge that "fitted [her] like a tight

chemise." Taking up the position of the native ethnographer authorized Hurston to "stand off and look" at folklore practices in which she had previously been immersed, thus opening up new avenues for understanding and relating to her own community's practices.

Hurston and Deloria confronted a tension between participation in and observation of community life, as their status as members of the communities they studied complicated the ways each writer participated and observed. Hurston's metaphor of the "spy-glass of anthropology" can be seen as a description of the power of intellectual practices of distancing to authorize and enable scientific forms of knowledge production—forms that were increasingly valued as anthropology emerged as a rigorous social science in the early twentieth century. Indeed, as anthropology professionalized, the opportunities that the new science seemed to open up for systematic cultural study appealed increasingly to members of the collectivities most often studied by white anthropologists in the United States—namely, members of Native American and African American communities. These intellectuals sought to harness the tools and techniques of scientific anthropology, acquiring for themselves the epistemic and rhetorical resources that systematic scientific study seemed to make available. In taking up the field of anthropology and locating themselves as professional researchers within that scientific community, Deloria, Hurston, and other "native ethnographers"[3] sought to gain access to a professional community in which their knowledge as cultural insiders could be transformed into a form of cultural capital more readily exchanged for material and epistemic resources. As they did so, however, both writers generated knowledge through writing practices that resisted the abstraction and decontextualization that underwrote anthropology's claims to epistemic authority.

Securing a professional identity was not easily accomplished by Deloria or Hurston, who found that their identities as Native American and African American intellectuals complicated the practice of ethnography they were called upon to perform as anthropologists. As Deloria reminds Boas, for her to conduct her ethnographic practice *as though* she were white would undermine both her effectiveness as a researcher and her standing within a community that she not only studied but also *belonged to*. Her position as a Dakota woman required her to gather folklore in a manner consistent with her insider status.[4] The necessity of maintaining relationships of reciprocity as she goes about her research confounds the scientific premise that distance and impersonality generate accurate knowledge. Hurston, too, adopts in *Mules and Men* an approach to ethnographic knowledge-making that contradicts the "spy-glass" approach she prizes in her introduction, instead grounding knowledge in the relationships she shares with specific members of the community she studies. As Hurston and Deloria take up the tools and methods of professional anthropology and tune their research practices toward their home communities, these writers also demonstrate that their insider identities complicate the practice of anthropology in fruitful ways.

These negotiations are manifested in the genres that Hurston and Deloria took up in their anthropological work. Within professional communities, genres serve as sites of disciplining, where writers learn to enact sanctioned strategies and confirm community norms.[5] Nevertheless, because individual users enact a range of purposes through the genres they take up, genres often serve as sites of contestation and innovation as well.[6] Consequently, although taking up a genre frequently compels writers to occupy a certain subject position in relation to their audience, positioning them "within the power relations of institutional activity," writers also make rhetorical choices that have the capacity to revise the ways a genre routinely functions.[7] In the case of Hurston and Deloria's anthropological writing, I suggest that by taking up the folklore collection genre *differently*—by writing from an overtly racialized and gendered position, as well as enacting other kinds of disruptions—these writers remake the knowledge that genre enacts. As they make rhetorical use of their complex positions as insider-outsiders, these writers repurpose the actions and arguments typically located in academic folklore collections, revising mainstream ethnographic practices and widespread representations of their home communities.

The practice of folklore collection as a colonial project is deeply implicated in the construction of indigenous and African American communities as static, fixed, and vanishing. Academic folklore collections obscure the asymmetrical power relations upon which the genre is premised. In taking up this genre from the complex position of the native ethnographer, Deloria and Hurston foreground and shift the relations of power the genre typically instantiates between subjects and objects of knowledge, between ethnographers and the communities they study. Deloria and Hurston's enactment of the folklore collection genre accomplishes both professional and public rhetorical aims. Each writer's work in this genre establishes her professional identity as a legitimate researcher, capable of deploying the epistemological tools of anthropology and invested with authority as a trained observer. At the same time, these writers make disruptive use of the genre as well: they foreground relations that folklore collections typically obscure, critique the ostensible objectivity of typical ethnographic work, and represent their home communities as vibrant and persistent. Through their revisions to the folklore collection genre, Deloria and Hurston reposition anthropologists, readers, and members of Dakota and African American communities into shared spaces of exchange, interaction, and mutual responsibility.

Academic Folklore Collections and Colonial Practices

Several factors led both Deloria and Hurston to adopt the folklore collection genre for their intellectual work in the 1930s. The two shared a mentor, Franz Boas, who was not only one of the most famous anthropologists of the early twentieth century but also the most powerful anthropologist to routinely encourage Native American, African American, and white women researchers to participate in anthropological work. His emphasis on the collection of folkloric materials for both cultural and linguistic analysis shaped Deloria and Hurston's early forays into anthropological research. Furthermore, in the early twentieth century, the folklore collection genre itself seemed vital to the political and historical aims of anthropology; charting historical processes of human change through the collection and analysis of folklore was seen as a crucial part of the antiracist project of Boas and many of his students.

Against scientific racism, which reified human difference as inherent and absolute, Boas advocated historical study of the myriad forms of human variation—physical, religious, cultural, and so on—as these differences developed over time. For instance, to counter the pervasive belief at the turn of the twentieth century that immigrants from southern Europe arriving in the United States brought inherent physical inferiorities with them, Boas conducted long-term anthropometric studies that demonstrated the plasticity of physical variation and emphasized the rapidity with which physical characteristics within a community changed in new environments.[8] According to Boas's way of thinking, no variation was predetermined and no apparent difference between groups of people was inherent. The task of historical study, Boas believed, was to investigate the variation that did exist among human communities and to put to rest pervasive beliefs about the inherent superiority or inferiority of specific human groups. Seeking to historicize rather than fetishize difference, Boas asserted in 1887 that "every phenomenon [is] worthy of being studied for its own sake. Its mere existence entitles it to a full share of our attention; and the knowledge of its existence and evolution in space and time fully satisfies the student."[9] This foundational belief motivated Boas' studies of indigenous communities and other groups. As Matti Bunzl argues, "rather than focus on their inherent Otherness (in an act of reification), he sought to understand them as the products of particular historical developments. Ultimately, it was not their difference that made them interesting, but the fact that they contributed to the plenitude of humanity."[10] As part of the broader, four-field discipline of anthropology that Boas advocated, folkloric studies were meant to contribute to the full picture of human variation.

Yet the discursive practices that anthropologists adopted in their efforts to professionalize ultimately worked against antiracist aims. First, any progressive project was undermined by anthropology's embeddedness in colonial logics and epistemologies. Despite the explicit antiracist agenda of Boas, Ruth Benedict, Melville Herskovits, and others, "the discourses of cultural difference that they developed . . . constituted a form of knowledge production that inevitably relegated the Others of the West to the status of objects and often erased or ignored the asymmetrical power relations that enabled this objectification."[11] The scientific discourses anthropologists adopted as they professionalized further enabled such objectification. To professionalize folklore studies along with the broader field of anthropology, Boas and folklorist William Wells Newell worked in the early twentieth century to systematize the collection of folklore material, to train fieldworkers in techniques of phonetic transcription to ensure accurate collection and translation, and to shore up publication standards for the *Journal of American Folk-Lore,* which Boas edited from 1908 to 1924.[12] None of these efforts was innocent of political import; as they worked to make folkloric study more systematically scientific and more rigorously technical and objective, Boas, Newell, and others contributed to the processes of divesting indigenous groups of epistemic authority and replacing it with the authority of professional science. Furthermore, the possibility of not merely studying but actively intervening in the settler–colonialist system that enabled the dissolution of indigenous communities was often foreclosed by anthropologists' scientific priorities and pretensions. As a result, anthropologists in general occupied themselves with the practice of "preserving cultural traditions by textual means without questioning the inevitability of their passing from the living repertoire of the people from whom they were recorded."[13] Pursuing the agenda of professionalized science in folklore studies mitigated against the efforts of some anthropologists to advance activist and antiracist claims.

The colonial entailments of anthropological discourse are activated within folklore studies by two related impulses: the impulse to *collect* in order to preserve phenomena as decontextualized data, and the impulse to mimic the methodologies of physical sciences by *objectifying* the phenomena under investigation. Both of these impulses are epitomized in Otis Mason's 1891 essay, "The Natural

History of Folk-Lore," in which Mason argues analogically from the practices of mineralogists and other physical scientists to prescribe research practices for folklore studies. Mason emphasizes the necessity of systematic collection of folklore material, asserting that "no physicist or mineralogist is more careful than [anthropologist and folklorist] Dr. Dorsey and his colleagues," even as he characterizes folklore as a field of study that does not require contextual information for its interpretation.[14] For instance, Mason posits that folklore material can be collected, moved, and removed from its original context without losing its richness as a source of data for future analysis; a great "advantage" of folklore is that "no bungling or malicious analyst can destroy it by dissolving it into its elements."[15] Furthermore, Mason asserts that "objectivity" in folklore studies can be garnered as readily as in any other science, by recognizing and eliminating what Mason terms "the personal equation," or the tendency of any individual observer of phenomena to observe and interpret in a routinely biased way. This individual bias shapes results predictably, meaning that any scientist's "personal equation" can happily be measured and eliminated: "I see no reason why the modern collector may not . . . carefully study out his own personal equation, and save the reader the trouble by eliminating it himself."[16] Regna Darnell notes that "accurate collection of materials for later study was a greater priority than immediate comparison of inadequate materials" during the early twentieth century;[17] accuracy was ensured through practices that mimicked the practices of other sciences. This approach, advocated by Mason and adopted by scholars including Boas and his many students, treated folkloric material "objectively" by representing it as a mass of texts that could be interpreted and reinterpreted by scholars regardless of the relations between those texts and the contexts and communities where folklore was created and used.

The academic folklore collection genre that resulted from such assumptions enabled colonial practices in several ways. Folklore collections, as I demonstrate in the brief analyses that follow, enact colonial power by *isolating* folklore from its contexts of use, *abstracting* both texts and individuals into generalized types, *preserving* material through an elegiac tone that implies its inevitable disappearance, and *authorizing* anthropologists as experts at the expense of those who produce folkloric material. Each of these practices are repeated routinely in academic folklore collections, cumulatively creating this genre as a site for the enactment of anthropological domination over indigenous and African American cultural productions. These features of the genre enable folklore collections to accomplish the colonizing ends of fixing indigenous communities in time and space, freezing their cultural adaptations into a decontextualized moment of preserved authenticity, and isolating those communities from ongoing processes of economic, social, and cultural exchange and transformation.

Isolation of Folklore from Context

Authors of academic folklore collections persistently isolate folkloric material from the contexts where that material is generated, altered, and used. Isolation of texts from their contexts happens primarily through erasure; almost no information about performance is included in academic folklore collections, neither about the places and times in the life of a community when a story is typically shared, nor about the specific context in which the anthropologist collected folkloric texts. Such omissions minimize the significance of storytelling context, subordinating it to the collected textual artifact, which is portrayed as something *found* that retains its fundamental integrity despite its removal from its original context of circulation. Writers of folklore collections occasionally specify in an introduction the methods by which the anthropologist *secured* or *captured* or *took down* texts included in a publication. Yet the absence of attention to the settings within which members of a community share folkloric material with one another suggests that anthropological contexts are the settings where folklore matters, not the manner in which people actively use storytelling to constitute political communities capable of ongoing action in the world.

The pages of academic folklore collections are typically filled with stories, tales, songs, and myths presented without information about when these stories might be spoken, among whom, and for what uses. In a typical instance, in his 1928 collection, *Bella Bella Texts,* Boas identifies a text simply as "Speech" and reproduces the text both phonetically in its original language and in English translation.[18] In "Speech," an unidentified speaker gives advice to young couples about how to ensure that their married life is harmonious: "I advise you young couples, young men, that you do as I was advised by the priest who married me. He said that I should be ready when morning comes, that I shave kindling wood in the house and that I split kindling wood, else my wife would not be happy. I do this and now my wife cooks my food. If I should not act thus, then I should be married badly. It is well if you do thus, young couples."[19] The speech continues in this mode, recommending specific ways of dividing labor to accommodate household responsibilities. Yet information about the context in which such a speech would be delivered is entirely absent. Was this spoken loudly, ceremoniously, to a hall crowded with people of different ages, each interpreting the advice according to their own relationships? Was it addressed only to a small group of new couples, each personally known to the speaker, so that the particular advice given here reflects the speaker's knowledge of the troubles these specific young couples are likely to encounter with each other? Does this speech represent routinely offered and mostly invariable advice, or was the advice made up on the spot by a specific speaker, whose performance conforms to a general pattern of speech-making but varies in the particular advice offered? Was the speaker's later advice that a woman should have a wash basin ready for her husband when he returns home delivered in an epideictic mode, to affirm widely shared values, or was this specific value subject to debate and disagreement? As a decontextualized artifact of folklore, "Speech" can tell us none of these things.[20] Treating stories, tales, myths, and other texts as objects that retain their meaning apart from their contexts of use allows anthropologists to consider such questions irrelevant to the analysis of folkloric material.

Academic folklore collections further isolate texts by eliminating textual traces of the act of collection as well: that is, the context of exchange between a native informant, an anthropologist, and, often, a bilingual interpreter who mediates between the two. When information about an informant's performance is included, it typically occurs in footnotes, subordinating such information and marking it as separate from the essential text that concerns the anthropologist. In Ruth Benedict's *Tales of the Cochiti Indians,* for instance, Benedict records in a footnote a momentary exchange between the anthropologist-recorder and the Cochiti speaker, who is identified only as Informant 1. The informant describes a conversation between a priest and two messengers in which one man points out a woman, saying about her, "She is punished because she did not like her husband in this world."[21] A footnote here leads to two quotations, unmoored from speakers but presumably not meant to be read as part of the Cochiti tale: "Because she had taken another lover?" "It doesn't say."[22] Such a footnote simultaneously evokes and elides the actual context in which this story is being told, that is, the encounter between Benedict as anthropologist and the unidentified speaker who is telling her this story. As footnote, the exchange—with Benedict seeking more explanation, and her speaker indicating the limitations of what the story can provide—is rendered as marginal rather than integral, even though the anthropologist's desire to elicit tales motivates this exchange.

In other folklore collections, informants' own explanations of or comments on the stories they are sharing are positioned in footnotes, placing such commentary *apart from* the text itself. For instance, John Harrington, discussing a character who travels naked despite the cold, moves into a footnote his informant's explanation: "They used to think it was good to go around that way. Nothing could make those old-time Indians wear clothes."[23] This material, subordinated by Harrington and separated from the rest of the text, reminds the reader that the person speaking is *speaking to an audience,* and more precisely an audience that lacks familiarity with what "they used to think" and do among the Karuk. Such marginal traces of the exchange between anthropologist and speaker—what anthropologist Roger Keesing calls the "elicitation situation"— demonstrate the efforts of anthropologists to reduce or eliminate from their texts the evidence of their intercultural encounters, preferring to represent collected texts as artifacts that are not influenced by such a context of exchange.[24]

Not only do discursive practices of isolation remove texts from their contexts of use, they also actively circumscribe the efforts of informants to enact survival and resistance and to assert political critique through the telling of folklore. The footnoted explanation by Harrington's Karuk informant hints at such uses. In the telling of this story, the Karuk speaker inscribes resistance through his commentary. He uses the folk story to mark a generational difference between him and earlier members of his community, as well as to remind his audience—in this case, a white anthropologist—that "nothing could make those old-time Indians" do something they did not want to do. Other commentaries that are relegated to footnotes often try to teach something about the speaker's culture—to describe customs, physical artifacts and their use, motivations of characters within the story, and so on. When anthropologists demote these explanations from their status as part of a text to a footnote, they suggest that teaching is not a central or permissible use of folkloric material; they reduce the role that folklore is represented as capable of playing in the lives of the communities that generate it. Indeed, explaining older customs, even to indigenous listeners, *could* be a vital function of such storytelling practices. But the textual practices of folklore collections work against recognition of that potential use.

A clear example of how these omissions serve the colonial project of limiting indigenous political possibilities emerges in Pliny Earle Goddard's *Jicarilla Apache Texts*. As in the examples above, Goddard removes to a footnote a full paragraph of spoken material that, he explains, was "addressed to the author and is not part of the myth."[25] But the political critique inscribed in this long footnote that Goddard claims is "not part of the myth" is striking. In the midst of a description of the promises and premonitions of a sacred figure, Naiyenesgani, the speaker explains:

"You shall live right here," he [Naiyenesgani] told them. "If they take you away from this place, to another, where the surroundings are not your own, you will perish."

We are dying off because the Americans have taken us to a place not our own and have forced us to live by means not ours. They have taken us away from the world which our father made for us to live in and we are dying in consequence. Some of the Indians who are intelligent do not like it. We are dying every summer. When we were living in our own country the people did not die as they do now.[26]

The critique of American settler colonialism this speaker voices is both pointed and poignant; the causes of Apache death, both physical and cultural, are named explicitly and repeated for emphasis. That this part of the speaker's performance was "addressed to the author" highlights the agency of this Jicarilla speaker, who uses the occasion of this encounter to confront with pointed critique the white American anthropologist who is "collecting" folklore from him.

Goddard ignores the speaker's overt critique of settler colonialism and Apache relocation and instead reframes the speaker's "addition to the myths of material pertinent to modern conditions" as an expression of religious fatalism. Goddard writes that the Apaches "hold that there is a definite cause for the evils which have come upon the tribe. They have been removed from that portion of the earth where the sacred rivers and mountains, filled with supernatural power for their help, were situated. There is no remedy, for it is a fate foretold long ago. Yolgaiisdzan and her grandson, while powerless are not unsympathetic; they will return to share the fate of extinction."[27] There is no indication in the recorded text that this Jicarilla man spoke with the fatalism that Goddard ascribes to him; in fact, Goddard's reframing *adds* to the speaker's text several elements that are notably absent, such as the resignation that "there is no remedy" for the "evils which have come upon the tribe." Through these discursive practices, Goddard dislocates the political critique his informant embedded in his own text and replaces that critique with a resigned acceptance of conditions wrought by settler colonialism.

Isolating folkloric texts from both contexts of use and contexts of collection serves several ends for anthropologists. Portraying texts as isolated artifacts helps anthropologists represent their practice as scientific. If folkloric material is merely found, like a fossil picked up from a beach, then the messy interpersonal relationships required to elicit folkloric material from living human beings can be set aside as irrelevant. The "personal equation" that Otis Mason warned against can be minimized if only technical proficiency in phonetic transcription is required to collect textual artifacts for later analysis. To call attention to the context of exchange would mitigate the perception of scientific objectivity that folklore collections seek to create. Contextual elements surrounding the elicitation situation—such as the presence of interpreters, the conversations and (perhaps) financial negotiations by which an anthropologist elicits a myth or a tale, the various imperfect technologies for recording speech, and so on—certainly shape the knowledge that ethnographic research produces. Yet erasing this contextual information enables anthropologists to assert their adherence to scientific values of objectivity and disinterested investigation.

Abstraction of Storytellers and Informants

Writers of academic folklore collections often erase the names of the specific individuals who spoke or wrote the folkloric texts comprising their collection, a practice that renders those individuals in abstract terms. Ruth Benedict, for instance, erases the specific identities of the Cochiti people who shared cultural material for *Tales of the Cochiti Indians,* identifying each informant only by a number and such broad characteristics as age, gender, and social position: "Informants 1, 2, 7, and 8 . . . were women, all of them well-known native narrators. Informant 2 held an important ceremonial position. The other informants were men. Informant 3 was a priest of importance."[28] Frank Speck, in *Catawba Texts,* elides the identities of his informants by naming each informant briefly in the introduction and then assigning each a number throughout the rest of the text.[29] Some anthropologists justified these abstractions as protecting informants from censure for sharing community information with outsiders. Elsie Clews Parsons, for instance, argues in her 1926 book, *Tewa Tales,* that prohibitions against sharing information led her to disguise the identities of her informants, remarking that she refers to informants by number "in consideration of the story tellers; story telling is not always a harmless pastime in the Southwest."[30] Yet "consideration of the story tellers" did not prevent Parsons and other anthropologists from actively soliciting information they knew to be sacred or secret. Instead, they deployed discursive practices that masked the identities of the individuals who had served as informants and sometimes—as Parsons did upon the publication of her 1936 book *Taos Pueblo*—worked to keep their publications out of the hands of those members of the community who might discern informants' identities.[31]

Transforming individual speakers into numerical abstractions also heightens the impression that the information gathered from them is scientific and generalizable. By dissociating speakers' identities from folkloric material, anthropologists characterized stories as typical, even archetypal, rather than as the idiosyncratic performances of specific individuals. Benedict guides readers toward this interpretation explicitly in her introduction to *Tales of the Cochiti,* explaining that although the texts have been collected from eight different informants by two different recorders (herself and Boas), nevertheless "they give the literary style to which all the stories in Cochiti conform."[32] Removing identifying information about speakers allows Benedict to emphasize the typicality of their tales. Such practices of abstraction suggest that folkloric material, like other scientific data collected by trained researchers, can be used as a basis for generalizations, removed from association with specific identities, idiosyncrasies, and purposes.

Furthermore, the practice of abstraction in folklore collections also constrains indigenous ownership over the materials anthropologists collected, published, and inserted into systems of academic value to garner material and social capital for themselves. That is, presenting informants as abstract numerals eliminates those individuals' claims to authorship and therefore ownership over these stories and tales. This purpose is evident, for instance, in John Swanton's *Myths and Tales of the Southeastern Indians,* where Swanton characterizes texts as "collected by the writer," some as "secured by W. O. Tuggle" and "preserved" at the Bureau of American Ethnology, others as "obtained from a few speakers of the Hitchiti language in the northern part of Seminole County, Okla., part of them having been recorded directly, while part were written down in the original by an Indian," all having been "taken down at various places and from various persons."[33] Swanton's verbs throughout the introduction position the texts themselves as subjects, far more important than the identities of those from whom they are "secured," "recorded," and "taken down." Such linguistic practices divest speakers of their own connections with these tales, instead portraying each story as an artifact, readily circulated within scientific networks once it has been "secured" by an anthropologist, while the uses made of these tales by the people who shared them are laid aside.

Authorization of Anthropologists

Indigenous ownership of folkloric material is further contested through a set of practices that writers of folklore collections use to inscribe their authority as anthropologists over the material they "secure" from informants. Many of these practices are seemingly minor yet widely practiced within folklore collections, making their cumulative effects quite significant. For instance, writers of folklore collections repeatedly use intertextual citations of other anthropologists to generate confirmation of or contrast with a specific collected text. The intertextual footnotes in Benedict's *Tales of the Cochiti* are typical, directing readers to "See Goldfrank, Esther Schiff, The Social and Ceremonial Organization of Cochiti, Mem. Amer. Anthrop. Assn., No. 33, p. 71, where this is spoken of as a shrine where one asked for success in courtship."[34] Similar intertextual citations in Frank Speck's *Catawba Texts* confirm the historical provenance of an informant's tale by asserting "a similar tale is found recorded in 1737 among the Indians of North Carolina, by John Brickell (The Natural History of North Carolina. Dublin, 1737, p. 371)."[35] The majority of footnotes in collections by Parsons, Goddard, Boas, and many others take similar form; the effect of these citation practices is to distribute authority among anthropologists, confirming their discipline's status as the ultimate arbiters of folkloric material.

Other textual practices further reinforce the sense that folkloric material is arbitrated—and authorized—by anthropologists, rather than the communities from which it is collected. For instance, the practice of assigning Latin botanical names to flora and fauna referred to by speakers in indigenous languages asserts the primacy of Western knowledge-making practices over those of Native communities. Frank Speck, for example, translates a Catawba phrase as "terrapin-with-the-big-head," then follows this translation with the English common name "the snapping turtle" and a footnoted Latin name, "Chelydra serpentina."[36] This common practice in folklore collections positions Native knowledge within the frame of Western epistemic authority. Likewise, when anthropologists rearrange the narrative sequence of a tale, as when Speck notes that "This section does not belong in the story but is a part of" a different text,[37] they assert their authority over the texts produced by indigenous people. In other instances, anthropologists explicitly call into question the accuracy of the knowledge their informants are sharing. Benedict, for example, questions the narrator of a text titled "The Deer and the Lost Child" in a footnote that asserts, "There is a gap here. According to parallel tales there should be an incident telling how he recognizes his son who gives him a signal."[38] The relation between anthropologist and informant that such textual practices construct is one in which anthropologists are authorized to judge the validity, accuracy, and value of folkloric material while informants are portrayed merely as vessels that vary in quality as conveyors of information.

Practices that undermine the authority and ownership of indigenous people pervade academic folklore collections, only occasionally expressing overtly the racist attitude they imply. One such overt example emerges in Frank Speck's treatment of the Catawba informants who produce the texts he publishes in *Catawba Texts*. Speck laments that one informant, Mrs. Margaret Wiley Brown, would have had "a far deeper memory heritage of native institutions had she been a woman of better mentality." He reflects that although anthropologists some-times find themselves "recording information... [from] individuals endowed with qualities really intellectual, so far as unsophisticated groups can nurture such qualities, and still more often with those who are extremely intelligent," nevertheless, "truth compels me to confess that Margaret Brown fell into neither of these categories. This condition had its effect upon the text narratives record-ed from her." The "condition" that limits Margaret Brown's ability to produce complete tales of Catawba folklore for his dictation means for Speck her inher-ent lack of intelligence—not her isolation from a sustaining community, the disruptions of which Speck merely glosses in the previous pages, not her identity as one of "the one hundred remaining members of the tribe now living on and around the reservation." The anthropologist's authority is doubly asserted here, as Speck bemoans the limited intelligence of his informants and its influence upon their productions, yet also asserts that nevertheless, "the characteristics of staccato style and poorly united expression, so apparent in the narratives, are typical of Catawba thought complexes covering a period of at least fifty years. I reach this conclusion after an examination of the linguistic material recorded by Dr. Gatschet in the 80's, from the standard of which my material seems not to have deviated to any considerable extent." Speck simultaneously determines that his informant is a woman "of unusually low intelligence"[39] and yet remains authorized by his anthropological training and earlier anthropologists' work to assert that the folklore collected from this informant is still typical of the Ca-tawba community at large. Such assertions are enabled by discursive practices, widespread in folklore collections, that repeatedly position anthropologists as authoritative producers of knowledge while divesting indigenous communities of ownership over the knowledge their stories are used to generate.

Preservation of "Vanishing" Communities

Writers of folklore collections—like much anthropological work from this period in general—generate a sense of urgency about their knowledge-making projects by portraying indigenous communities as teetering on the brink of extinction. The representation of indigenous communities as declining, disin-tegrating, or losing their cultural uniqueness is a widely shared topos throughout this genre. For example, Boas writes in *Bella Bella Texts* that by 1923 when he collected the bulk of the material in the volume, "the whole culture of the Bella Bella has practically disappeared and information can be obtained only by questioning. It was remarkably difficult to obtain any kind of connected texts."[40] Similarly, Frank Speck writes that by 1910, "the last of the Catawba men of the old regime . . . had died, and the remaining members of the tribe who were still conversant with the language were not rhetorically fluent in their native idiom."[41] Speck uses this characterization of Catawba decline to generate urgency for his own research, asserting that when he began his study, "by the turn of fate, the language had neared the precipice of oblivion which it has now practically reached." Speck portrays his text-collecting activity as an act of heroic salvage, rescuing what he calls a "last feeble voice from the grave of a defunct native culture" from its "precipice of oblivion," which gives him "a certain after-sense of satisfaction" for "having had the opportunity to preserve [these texts] for future students of human achievement in its simpler phases."[42] Not only is the persistence and survival of Native communities ignored, but furthermore, language decline is portrayed with intensely romantic overtones as a problem that motivates anthropological *collecting*—rather than a disruption enabled by colonialism that could prompt activities other than collecting to forestall linguistic losses.

Anthropologists' repeated use of the vanishing topos in folklore collections has several implications. For instance, this topos constructs indigenous communities primarily as *anthropological material* rather than as sovereign communities with inherent rights to linguistic, cultural, religious, and economic self-determination and survival. Speck demonstrates this tendency when he historicizes the Catawba people exclusively in terms of anthropological research. He explains that this group has "been a center of interest for American linguists and ethnologists for almost a century," and points his readers to work by Albert Gallatin in 1836, Albert Gatschet in 1881, A. F. Chamberlain in 1886, J. O. Dorsey in 1891, and J. R. Swanton in 1900.[43] The focus on preservation also significantly circumscribes the agency and ongoing survival of the contemporary indigenous communities that anthropologists repeatedly construct in the past tense. John Swanton, for instance, in *Southeastern Indians,* writes that "the native attitude toward these [collected myths and stories] was, of course, various, some no doubt having been originally sacred legends embodying actual beliefs, while others were told for amusement. Only in the Natchez series have I any absolute clew [*sic*] as to which were considered sacred and the reverse."[44] Swanton's use of past-tense terms—that stories *were* told for certain purposes and *were* considered sacred or not—suggests that, whatever the stories were once used for, they no longer retain any such use, nor function as active components of the life of a community.

These discursive practices of abstraction, isolation, authorization, and preservation have spatial and temporal dimensions. For instance, when anthropologists portray indigenous communities as vanishing, they foretell the absence of indigenous people from the future spaces of the United States; at the same time, such portrayals also work to enact that absence by shaping the material and social world in ways that justify ongoing formations of colonial power. Likewise, dislocating folkloric material from the social and material spaces where it is generated and used enables anthropologists to *reposition* that material as isolated, decontextualized data; instead of being rooted by its use within a specific social and material space, this data becomes available for anthropologists to circulate within their own institutional systems, garnering professional status and rewards while denying such benefits to indigenous producers of "data."

Some of these spatial and temporal dimensions of academic folklore collections can be captured through the concept of the chronotope. Bakhtin identifies chronotopes as normative orientations toward space and time, orientations that are generated by and maintained within genres. These value-laden orientations are often masked, even as they constrain the capacity of readers and writers to question the attitudes toward space, time, and human agency that a genre enacts.[45] As Schryer explains, "every genre expresses space/time relations that reflect current social beliefs regarding the placement and actions of human individuals in space and time" and that allocate agency differentially among individuals.[46] In folklore collections, discursive practices of isolation and abstraction persistently orient readers toward Native communities as objectified material for scientific analysis, while related practices authorize anthropologists as makers of knowledge, positioned powerfully to scrutinize, arbitrate, and survey the spaces of indigenous life. Such a normative orientation toward indigenous communities as *objects* and anthropologists as *subjects* of knowledge also allows anthropologists to dislocate their own practices from the systems of colonial domination that enabled them; as makers of *science,* anthropologists can claim to occupy a stance that is distant from rather than embedded in systems of social, political, and ethical relations. Ultimately, such discursive practices collectively construct Native individuals and communities as existing in the past, in temporal and spatial isolation, while constructing anthropologists as objective, ideally positioned observers of Native life.

Professional Positions of Native Ethnographers

In taking up the folklore collection genre, Hurston and Deloria encountered a site where anthropological discourse tended to authorize white anthropologists as owners of folkloric material, to isolate folkloric material from its contexts of use in ways that circumscribed its political potential, and to portray indigenous and African American communities as in need of "anthropological salvage" to combat their inevitable loss of authenticity and vitality.[47] They confronted in this genre orientations toward space and time that positioned indigenous and African American communities in a pre-modern past and anthropologists in the present, in positions of power and authority. What resources and opportunities, then, did this genre offer to Deloria and Hurston to prompt them to take up a genre so frequently used to circumscribe the agency of their home communities?

One significant resource this genre offered to Deloria and Hurston is its capacity to secure a writer's identity as a member of the profession of anthropology. In many ways, the professionalization of anthropology opened up this field of scientific study to writers like Deloria and Hurston. In the 1920s and 1930s, "real logistical limitations that accompanied new fieldwork methodologies" as well as the "increased need for native language proficiency and the increasing resistance of native informants to outsiders" created conditions of possibility for the participation of native ethnographers in anthropology.[48] When Deloria and Hurston began working formally with Boas in 1927, the heightened demand for linguistic expertise and intensive, long-term field study placed a greater value on the language skills of community insiders, while the increased emphasis on professional training and university credentials seemed to provide clear mechanisms for initiating those community insiders into the *anthropological* community as well. If they were trained as researchers rather than cast as informants, the intimate, insider status of native ethnographers like Hurston and Deloria seemed to offer enormous opportunities for the advancement of professional anthropology.

Yet at the same time, the epistemic authority of native ethnographers was circumscribed by the emergence of the Malinowskian ethnographic mode, which depended upon the distinction between an "ethnographic Self" and a "native Other" that were "constructed as irreducibly distinct through the very epistemological clarity afforded the anthropologist in the ethnographic encounter."[49] The "native ethnographer" is an impossibility in Malinowski's version of fieldwork: "if natives obeyed the tribal code without comprehending it [as Malinowski argued], they were inherently excluded from the subject position of ethnographer," lacking recourse to the "foundational difference" that produced ethnographic insight.[50] Thus, Deloria and Hurston had to contend with ideological and institutional structures that sought to position their work as what Kirin Narayan refers to as "virtual anthropology": a marginalized form of knowledge, never as fully authorized or reliable as that of a white Euro-American observer.

These tensions made securing a professional identity an uneasy accomplishment for both writers. For instance, Deloria's earliest affiliations with Franz Boas positioned her not as a student who might pursue graduate study in anthropology, but as an informant. While Deloria was briefly enrolled at Columbia's Teacher's College in 1916, she assisted Boas in a series of lessons on Dakota language in his graduate course in linguistic anthropology, earning eighteen dollars a month for her assistance.[51] Boas provided her with some cursory training in phonetics and linguistic analysis at that time, but apparently did not encourage her to pursue an anthropological degree, neither in 1916 nor when their professional relationship resumed more than a decade later in 1927, when Boas wrote to Deloria proposing to work together for a couple of weeks "to get some good material on Dakota" as he passed through Kansas on his way west.[52] At that time, Deloria was working at the Haskell Institute in Kansas as a physical education and drama teacher, but was seeking a profession that would make fuller use of her talents and provide higher and more reliable pay.

Deloria's background as the college-educated daughter of a prominent Dakota minister led Boas to believe she might become a valuable collaborator, but he treated Deloria as a paid field researcher rather than an independent professional. That Boas failed to relate to Deloria as a colleague is especially evident at the onset of their long-term collaboration in 1927, when Boas tended to direct Deloria's linguistic work very closely and to offer minimal payment for the completion of discrete tasks. For instance, Boas agreed to pay Deloria fifty dollars for a month of work if she would write out Dakota linguistic material with interlinear translations and correct the text of a manuscript describing the Sun Dance.[53] Certainly other anthropologists who Boas officially trained did not face the same degree of oversight that characterized his working relationship with Deloria in the 1920s. Graduate students undertaking field research under Boas's direction were typically allocated several hundred dollars for a season, to spend according to their discretion, and the ethnographic or linguistic material that resulted from such research was understood as the intellectual property of the researcher, to shape into publications as he or she saw fit. In contrast, Deloria's arrangement with Boas included a higher level of scrutiny over Deloria's expenses and a sense that Deloria's work would provide *Boas* with material.

Deloria challenged this scrutiny repeatedly during her long affiliation with Boas, attempting to regain control over her own knowledge production in ways that prefigured her efforts to reshape these relationships in her published folklore collection, *Dakota Texts*. For instance, although Boas admonishes Deloria that she must become more prompt about sending in her material to him, she tries to explain that she wants to keep her materials together so she might *work on* them rather than merely collect and submit them.[54] She attempts to change Boas's perception of her as merely a collector by insisting on her status as a researcher. When she sends in four hundred pages of ethnological material in 1934, she challenges the practice he has insisted on and instead describes a process much more similar to that used by other anthropologists: keeping her own material to work up, rather than sending it bit-by-bit to someone else to use. She explains, "I know I have been remiss in sending my data, but it seemed clearer in my mind if I wrote my material up as I went, and I felt as though I wanted to retain most of it, for reference, from place to place." She also attempts to reframe her work as *ethnographic observation,* not merely collection of texts, noting that her material is sometimes slow to arrive because "there is so much to watch, in the way people behave . . . all of which I shall include in my next papers."[55] Being positioned as a collector or a linguistic consultant diminished Deloria's opportunities to turn her research into publications, a crucial form of intellectual currency, and consequently compounded her professional marginality.

Deloria's rhetorical efforts to regain control over her material circumstances and research practices in her correspondence with Boas likewise anticipate her work in *Dakota Texts* to establish community-based ownership over "anthropological" material. Deloria repeatedly attempted to counterbalance the inequities that limited her funds for field research and constrained her ability to conduct research under her own direction. She chafed at the slowness of payment arrangements that required her to submit material by mail to Boas and then wait for a check from Columbia to arrive; this was not only a source of worry for her personally, but she tried to impress upon Boas the inefficiency of this arrangement, explaining that it left them "both at a decided disadvantage," for while he waited each month to receive her material before sending her a check, she was "always held up the first ten days at least of every month, because I cannot get anywhere and get any material or find an informant without money to do it with."[56]

Even several years into her collaboration with Boas, she still struggled to enact equitable financial relations. For instance, both Ruth Benedict and Deloria wrote to Boas regarding a disagreement the two had, in Boas's absence, over Deloria's payment for field research. Benedict complained that Deloria forced her "to pay her when she had as yet done no work for me" and remarks revealingly that "such are the difficulties of working with Indians." In her own letter to Boas, Deloria reports that Benedict "told me that she and anyone else who went in the field did it at their own expense, and made me feel uncomfortable. I think if she and Gladys and others do go out on their own, it is because they wish to . . . I know Dr. Klineberg had a salary and travel fund, because I was with him."[57] In this way, Deloria insists upon her status as a professional—a trained expert who expects payment for her work. Deloria's correspondence with Boas repeatedly demonstrates her insistence on equitable compensation and Boas's apparent inability to accomplish or understand that need. As Deloria negotiates and renegotiates payment for her work as a translator, collector, editor, and ethnographic fieldworker over the course of her career, these negotiations concern not only financial relations—which were centrally important to Deloria, who lacked a secure institutional position—but also relations of authority and ownership over Deloria's intellectual productions.

Although their relations to professional anthropology differed, Zora Neale Hurston faced a similar set of struggles in her efforts to achieve full professional status.[58] Hurston also studied briefly with Boas at Columbia, though her connections with the broader artistic community that comprised the Harlem Renaissance mitigated her commitment to anthropology as a career. Hurston's complex relationship with anthropology as an academic discipline underscores her desire to use the tools of anthropology—the field's discursive practices, research methods, and epistemic resources—for her own widely varying intellectual and social ends. When Hurston arrived in New York City in 1925 at age thirty-four, she made an immediate splash, publishing in important periodicals and becoming connected to prominent male figures in the Harlem Renaissance, including Alain Locke and Langston Hughes, who was a close friend and collaborator of Hurston's for several years.[59] Despite Hurston's wide-ranging artistic ambitions, she invested significant time and energy in folklore research; her fiction has earned her designation as the "founding mother" of an African-American women's literary tradition, yet "folklore was the passion of her life and informs all of her work."[60] Hurston published collections of black music for the Library of Congress, won a Guggenheim to study folklore in the West Indies from 1936 to 1938, and was a member of the American Folklore Society, the American Anthropological Association, the American Ethnological Society, the New York Academy of Sciences, and the American Association for the Advancement of Science.

Despite these engagements with the professional apparatus of anthropology, Hurston's financial difficulties, like Deloria's, were ongoing. She, too, never attained a long-term, stable professional position, and financial insecurity significantly shaped her working life, prompting her to take on remunerative work that did not always offer intellectual satisfaction and generating instability that made it difficult for her to carry out the work that mattered most to her. Hurston's letters to her many correspondents demonstrate the extent to which her insecure financial position was an enormous source of anxiety; financial difficulties prompted Hurston to enter into financial arrangements that limited her ownership over her own materials and positioned her at times as a subordinate fieldworker rather than a researcher in her own right. Most notably, Hurston's arrangement with her patron, Charlotte Osgood Mason, impeded her research training. According to the contract Hurston signed with Mason in late 1927, Hurston was paid two hundred dollars per month for her folklore collecting throughout the South from 1928 to 1930, and a slightly lower stipend for intermittent research until 1932, but the material was stipulated as belonging to Mason, not Hurston. While Mason funded Hurston's fieldwork over the next five years, she insisted that the material Hurston collected be considered Mason's exclusive property and prohibited Hurston from identifying Mason to anyone, including to her faculty at Columbia.

The repercussions of this arrangement for Hurston's academic progress were significant. As part of her graduate training, Boas had arranged for Hurston to work with Otto Klineberg on psychological studies in New Orleans in 1929, only to receive scant and cryptic correspondence from Hurston from the field; eventually Hurston admitted to Boas that she was being employed by a patron who would not permit her to enter into other arrangements, despite Hurston's efforts to follow the plan of research with Klineberg that she and Boas had initially agreed upon. In response to Boas's insistence that Hurston should try to cause her patron to see that completing research toward her degree would be exceedingly advantageous, Hurston explained that her patron was "cold towards the degrees. . . . I have broached the subject from several angles but it got chill blains no matter how I put it."[61] Despite Boas's encouragement and Hurston's promise and energy as a researcher, she ultimately did not complete her PhD.[62]

Deloria and Hurston both sought the resources—rhetorical, epistemological, and material—that the discipline of anthropology seemed to make available for the study of human communities. But the identity of the professional researcher was only partially secured by these two women of color, and then only through their complex rhetorical negotiations, in their publications as well as in their correspondence. Deloria and Hurston's ethnographic writing, especially the collections of folklore both writers published in the 1930s, revises the social actions embedded in typical folklore collections, suggesting that in taking up the folklore collection genre, these two writers revealed contradictions inherent in the premises and practices of professional anthropology. In what follows I argue that Deloria and Hurston's folklore collections simultaneously assert their identity as professionals *and* subvert the ostensible authority of the white, "objective," outsider anthropologist who typically created knowledge of their home communities. Both Deloria and Hurston accessed the epistemological resources of scientific anthropology, while their positioning as native ethnographers disrupted the relations between anthropologists and insiders upon which anthropological knowledge was grounded.

They accomplished this disruption in part through simply being community insiders and writing ethnographically, consequently blurring distinctions between subjects and objects of anthropological knowledge. Although genres make available certain subject positions to those who use them, a genre's "façade of normalcy" can become "cracked by resistance, inappropriate deployment, unfamiliarity, or critical analysis."[63] By taking up the genre of the folklore collection and speaking simultaneously as anthropological insiders and as insiders within the communities they study, Deloria and Hurston disrupt the relations of power that traditionally governed the creation of ethnographic knowledge. In the field autobiographies I examined in chapter 2, writers inserted their gendered identities into accounts of research practices in ways that countered beliefs about those practices as gender-neutral and objective; similarly, Deloria and Hurston inscribe their insider identities in ways that reframe practices of collection, counter static representations of their home communities, and reconfigure the relations of power, authority, and expertise that typify the folklore collection genre. The complex positioning of these two writers shifted the function of the genre they adopted. Publishing folklore collections supported their efforts to secure a professional identity for themselves, but their insider-outsider positioning also rendered their use of this genre subversive, specifically by foregrounding relationships between ethnographers and the communities they study and by performing and recontextualizing knowledge of their home communities.

Contextualizing Knowledge in *Dakota Texts*

Deloria recognized that her status as a cultural insider was simultaneously an advantage and a drawback in her profession. She often emphasized her language ability as giving her access to cultural information that would be difficult for nonnative ethnographers to obtain, explaining in a letter to Hugh Burleson that she was "very thoroughly convinced that you can not really get at the heart of a people without knowing their language. I think my knowledge of Dakota is a big asset there."[64] She stated frankly to Boas that she was skeptical of the value of research conducted by outsiders with little or no knowledge of Dakota languages, writing that she did "not see how non-Dakota speaking workers get along as well as they do."[65] In these exchanges, Deloria argues that her insider status enables her research to be *more* scientific: more reliable, valid, and accurate, as well as more precisely attentive to linguistic variations among Dakota, Lakota, and Nakota dialects. Yet she also acknowledged that her identity as a Dakota insider constrained her fieldwork practice and shaped how both informants and other anthropologists viewed her work. Although she "drew on stories told to her by her grandfather as a guide for questioning informants about tribal myths, history, and practices,"[66] for instance, Deloria also expressed concern that her insider status could lead her to exploit her informants unfairly. Because she worried that her social kinship relations with her informants might make them feel obligated to share information with her that they would rather not see printed, she was careful not to ask her informants about information that she knew they would prefer to keep secret.

Deloria's correspondence with Boas makes clear her investment in accessing the resources available to rigorous, trained scientists during this period. However, in her published folklore collection, *Dakota Texts,* Deloria counters the practices of isolation, abstraction, preservation, and authorization that typify this academic genre. Using strategies that contextualize Dakota folklore and characterize its ongoing use among Dakota people, Deloria enacts rhetorical purposes that exceed the genre's boundaries.

Against the tendency of folklore collections to isolate folklore from context, *Dakota Texts* foregrounds rather than effaces the relations between ethnographers and informants that enable anthropological knowledge production. Deloria especially draws attention to the storytelling *performance,* a performance for which both the storyteller and Deloria, as listener and recorder, must be present. She notes, for example, that "every so often a narrator, in inserting a sentence of an explanatory nature, will let her voice down perceptibly. I have made such sentences parenthetical, for so they seemed to me in the telling." Deloria also translates meanings both denoted and implied by a speaker's commentary, remarking, for instance, that one speaker's expletive "*sika*" means "pitiful one," and is spoken as "something of an aside, by the person telling the story, to stir pity in the hearers for a character in the tale."[67] Deloria here does not only translate the meaning of the term, but comments on the *use* of this term within the context of a storytelling performance, in which the storyteller aims "to stir pity in the hearers." In contrast to the typical practice in folklore collections in which the anthropologist simply erases or moves to a footnote any spoken material that appears explanatory, here Deloria inscribes those explanations *within* the recorded texts. Though she renders these explanations as parentheticals, marking them as distinct from the story proper, she also highlights their function within a specific performance, rather than removing them as traces of the context of collection that the anthropologist would prefer to obscure.

In other ways as well, Deloria draws attention to the telling of folklore as a performative event that occurs in a specific place and time. Deloria includes footnotes that frequently describe some aspect of the speaker's performance that would otherwise be erased. For instance, she notes that "generally Ikto is quoted, in a voice curiously nasal and twangy, and with a disdain for enclitics and particles." She records not only routine characteristics of the performance of folklore, but also specific embodied actions performed by her particular informants, as when she explains in a footnote that "the informant took a handful of sand in his right hand and threw it over his left shoulder; and then some in his left, and threw it over his right shoulder, as he said, 'in this manner.'" Perhaps most importantly, Deloria records information about the way an audience *responds* to the storyteller's performance, noting that "during the telling of a story there are little asides or comments made constantly by the story-teller and hearers, concerning the folly and stupidity of the [characters in the story] who believed in him."[68] As she repeatedly calls her readers' attention to these performative aspects of folklore, she counters portrayals of folklore as isolated, decontextualized objects. Acknowledging that storytellers and their hearers comment "constantly" on the text being performed, Deloria reminds readers not only of the anthropologist's "context of elicitation" but also of the presence of a *non*anthropological audience, an audience that engages with rather than merely records the speaker's performance. Consequently, Deloria resists the implication that folklore exists *for the purpose* of anthropological collection and analysis.

Deloria further highlights the use of folklore within the Dakota community through her frequent reference to the contextual cues that the intended hearers of these stories would certainly catch, thus encouraging her readers to view folklore as cultural material typically circulated within rather than outside the community that produces it. She explains to her readers clues about the trickster figure Ikto, for instance, that most Dakota hearers would not need, as in her footnote clarifying that "there is normally a strict avoidance between a son- or daughter-in-law and the mothers- and fathers-in-law, and a trifle stricter where opposite sexes are involved. But it isn't surprising to find Ikto attempting to break it. He is immoral always." Elsewhere, Deloria interprets the significance of a moment when norms of social kinship are breached, explaining to her readers that "this sentence is enough to tell us the outcome of the brothers' encounter with this person. She enters and accepts food without any word. She doesn't relate herself to them, and she takes their food without acknowledgement." In contrast, another character's behavior in a different story prompts Deloria to explain that "the woman's reply tells us at the very outset that here is introduced a character that will be good."[69] On this and many other occasions, Deloria explains for her readers the significance of cultural norms they might otherwise miss, norms that the speaker encodes implicitly rather than identifying overtly because the speaker addresses an audience that *shares* these norms. Such explanations draw attention to the typical context of folkloric performance, in which an audience shares sufficient cultural knowledge that cues carry immediate and obvious import. As Deloria supplies the cues for her own audience, she alters *where* meaning resides in folklore, locating meaning in the context of folkloric performance.

Furthermore, Deloria's explanatory asides also remind her readers that *she* occupies a position as an insider in the community that produces and shares this folklore. Because the speakers whose stories she records are speaking to Deloria herself, and because they recognize her as a member of their community, they refrain from explaining cultural clues that an insider would not require. As Deloria provides those clues to her own readers, she indicates the different relations that inhere between herself and her readers as audiences for folkloric performance—and encourages her readers to view these differences as factors that powerfully shape that performance. This contrasts significantly with Mason's proposal that folkloric material, like objects of natural history, can be picked up by anyone, interpreted readily, and understood easily apart from its context.

Deloria's emphasis on the specific practices of certain storytellers in their performative context supports the work she does in *Dakota Texts* to counteract generalizations as well. She accomplishes this in part through detailed attention to linguistic differences that mark the distinct dialects of Teton, Yankton, and Santee groups, as when she notes that the term *winu'hcala,* used by a character in a folk story, is "the current Santee word for a woman of maturity; Teton and Yankton use it as a direct term of address to one's wife." In addition to registering differences in usage that distinguish dialects, she also grounds her study in specific places and contexts by noting less formal linguistic variations as well. For instance, she remarks that the expression "*mak'i'li,* I am quite the clever fellow," is "distinctly colloquial, heard, so far as I know, only among the Standing Rock people." Elsewhere, discussing a Teton term that means "it is said" in contrast to a Yankton term that translates as "they say that," Deloria remarks that this variation in usage is not only related to dialect but reflective of cultural differences between the Yankton and Teton groups, as she explains that "the Yankton consider the word *sk'e,* too indefinite; they consider it a gossip-help, useful because the authority for the gossip is vague to the point of lacking entirely." Her focus on the specific context of a speaker's performance helps her guard against excessive generalizing; for instance, she remarks that a term used in a certain folk tale is especially uncommon, noting about the expletive *husti* that "I have only heard it perhaps twice. . . . I believe the *h* was omitted once when I heard an old man named Little Bear use the word."[70] Through such rhetorical practices, Deloria draws attention to distinctions between Dakota groups and repeatedly reminds her readers that these texts were performed in a specific time, place, and cultural context, grounding her study in their specificity.

Deloria's practice of including—and naming—specific speakers whose language or storytelling practices differ from others' overtly counteracts the practice of anthropologists like Speck. For instance, though one speaker's performance of an Ikto story represents Ikto as using "raccoon fat to grease his arrows," Deloria notes, "However, Standing Bear of the Standing Rock Reservation said arrows did not need greasing." She identifies her own father as a resource who contradicts at points the information she has gathered elsewhere; she notes, for example, that although the verb *ksa'pa* is "a neutral verb in Teton," she has "heard my father, a Yankton . . . making an active verb out of it." Similarly, Deloria identifies other informants by name who have taught her something she did not already know as an insider: "Mrs. Frank Fiske, of Fort Yates, N.D., who has a Dakota grandmother, pointed out to me that when a Dakota woman tells you the road somewhere, she doesn't say, 'Go until you come to the third road branching off to the left;' rather, she will say, 'You will go on for a while, and soon there will be a road branching off to the left; but that's not it. Farther on, there will be another; but that's not it. Soon after, there will be a third; and that's it!' I tested it out and found she was right in every instance in which I questioned an old-time Dakota who had never learned English."[71] This practice in *Dakota Texts* inscribes specific linguistic and cultural variations into the folklore collection and ties those variations to specific identities, counteracting other folklorists' tendencies to generalize about an entire community based on the performances of very few speakers.

Deloria also counters the impulse typical of the genre to authorize anthropologists as knowledge producers while divesting indigenous communities of their ownership over their own cultural productions. She does this in part through repeatedly referring to herself as a member of the Dakota communities she studies, thus positioning herself as an authority *because* of her insider status as a Dakota person, embedded in—rather than outside of—the kinship relations that structure this community. As Janet Finn argues, when Deloria speaks simultaneously as an anthropologist and a Dakota person, she "give[s] voice to [her] embodied contradictions and transform[s] them into resources for cultural engagement and understanding."[72] Deloria explains in her introduction, for instance, the different categories of story circulated among the Dakota: "To our minds, [the stories in one category] are a sort of hang-over, so to speak, from a very, very remote past," while others "are accepted as having happened to our people in comparatively recent times, perhaps in the lifetime of the aged narrator's grandfather or great-grandfather." Deloria emphasizes her participation in this community by referring to the stories as emerging from "our people" and having significance "to our minds." Her ongoing presence within this community solidifies her authority, as when she notes, for instance, "When I used to play with my little friends from the camp, on the reservation, if we strayed near the woods, someone was always sure to warn us that the Double-face might get us. Nobody knew what that was, but we were all afraid of it." Moreover, this insider authority allows her to describe the way these stories are *used* within the community that owns them, as when she notes that within her community, "constant allusion is made to [this category of story]; similes are drawn from them which every intelligent adult is sure to understand."[73] In contrast to the suggestion, both implicit in many folklore collections and explicit in Speck's remark that folklore is the "feeble voice . . . of a defunct native culture,"[74] Deloria speaks from her authority as an insider to confirm the ongoing importance of folklore as a resource for cultural and linguistic invention within her community.

Situating her authority as something that emerges from her insider status,

Deloria prioritizes the insights gained through her community affiliations over the knowledge-making techniques learned through anthropological study. She footnotes discussions of Dakota expressions that cannot be readily translated into English, explaining that a particular phrase "is a figure of speech in Dakota and graphically expresses a nervous state wherein a person looks about quickly, as a puppet might, if the strings were worked fast. It is difficult to render the exact picture by any English phrase." Such instances could be seen as merely offering disclaimers typical of translation, yet because Deloria registers her own understanding of these complexities of meaning, she also outlines the limitations of what an outsider could know. Through disclaimers, such as her explanation that "this is an idiomatic expression and conveys very vividly in Dakota that one is making a great big fool of oneself. The translation here given is literal, and lacks the force of the Dakota," Deloria prioritizes the diffuse cultural knowledge that a linguistic and cultural insider like herself enjoys, while marking the inadequacies of the approximations rendered by less fluent speakers.[75] Pointing out the limitations of understanding when a whole cultural context is not provided, Deloria challenges implicitly the very basis of the kind of folklore collecting Boas and others often did.

This purpose is also reinforced when Deloria corrects mistranslations that have gained currency in other scholarly works. She writes, for instance, that the term *woha,* which is part of the term *wic'a'woha,* meaning to be a son-in-law, "has been translated as meaning 'hidden' (from *wo'ha,* a cache) with the idea that a son-in-law must keep out of the way, because of avoidance rules. But that is not correct. The word for daughter-in-law . . . throws light on the problem."[76] Deloria then describes several contexts in which the phrase in question is typically used, in order to demonstrate that *attraction* rather than *hiddenness* is the salient characteristic of these various contexts. In this way, she highlights the mistakes that emerge from anthropological study undertaken with little or no knowledge of the local dialect, and authorizes the knowledge in *Dakota Texts* through reference to her fluency as a native speaker of Dakota.

Furthermore, Deloria also inscribes in *Dakota Texts* moments when her deep knowledge of her native language reveals the idiosyncrasy of the choices made by a particular speaker. She reflects on the text collected from one speaker that she "should expect," in the context of the story, a different word; she proposes "a more likely word, also meaning, 'to hold,' . . . which would fit in here more naturally. . . . is what I should say."[77] Here her authority comes from knowing and speaking this language, enabling her to point out even when a linguistic choice made by a speaker strikes her ear as odd. In this way, Deloria's insider knowledge as a native speaker counteracts the tendency of anthropological collection to treat as *typical* certain choices that may be idiosyncratic, the product of a specific person speaking at a specific moment rather than a general pattern of thought or expression.

A further implication of Deloria's efforts to position her authority as an insider is that she resists the practice of divesting indigenous communities of ownership over their stories. Ongoing indigenous ownership over certain stories is asserted in particular when those stories are associated with a specific locality; for instance, Deloria acknowledges that "each locality, each band, has its own stories of this nature. These particular ones belong to the Pine Ridge people who told them to me on my first visit in 1931."[78] Positioning her folkloric material as still belonging to those who created it diverges fundamentally from the exercise of intellectual dispossession typical in this academic genre.

Deloria's rhetorical choices also counter portrayals of indigenous life as static and vanishing. This task was crucial to her overall intellectual project; she wrote, for instance, in *Speaking of Indians* that "reservation life has never been a 'still.' It is a moving picture of continuous change."[79] *Dakota Texts* similarly focuses readers' attention on the ways in which folklore is used within a living Dakota community. For instance, the bulk of Deloria's notes in *Dakota Texts* are linguistic, explaining connotations and usages of specific phrases and idioms; as critic Janet Finn argues, in an era of violent repression of indigenous languages and cultures, "Deloria's very dedication to language can be seen as an act of resistance."[80] Indeed, Deloria's notes suggest that she *assumes* linguistic survival. As she remarks, for instance, that "the way [a particular term] is used here is heard often,"[81] Deloria reminds readers that language is not static but perpetually remade, and draws attention to relationships between contemporary and historical language use among the Dakota in a way that assumes her community's linguistic survival.

Even when folk stories concern past ways of behaving, Deloria often emphasizes present practice among the Dakota. For instance, a historical account of parents who loved their son deeply provides Deloria with an occasion for reflecting on parental relations at present among Dakota people: "When a son or daughter has arrived at years of discretion the father and mother fall very naturally into a subordinate place, willingly, proudly, for having raised such a son or daughter. The dominating parent, that wants to hold the reins forever, is generally missing among the Dakota." She frequently remarks in footnotes upon present Dakota practices as related to but distinct from the prior practices often recorded in folklore. She notes, for instance, spatial configurations of privacy that were typical in Dakota homes in the past and in the present: "In a Dakota lodge, the space reserved for each grown-up member of the family was as much respected as a room in a house occupied by an individual. Up against the rear, piled up in a neat array, were the belongings of that person, in beaded saddle-bags, (so-called), rawhide cases, and latterly, in leather suit cases." The materials containing someone's belongings have changed, from saddlebags to rawhide cases to leather suitcases, but the practice of organizing individual belongings within the open space of a Dakota home has been ongoing. About other practices—such as pouting, which is represented as an appropriate activity for grown women in one folk tale—Deloria remarks that it is "out of style for adults now."[82] Such comments use Dakota folklore to reflect on—and instruct her readers in—contemporary cultural and linguistic practice, rather than relegating Dakota stories to a rapidly receding past.

In sum, Deloria's rhetorical choices in *Dakota Texts* treat folklore as a performative act, shared by a community that develops linguistic resources for their own purposes and uses shared stories for their own ends. The folklore collection genre provides Deloria with a location where she can speak to her colleagues in a way that is both conventional and simultaneously deeply challenging to the portrayals of indigenous people that academic anthropologists typically perpetuated.

Narrating Knowledge-Making in *Mules and Men*

Although both Hurston and Deloria used folklore collections to negotiate their professional status and revise cultural scripts about their home communities, the texts they produced differ in significant ways. *Mules and Men* is far more formally experimental than *Dakota Texts* and adheres less closely to academic norms. Though it includes many features of academic folklore collections, including footnotes, a glossary, an appendix, and an introduction that discusses Hurston's methods and thanks the sponsors of her research, *Mules and Men* was published by Lippincott, rather than a university press, increasing its general readership significantly. Its most crucial departure from academic norms comes from the "connective tissue" that Hurston wrote to weave the individual pieces of folklore into a narrative. Through this connective material Hurston narrates her process of entering town, finding willing speakers, and negotiating social conventions to elicit tales. She describes the conversations, arguments, parties, and social settings in which she participates over the course of her research, so that each tale in the collection is spoken by a particular character, in the presence of other specific characters, and in response to Hurston's or another's prompting.

This unusual formal structure was necessitated, as Hurston explained to Boas, by her difficulty finding a publisher for the original manuscript, which *did* conform closely to academic norms. When Hurston offered only the folklore itself, no publisher was interested, but after writing a narrative thread to connect the folktales, multiple presses asked to publish the manuscript. Hurston wrote that she hoped this "unscholarly" presentation would not prevent Boas from writing the preface, as planned.[83] He responded that he needed to review the manuscript for accuracy before he would agree.[84] Scholars note that Hurston's "highly visible, intensely subjective, and active narrator [constitutes] a willful violation of long-held and persistent attitudes to social-scientific writing"—attitudes that Hurston's training with Boas made her well aware of.[85]

The narrative that links individual pieces of folklore and describes Hurston's research process also functions to counteract many of the colonizing effects of academic folklore collections. By embedding specific pieces of folklore—ranging from elaborate John-and-Old-Master stories to brief, rapid-fire exchanges of jokes and verbal sparring—in an overarching narrative of her research process, Hurston *situates* rather than *abstracts* the material included in her collection, resulting in a text that avoids portraying folklore as isolated, abstract, and properly under the authority of anthropologists.

One of Hurston's most crucial renovations to the folklore collection genre involves her representation of folklore—both its circulation within a community and its performance for the sake of anthropological study—as a richly contextualized practice. Folklore in her collection is told in specific settings: during a walk to and from a fishing hole, early in the morning while a group of men are waiting for work at a lumber mill to begin, late at night around a bonfire as a party winds down. These jokes and stories are told by and to specific individuals: by Charlie Jones and Gene Brazzle, Joe Wiley and Jim Pressley, and dozens of other individuals who are named and known to Hurston and whose interactions and relations shape the stories they tell and the reasons they tell them. The tales in *Mules and Men* are not collected from a generalized African American community and then isolated as textual artifacts; instead, Hurston retains their specific contexts, reminding her readers that speakers and audiences together shape a story, its performance, and its use.

Hurston recontextualizes folklore in part by revealing how the storytelling context prompts certain kinds of tales. She depicts, for example, a group of lumber workers sharing jokes and tales while waiting for a "swamp boss" who is late in assigning the men their duties for the day. The men comment that there "must be something terrible [going on] when white folks get slow about putting us to work," and then exchange a series of tales about John, the legendary slave who perpetually evades work by outwitting the slaveowner "Old Master," and a series of jokes about the meanest boss they've ever worked for, such as a boss who "was so mean and times was so hard till he laid off de hands of his watch."[86] Situating these stories in a specific context significantly changes how Hurston's readers encounter the tales; instead of offering decontextualized artifacts, she underscores the inventive and purposeful use of folklore within this community, emphasizing, for instance, how contemporary workers use folklore to connect their labor to a long history of racialized exploitation.

Situating storytelling within specific contexts also allows Hurston to emphasize folklore's performative aspects in settings where specific audience members and speakers show off their verbal virtuosity and negotiate their own status. For instance, after a man at a party tells a humorous, rhyming story about pursuing three women at once, a woman in the audience, Shug, responds by offering a story about three men courting one woman at once. Shug's step-brother Bennie objects, crying "Dat's bogish" before Shug can begin. Shug and Bennie swap gibes, with Bennie threatening and repeatedly asking "Whut you gointer do?" and Shug retorting that she's talking to Zora, not to Bennie anyhow. Hurston remarks to the reader that the two "had a lawsuit over the property of his late father and her late mother, so a very little of Bennie's sugar would sweeten Shug's tea and vice versa." After Bennie falls asleep, another member of the audience prompts Shug to proceed with her story, and the round of tales continues. Shortly afterward, a young man named Little Julius Henry, who "should have been home in bed," announces that he wants to contribute a John-and-Old-Master story, prompting the older men in the group to tease him for his boldness and his youth. When he finishes his tale, an especially long one, he earns laughing praise from the audience, which pronounces it "a long tale for a li'l boy lak you" and an "over average lie."[87] These scenes highlight the status of storytelling within this community, where telling a story marks one as a participant but also requires the speaker to negotiate his or her relations with the audience. As the negotiations attending Shug's and Julius's stories indicate, these relations are shaped by gender, age, and by specific familial and personal histories. By highlighting these negotiations, Hurston's text counteracts the anthropological practice of isolating and abstracting folklore, insisting instead that its meaning arises through its performance and exchange.

Situating folklore within these contexts gives Hurston the opportunity to demonstrate as well the wide array of uses that African American speakers make of their folklore performances. Speakers in *Mules and Men* use their performances of folklore not only to negotiate interpersonal relationships but also to comment on gendered and racial dynamics. Several speakers, for instance, tell stories that critique religious divisiveness; in one, Hurston's friend Armetta describes a Baptist and a Methodist preacher who, both being black, are in the "colored coach" just behind the engine of a train. When the engine explodes, both preachers are blown up, but the Baptist preacher yells to the Methodist, "Ah bet Ah go higher than you!"[88] The humorous story carries an edge of critique, reminding Armetta's audience that despite internal tensions within black communities, a broader structure of power positions African Americans collectively in places like the "colored coach," where religious differences do not prevent black Baptist and Methodist preachers from sharing the consequences of their shared lack of power.

Similarly, Hurston includes many examples of speakers using folklore to comment on gendered power dynamics as well, as men and women—sometimes playfully, sometimes seriously—critique the gender order and assert counter norms. One evening, Gene rolls his eyes after a woman named Gold tells a story, prompting a long back-and-forth between the men and the women in the party regarding the extent and the source of women's power. Mathilda Moseley argues that women have "too much sense to go 'round braggin' about it like y'all do" and that they've "got the advantage of mens because God fixed it dat way." When a man in the party, B. Moseley, counters, "We got all de strength and all de law and all de money and you can't git a thing but whut we jes' take pity on you and give you," Mathilda replies with a long story about a time when men and women were equally strong, so balanced that they would "get to fussin' 'bout who gointer do this and that and sometime they'd fight, but they was even balanced and neither one could whip de other one." After the man asks God for more strength, the woman persuades God to give her a set of keys—to the kitchen, the bedroom, and the cradle—which the devil teaches her gives her more strength than a man; as long as she keeps these, he says, man will have to "mortgage his strength to her [in order] to live."[89] Including the context surrounding this story, where male and female storytellers and audience members exchange gibes and jokes, Hurston underscores the role of this instance of folklore in an unfolding discussion of gender, strength, and social and sexual relations. The message of any particular story becomes more pointed when positioned within the live social environment that called it forth and to which a speaker responds by telling a story.

Hurston's choice to situate folklore in these ways allows her to portray folklore collection not as the *preservation* of material that is about to be lost, but as a record that can generate greater appreciation for the rich, creative cultural productions of a living community. For instance, when she first arrives in Eatonville she explains to her friends what she's looking for:

> "Ah come to collect some old stories and tales and Ah know y'all know a plenty of 'em and that's why Ah headed straight for home."
>
> "What you mean, Zora, them big old lies we tell when we're jus' sittin' around here on the store porch doin' nothin'?" asked B. Moseley.
>
> "Yeah, those same ones about Ole Massa, and colored folks in heaven, and—oh, y'all know the kind I mean. . . . They are a lot more valuable than you might think. We want to set them down before it's too late."
>
> "Too late for what?"
>
> "Before everybody forgets all of 'em."
>
> "No danger of that. That's all some people is good for—set round and lie and murder groceries."[90]

Here Hurston registers the preservationist impulse among the "we" who want to "set [folklore] down before it's too late," but this impulse is immediately challenged by the people surrounding her, who ensure there's "no danger" that the stories will be forgotten, because they're so thoroughly *in use*. And indeed, throughout the collection Hurston portrays so many contemporary contexts for and uses of folklore that she reinforces this speaker's assertion, showing us folklore not as preserved specimens but as performances through which people participate in their community's life. As Hurston explained in a 1934 essay, "Negro folklore is not a thing of the past. It is still in the making. Its great variety shows the adaptability of the black man: nothing is too old or too new, domestic or foreign, high or low for his use."[91]

In addition to portraying this "great variety" in *Mules and Men,* Hurston also repeatedly points her readers toward the context of elicitation, in which an anthropologist actively seeks out material to study. Hurston, for instance, must *ask* for folklore; she must ask to be included in situations where folklore is likely to be told, and she has to negotiate, even with people she knows well in Eatonville, to have the opportunity to record the stories she seeks. Representing rather than omitting these many negotiations counteracts portrayals in academic folklore collections that treat folklore as static artifacts, always ready at hand. For instance, on Hurston's first afternoon back in her hometown of Eatonville, she asks a group to visit her that evening at the house of her close childhood friend, Armetta, to tell stories for her to record. Many agree to come, but when Hurston greets the first two visitors to arrive that evening, Calvin Daniels and James Moseley, she learns that most of her potential "informants" will be attending a party in nearby Wood Bridge instead. Calvin and James invite Hurston to join them, reassuring her that no one else is planning to visit her that evening because they are "all 'bout goin' to Wood Bridge, too." Hurston negotiates with Calvin and James to tell her a story while she decides whether to join them; after the first story, the two men in turn negotiate for a corner piece of gingerbread before they agree to tell another. A group of cars then pulls up outside Armetta's house to confirm that all Hurston's potential informants are attending the party; they call out to Hurston, "We kin tell you some lies most any ole time . . . Tell 'em tomorrow night."[92] Hurston consequently relinquishes her plans for how her first evening of research will proceed and adapts to the lives and schedules of the people around her.

In choosing to inscribe this sequence of events into *Mules and Men,* Hurston reinforces the agency of her informants to *choose* whether to tell their stories to her, and when, and for what sorts of recompense. Indeed, throughout *Mules and Men* Hurston has to negotiate to get material: she provides transportation, shares food, dances, socializes, and actively participates in this community's life. These are negotiations, of course, that other anthropologists must conduct in order to access cultural material as well, although such exchanges are routinely excised from anthropologists' publications. In contrast to collections that thank informants in the introductory pages but remove those informants from the collection itself, Hurston here acknowledges that storytellers fit their tales into their ongoing lives—and that they are not always willing to conform to a schedule imposed by an anthropologist. In organizing *Mules and Men* as a narrative of her research process, Hurston resists erasing her own presence as an anthropologist within a context of collection, and consequently inscribes rather than omits the interpersonal relations that enable or constrain an anthropologist's work. For instance, when she arrives in Eatonville, she goes immediately to the house of an old friend, calling on social ties to support her presence in this town and simultaneously registering within the text itself that she is fed and sheltered by a particular person. Although such relations are necessary to sustain the presence of any anthropologist in the field, they are persistently obscured in academic folklore collections.

Hurston also counteracts the tendency of folklore collections to share authority among anthropologists and to objectify the knowledge embodied in informants. Authority in *Mules and Men* is distributed among participants and often negotiated within the storytelling scene. Some storytellers, for instance, lay claim to their ownership over the story they share, as when John French admonishes Hurston before he begins speaking, "Zora, Ah'm gointer tell one, but you be sho and tell de folks Ah tole it. Don't say Seymore said it because he took you on de all-day fishin' trip to Titusville. Don't say Seaboard Hamilton tole it 'cause he always give you a big hunk of barbecue when you go for a sandwich. Give ole John French whut's comin' to 'im."[93] When he asks for "whut's comin' to 'im," French refers to attribution of the story he is about to tell; his remarks draw attention to the value of attribution in the kind of academic work Hurston is engaged in. Having his name attached to his contribution has a value, especially as Hurston's text circulates more broadly; John French only retains a claim to ownership so long as his name remains attached to his version of the story he tells. His teasing gibes that Hurston might attribute the story to someone else in exchange for favors, like a "big hunk of barbecue" or an "all-day fishin' trip," underscore the reality that in academic circulation, confirmation of ownership through attribution is a currency with significant value.

By narrating her research process as she collects folklore in multiple locations—first Eatonville, then Polk County to the southwest, then finally New Orleans—Hurston includes information about *how to do fieldwork*. In moving between these research sites, Hurston demonstrates the process by which an anthropologist must negotiate with a community of informants in order to achieve access to cultural productions. For instance, the long middle section of the book describes Hurston moving on from her hometown, Eatonville, where she began her research, and entering a new county, where she's been told the folklore will be rich but where she lacks familiarity with community members. What she recounts is a series of lessons regarding how she manages to gain a place for herself in an unfamiliar community. The initial welcome she receives in Loughman, Florida, is cool, and Hurston describes herself "figuratively starving to death in the midst of plenty," surrounded by "a rich field for folk-lore" but unable to enact the right relations with new informants that would permit her to access that material.[94] Those relations are shaped by Hurston's embodied choices, such as the expensive dress she wears to a party and the fact that she drives a car, which have marked her as an outsider and caused members of this lumber-mill community to keep their distance. As she develops a friendship with Babe, a Loughman woman, Babe's son eventually feels "close enough to tell [Hurston] what was the trouble"—namely, that people in Loughman "were accustomed to strange women dropping into the quarters, but not in shiny gray Chevrolets. . . . The car made me look too prosperous."[95] As a marker of class difference, Hurston's "shiny gray Chevrolet" does not seriously impede her research in Eatonville, where Hurston's prior relationships with community members provide reassurance; yet in a new town, such a mark of wealth arouses suspicions that Hurston must work to allay.

Even after Hurston has gotten past these initial barriers, she still finds that she has to perform her similarity to the other people in Loughman in certain ways in order to achieve the relations that will enable her research. In particular, she rises to the occasion at a party when she has to show her own quick wit and her willingness to reciprocate in the "woofing," or mild flirting, that a bold member of the party engages her in, while a large group "stood around to see how I took it." She and Mr. Pitts trade arch remarks in front of a group of onlookers, and eventually people start asking her to dance, after her "laughing acceptance of Pitts' woofing had put everybody at his ease." Finally, Hurston establishes a relationship with this community by singing John Henry verses at the party; she asks James Presley, the musician, to play "John Henry" and he agrees to play only if Hurston will sing. Hurston writes that she "started to sing the verses I knew . . . Joe Willard knew two verses and sang them. Eugene Oliver knew one; Big Sweet knew one. . . . By the time that the song was over, before Joe Willard lifted me down from the table I knew that I was in the inner circle."[96] These performances—in the "woofing" outside the party and the singing inside it—are not simply tests that Hurston must pass to gain informants' trust, but also opportunities for Hurston to inscribe herself as a *participant,* not merely an observer.

By depicting her arrivals in both Eatonville and Loughman, Hurston underscores the complexity of African American communities. Though these two research sites are separated by only thirty miles and are both small, all-black Florida towns, the social relations and research opportunities available to Hurston in the two towns differ dramatically, as do the techniques Hurston must use to insert herself into a network of relations before her research can begin. Staying with her old friend Armetta in Eatonville, Hurston is able to take up the former relationships she created in her hometown long before she began working as an anthropologist; she knows immediately who is likely to provide her with folklore, what situations are likely to prompt its telling, and how open she can be in her requests without alienating her potential informants. In

Loughman, Hurston stays at a boarding house, watching from the periphery for days until the opportunity arises for her to take up a more active role within Loughman's community life. Depicting the differences between these two situations, Hurston provides insight into the complex challenges facing a native ethnographer and puts the lie to decontextualized research that masks these challenges by representing folklore research as a simple act of "securing" texts from tractable informants. Focusing our attention instead on the processes by which she forms relationships and constructs scenarios in order to record these tales, Hurston offers what Boxwell has called a "metaethnography," one attentive to the *different* relations that inhere between a researcher and the various specific communities where she undertakes research.[97]

Performing and Contextualizing Knowledge

Academic folklore collections routinely denied authority to local communities, isolated folkloric practice from specific contexts of performance and use, and preserved folkloric texts as artifacts rather than living cultural productions. These discursive practices underwrote inequitable power relations as they reinforced the epistemic authority of anthropologists and diminished the authority of indigenous and African American communities. Such broad imbalances of power were further manifest in the circumscribed opportunities for full participation in professional anthropology that Deloria and Hurston each experienced. As "native ethnographers," deeply involved with the communities they studied, their authority as anthropologists remained significantly circumscribed.

Unchosen ascriptions of race and gender that positioned Deloria and Hurston differently in relation to the practice of anthropology also shaped the knowledge they created in their folklore collections. That is, their bodies and community affiliations position these writers at odds with many of their discipline's privileged epistemic practices. Both their complex professional positioning and their choices to contextualize and narrate their folklore research bear effects for the knowledge that their genre performances generate. Their texts remind us that taking up a genre from an alternative subject position can change that genre's function. Furthermore, their inclusion of elements typically omitted from the genre shapes the capacity of their texts to generate alternative knowledge-making practices—regardless of whether Deloria and Hurston aimed primarily to *use* or to *critique* anthropology's epistemic tools. As Deloria and Hurston ground their knowledge in contexts of performance and use, they underscore the role of folklore in the ongoing vitality of the communities it supports. Producing knowledge according to the presumption that folklore gains meaning through use generates substantial shifts in the relations of power such knowledge engenders. Ultimately these texts *reposition* Deloria and Hurston, their home communities, and the practice of anthropology, redistributing authority and ownership among these actors in the scene of anthropological knowledge-making.

Juxtaposing the folklore collections of these two writers makes it evident that dramatic revision to a scientific genre is not required for the social action accomplished through the genre to change substantially. Hurston's and Deloria's texts share the strategy of recontextualization even as the formal characteristics of *Dakota Texts* and *Mules and Men* otherwise diverge. Hurston's folklore collection *looks* formally innovative, with its narrative structure reinforcing its departure from standard academic presentations. Despite this structural dissimilarity with the genre's academic form, Hurston's book nevertheless collects, records, and recirculates folkloric texts for anthropological study, doing so in ways that insist upon context and performance as arenas of meaning-making. In contrast, Deloria's text looks formally indistinguishable from other academic folklore collections, with its apparatus of footnotes, its publication by the American Ethnological Society, and its absence of the kind of narrative that Hurston provides. Yet *Dakota Texts* also remakes anthropological knowledge according to an alternate set of relations and practices, insisting that folklore makes meaning not in isolation as an artifactual remnant of a diminishing culture, but rather through its circulation within a living community.

Adopting scientific discourse—adapting it, as Hurston and Deloria do—does not merely reinscribe these women scientists into discourses of power that ultimately constrain their capacity to challenge scientific norms, as other feminist science scholars suggest.[98] Instead, Deloria and Hurston's texts challenge scientific norms in myriad ways. In particular, by taking up a powerful genre but making knowledge within that genre differently—through insider identifications with their research subjects—Deloria and Hurston open up fissures in the authority that professional anthropologists sought to attach to their research and writing practices. Although texts like Mason's "Natural History of Folk-Lore" argued that the research practices of geologists and other physical scientists were readily suited to the study of human cultural productions, Hurston and Deloria contest this metaphoric association between geological objects and the living human communities where folklore is located. Furthermore, although metaphors drawn from natural sciences seemed to authorize anthropological research as *really* scientific, Deloria and Hurston's writing and research practices disrupt these associations by making knowledge they represent as accurate and valid out of relations of reciprocity rather than relations of exploitation and control. In this way they contest the inevitability of scientific practice as an exercise in epistemic domination. Instead, Deloria and Hurston's use of this genre suggests that objectification is neither inherent in nor required for knowledge production, opening up for critique and revision the discursive practices their colleagues adopted.

Ethnographic Novels

Educational Critiques and Rhetorical Trajectories

At that time . . . few anthropological monographs on Indian tribes had been
written, but it is doubtful if such publications are to be found in New England
village libraries even today, and it is more than doubtful that if they were in
the libraries anybody would read them; anthropologists themselves have been
known not to read them. Between these forbidding monographs and the
legends of Fenimore Cooper, what is there then to read?

—Elsie Clews Parsons, *American Indian Life*

INTRODUCING *AMERICAN Indian Life,* the experimental collection of
ethnographic fiction she edited in 1922, Elsie Clews Parsons bemoans the
wide gap between anthropological writing, which primarily took the form of
"forbidding monographs," and the kinds of "legends" about Indians that public
audiences primarily consumed. Despite anthropology's growth as a discipline
over the first decades of the twentieth century, Parsons writes, her professional
colleagues had not yet extended their scientific expertise into texts aimed at
popular consumption. This was an oversight that anthropologists needed to
correct, Parsons suggests, for anthropologists' failure to get factual, accurate
information into the hands of readers allowed most members of the public to
content themselves with sensationalist and inaccurate portrayals. Consequently, if anthropologists produce nothing but "forbidding monographs" that only
professionals read and reward, they leave readers outside of their discipline with
only the sensationalism of Fenimore Cooper—one writer of many in a long
tradition of "over-abundant lore of the white man about the Indian"—and no
way to learn accurately about Native American life.[1]

The urgency of bridging the gap between scientific and popular knowledge was felt widely enough that Parsons convinced the most prominent anthropologists of her generation, including Alfred Kroeber, Robert Lowie, Clark Wissler, Paul Radin, Edward Sapir, Leslie Spier, and even the venerable Franz Boas to contribute short pieces of ethnographic fiction to her collection. Ethnographic fiction attempts to engage broad readerships in anthropological knowledge by casting detailed cultural information into narratives that recount the experiences of fictionalized members of a particular community. For instance, Alanson Skinner's contribution to *American Indian Life,* titled "Little-Wolf Joins the Medicine Lodge," narrates the Menominee protagonist Little-wolf's initiation into "the Grand Medicine Society, a secret fraternal and medical organization, to which, in one form or another, nearly every Indian of influence in all the Great Lakes and Central Western region belonged."[2] Narrating Little-wolf's induction into the organization allows Skinner to depict prayers, meals, origin stories, songs, and other ritual occasions in detail. The typical concerns of the fiction writer, such as plotting and characterization, tend to play a subordinate role in ethnographic fiction, where writers instead aim primarily to devise plots capable of providing sufficient opportunities to convey ethnographic detail.

Of course, Parsons's call to anthropologists to write more accessible texts is not motivated exclusively by the desire to circulate more accurate knowledge about Native Americans. Other institutional factors, such as the need for public funding for anthropological research, are also motivating forces. Parsons acknowledges such motivations when she writes that, "appearances to the contrary, anthropologists have no wish to keep their science or any part of it esoteric. They are too well aware, for one thing, that facilities for the pursuit of anthropology are dependent more or less on popular interest."[3] Parsons—who was independently wealthy in addition to holding a PhD from Columbia—personally financed an enormous amount of anthropological research during the 1920s and 1930s, including paying for the continued publication of the *Journal of American Folklore* when lack of funds threatened to shutter one of the field's most important journals. Consequently, she was particularly attuned to the fragile status of this scientific discipline in the absence of material public support.[4]

Furthermore, Parsons's suggestion that information about Native Americans *belongs* to anthropologists as part of "their science" indicates an additional motivation for writing accessibly: performing boundary work to maintain anthropologists' authority over Native American lives. For anthropologists to continue to position themselves as experts on indigenous life, they needed a public willing to grant their claims to expertise and authority. In a sense, the very fact of public interest in Native Americans served as an exigence for anthropologists, whose claims that Native populations belonged to "their science" shored up their field's scientific status. As monographs became more important professionally *and* more removed from everyday, nonspecialist readers, the distance between professional norms and public engagement increased. Ethnographic fiction, Parsons suggests in this collection, could offer scholars a way to remind the public of anthropologists' expertise.

Yet changing the characteristics of anthropologists' knowledge-making genres could have repercussions not confined to the purposes Parsons outlined. Scholars in science studies have shown, for instance, that scientific popularization does not only repackage scientific knowledge, but often shifts the relations that inhere between creators and consumers of knowledge, enabling an alternative set of political and epistemic possibilities.[5] In very real ways, popular scientific texts transform scientific knowledge through the acts of redistributing, reframing, and refashioning knowledge for new audiences and purposes.[6] Likewise, scholars in rhetorical genre studies underscore the epistemic shifts that can be accomplished when writers repurpose and reshape a deeply institutionalized genre.[7] Consequently, moving ethnographic knowledge from the monograph genre into the new spaces opened up by ethnographic fiction does not only redistribute but significantly reshapes that knowledge. For instance, if, as Parsons warned, anthropologists' "classified data [in monographs] give the impression that the native life is one unbroken round, let us say, of curing or weather-control ceremonials, of prophylaxis against bad luck, of hunting, or of war," then changing the genre in which that data is cast as knowledge might enable writers to refashion these constrained representations as well.[8]

These goals for Parsons's collection of ethnographic fiction underscore the tensions anthropologists felt as they tried to craft knowledge capable of public interventions in the 1920s and 1930s. The ongoing and enormous public interest in Native American lives during the early twentieth century seemed to require anthropologists to participate in public discussions; yet such an impulse existed in tension with the insularity of science and the determination to speak primarily to *internal* audiences that had helped anthropologists establish their field's scientific status. Professionalization in the early twentieth century had helped anthropologists secure their authority over a specific field of knowledge (namely, the languages, histories, and practices of Native American and worldwide indigenous populations), position their discipline as a rigorous science among other social sciences, and secure institutional and financial resources from government agencies and philanthropic foundations. Yet the professionalization process did not simply end debate over the practices and purposes of anthropological knowledge creation. Instead, as chapters 2 and 3 have shown, participants in this new discipline continued to negotiate key disciplinary questions, including *who* could create legitimate anthropological knowledge, *what practices* enabled such knowledge production, and *what ends* that knowledge should advance.

Ethnographic novels emerged in the 1930s amid these disciplinary negotiations. This genre, in which writers use the tools of anthropology to create fictional stories promoted as scientifically accurate information about Native people, served as a site where writers questioned the insular ends of scientific anthropology. Although this genre was fleeting—emerging and then fading from practice within a decade—ethnographic novels were a prominent popular genre during this period. Following the high-profile success of ethnologist Oliver La Farge's *Laughing Boy,* which won the 1930 Pulitzer Prize against competition from nominees that included Hemingway's *A Farewell to Arms* and Faulkner's *The Sound and the Fury,* ethnographic novels were published by major presses such as Dodd, Mead and Houghton Mifflin nearly every year throughout the 1930s.[9] They were reviewed in prominent periodicals such as the *New York Times* and the *Nation.* In writing scientific texts targeting broad popular readerships, ethnographic novelists argued implicitly that anthropological research should attempt to achieve influence beyond professional arenas.

Thus, the emergence of this genre in the 1930s reflects ongoing uncertainty among anthropologists regarding the assumption that disciplinary insiders *should be* the primary audiences of their research. If professionalization enacted a more insular notion of audience among practitioners of anthropology, by the 1930s it seems clear that a number of writers were questioning this value as they published texts that sought to create and circulate knowledge for popular audiences. The ethnographic novels I examine in this chapter use anthropological knowledge to intervene in public discussions, countering the isolation of scientific discourse as popular texts meant to provide accurate and engaging ethnographic information. Consequently, ethnographic novels can be seen as spaces where the production of anthropological knowledge—both how and for what ends—was still being negotiated in the 1930s.

Writers of ethnographic novels advanced knowledge claims based on first-hand observation and ethnographic research techniques that distinguished their texts from the long history of "Indian fiction" written in the United States, although connections to that sentimental tradition persisted. Ethnographic novelists created fictional plots and characters to stage their presentation of ethnographic data, which typically included descriptions of ceremonial as well as everyday cultural practices, accounts of kinship relations, discussions of folklore, and descriptions of musical, artistic, and other creative productions. Emphasizing the accuracy of the cultural information conveyed in their ethnographic novels, these writers typically situated the authority of their depictions in the writer's firsthand experience observing, either formally or informally, the daily life carried on within this community. Thus, ethnographic fiction creates narrative structures for fictional characters to move through, yet also relies upon the discursive tools and epistemic categories developed within professional anthropology to ascribe authority to these fictional narratives as knowledge-making texts.

The writers who adopted this genre in the 1930s sought to intervene in public discussions or counter static portrayals of indigenous life, yet the narrative structures surrounding these interventions remained problematic. Writers of ethnographic novels engage "genre work," what Wendy Sharer describes as "strategic blending of typified and innovative textual elements"; the work accomplished through such blending varies significantly.[10] For instance, although many ethnographic novels use anthropological expertise to critique federal Indian policy, some of these same texts also attach the scientific authority of anthropology to narratives that plot trajectories toward Native death, as La Farge's *Laughing Boy* epitomizes. Sentimental and elegiac portrayals persist even within the genre's ostensibly accurate representations of indigenous life; this suggests a greater kinship between ethnographic fiction and the "legends of Fenimore Cooper" than Parsons would allow. Ultimately, the analysis that follows explores the complexity of rhetorical purposes enacted by writers who wove the discursive and epistemic techniques of professional anthropological discourse together with the fictional narratives of the novel.

To underscore the complex rhetorical purposes that writers take up in their ethnographic novels, this chapter proceeds through a series of contrasts. In the 1920s and 1930s, discourses that privileged social-scientific expertise and critiqued federal Indian policy were prominent, and ethnographic novelists both drew from and responded to these discourses. As a consequence, traces of antecedent genres persisted in ethnographic novels, in sentimental plot trajectories that reinforced a narrative of Native death and limited the efficacy of potential policy interventions by shoring up anthropological authority at the expense of Native people's rhetorical sovereignty. In contrast, Gladys Reichard's 1939 ethnographic novel, *Dezba, Woman of the Desert,* underscores the extent to which genre affordances do not determine genre uses. Reichard's inventive use of the spatial strategies available in this genre allowed her to critique boarding school education while also crafting a multivocal form of anthropological knowledge. In this way, Reichard contested the presumption of anthropological authority over Native lives and educational practices and underscored the generative rhetorical possibilities of genre work.

Expertise and Indian Education

Two pervasive discourses circulating at the national level shaped the context in which ethnographic fiction emerged: a burgeoning discourse that privileged expertise and sought to solve social problems with specialized knowledge, and a widespread discourse of dissatisfaction with federal Indian policy in general and with Indian educational programs more specifically. These discourses shaped the policy-making context of the interwar United States and were manifested in the ethnographic novels that emerged in the 1930s.

The first few decades of the twentieth century saw a marked turn among the U.S. public toward valuing expertise, specialization, and professionalization. The social sciences that emerged or flourished during this period—economics, public health, sociology, and political science, as well as anthropology—all drew upon these widely shared values as they created their disciplinary practice on a rigorously professional model. The enormous value of this expertise rested on the ability of specialists to generate what Gregory Clark and S. Michael Halloran call "morally neutral" knowledge, which "was considered the property of specialists whose job was to apply it to particular problems through a discourse of strictly logical argument among themselves."[11] This knowledge, though "morally neutral" and owned by insular communities of experts, was nevertheless meant to guide policy and to ameliorate social problems. These sometimes contradictory impulses could result, as Wendy Sharer has shown, in genres where writers sought to balance the ethos of rational professionalism with advocacy aims.[12]

For anthropologists, the social problem most obviously in need of their expertise was the "Indian problem": that is, the ongoing settler-colonial project of the United States, which attempted to consolidate American nationhood through colonization and usurpation of indigenous communities across the continent. Although Americanization policies, which sought to forcibly civilize, citizenize, and individualize Native people, enjoyed widespread support in the last decades of the nineteenth century, by the 1920s a national public discourse emerged that voiced deep dissatisfaction with these policies and skepticism about the model of Native education they enforced. For one thing, it was increasingly evident that boarding school education had not succeeded in separating Native students permanently from their homes and dispersing them as assimilated citizens. Although the "educational crusade" of boarding school education was "vast in scope, military in organization, fervent in zeal, and violent in method," as K. Tsianina Lomawaima argues, "as in many crusades, its leaders could not accurately predict all of its astonishing results."[13] Instead, Native students who had been educated in boarding schools retained strong ties to their home communities, wrote and spoke on behalf of those communities in local and national forums, and put their multilingual and multicultural talents to all sorts of uses not imagined by school officials.[14]

Ethnographic novels were not, of course, the only site where discourses of expertise and policy critique intersected; in particular, these discourses are strongly reflected in *The Problem of Indian Administration,* a nine-hundred-page 1928 publication that reported the results from a sprawling, multidisciplinary, two-year social scientific study. This publication crystalized ongoing public debates over Indian policy, and the study's findings were circulated widely, reviewed in dozens of social scientific journals, and reported extensively in the popular press, allowing this study to guide the sweeping revisions to Indian policy that took place through the 1930s. Referred to as the Meriam Report, after Lewis Meriam, the senior staff researcher at the Institute for Government Research charged with overseeing the project, this extensive survey of the Bureau of Indian Affairs (BIA) proposed to rectify the failings of federal Indian policy through stronger reliance on social scientific expertise. Critiquing boarding school education in particular as unsanitary, ineffective, and outdated, the Meriam Report called for educational practices more in line with the newest social science research and recommended sweeping changes to the structure of the BIA in order to achieve a more highly trained, specialized, professional staff throughout the bureau.

The pervasive belief that expert intervention and empirical knowledge should guide social policy was reflected in the staff hired to conduct the investigation, which included Fayette Avery McKenzie, a professor of sociology at Juniata College in Pennsylvania and an organizer of the Society of American Indians; Mary Louise Mark, a professor of sociology at Ohio State University who had worked previously for the Census Bureau and the Bureau of Labor Statistics; and Henry Roe Cloud, a Winnebago man who had earned several advanced degrees including a master's in anthropology from Yale. Furthermore, the report recommended repeatedly that the BIA would effectively administer its duties only when its staff was overhauled to include sufficiently trained "specialized workers" in accordance with current research in education, psychology, economics, and social work.[15] The writers of the Meriam Report proposed specific revisions to the minimum qualifications for many positions within the BIA. For example, the report recommended that the position of field matron, a generalized social worker role, be replaced by several more specialized workers, including public health nurses, home demonstration workers, vocational advisors, family case workers, and recreation leaders, each of whom needed specific credentials, specialized training, and formal work experience. In these recommendations, the writers of the Meriam Report echoed the arguments of professional anthropologists of the same period, as they asserted that Native communities *belonged* to the specialized terrain of scientific experts. Consequently, this discourse of specialized expertise further extended the authority of government and scientific experts over indigenous life.

In addition to arguing for more expertise in the administration of Indian affairs, the Meriam Report also critiqued severely the forms of education taking place in off-reservation boarding schools. These critiques targeted several widespread problems: the extent and kind of labor that students were required to perform, which the report found far exceeded any possible claims to vocational instruction; overcrowding in dormitories; insufficient allocation of resources for food and clothing, with some boarding schools reportedly spending only pennies per day on food for each of their several hundred students; and inhumane lapses in medical care, which permitted the spread of tuberculosis and other communicable diseases.[16] The report also critiqued boarding schools across the country for failing to attend to Native children as individuals. Instead, schools enforced conformity among their students through practices such as mandatory English-only instruction, extensive military-style drilling, and outdated curricula focused on rote learning that ignored differences among individual students and among tribes. Such practices, the writers of the Meriam Report contended, ignored the most recent social scientific research and thus were "at variance with modern views of education."[17] In their detailed critiques and proposed solutions, the team of social scientists who conducted the investigation into *The Problem of Indian Administration* argued forcefully to bring the practices of Indian education into closer alignment with the most current research.

Critiquing Education

Although an institutional genre such as the research report generally differs sharply in audience, purpose, and textual features from the genre of the novel, the ethnographic novels that emerged in the 1930s share with the Meriam Report these pervasive discourses of expertise and dissatisfaction with federal Indian policy. In particular, ethnographic novels depend upon two discursive strategies developed within professional anthropological genres: ethnographic realism and ethnographic holism. Through realism and holism, anthropologists position themselves as experts, assert the accuracy of their claims, and reinforce their authority to speak publicly about a specific culture or community. The closely related discursive modes of realism and holism, when employed in the emergent genre of the ethnographic novel, serve to transfer epistemic authority to the portrayals and critiques located within even these fictional texts, enabling ethnographic novelists to position their fictional portrayals as *knowledge*.

Ethnographic realism, as George Marcus and Michael Fischer demonstrate, is a strategy that involves "close attention to detail and redundant demonstrations that the writer shared and experienced this whole other world."[18] Realist ethnographic writing simultaneously asserts that a specific culture or community exists as represented and that a particular writer has observed that world accurately firsthand. Ethnographic holism emerges from the accumulation of realist detail, which writers organize in order to construct a more or less coherent cultural whole; through holism, ethnographic writing aims "not to make universally valid statements, but to represent a particular way of life as fully as possible."[19] These strategies work together by legitimating knowledge claims through amassing specific details that simultaneously reinforce the ethnographer's authority and lend an ethnographic text "a pervasive sense of concrete reality."[20] Ethnographic realism and holism function in early-twentieth-century anthropological discourse pervasively as strategies for reinforcing anthropological knowledge as valid, rigorous, and scientific. Drawing on the authority provided by ethnographic realism and holism, ethnographic novelists in the 1930s constructed cultural descriptions that, they suggested, were as reliable and accurate as monographs despite being located within fictional plots. That is, their deployment of realism and holism casts their narratives of Indian life as not merely stories, but accurate cultural accounts.

Ethnographic novelists call upon the epistemic authority of realism when they attest to their firsthand experience within the cultural setting they are depicting. John Louw Nelson introduces his 1937 *Rhythm for Rain* by citing his "ten years with the Hopi Indians" as evidence that his book, though fictional, presents readers with reliable ethnographic knowledge. Frances Gillmor, in her 1930 ethnographic novel, *Windsinger,* asserts she has "spent considerable time on the Navajo reservation, . . . far from railways and travelled roads. . . . I have travelled horseback at the foot of Black Mesa, where in my story Windsinger lives, I have seen sand painting in the making, a very rare privilege for a white person, and something which women, either white or Navajo, are seldom allowed to do." Citing her experiences among the Navajo as a source for her authority, Gillmor emphasizes her rare access to ethnographic information to elevate the epistemic status of her fictional story.[21]

Writers of ethnographic novels primarily assert the status of their texts as knowledge by inserting frequent and abundant cultural details into the frameworks of their fictional plots. Ethnographic novelists narrate marriages, births, deaths, and other significant ceremonial occasions as opportunities for conveying ethnographic knowledge. Gillmor's *Windsinger,* for instance, describes the ceremonial steps the protagonist follows in order to seek and receive a religious vision from his gods, and by centering her narrative on a Navajo chanter, Gillmor generates numerous opportunities to include detailed descriptions of Navajo medicinal chanting practices. Meticulous descriptions of artisanal production are typical as well, in realist language that often strongly evokes conventional anthropological discourse. Reichard's novel *Dezba, Woman of the Desert* includes close descriptions of weaving practices and traditional chants, while La Farge's *Laughing Boy* describes the weaving and metal-working practices of his protagonists. Following a long account of the processes involved in digging clay for pottery, Margaret Smith's *Hopi Girl* describes how an experienced potter makes clay workable: "When the clay was thoroughly pulverized, it was placed in a big hard-baked pot and allowed to soak for many hours. . . . A handful at a time was transferred to a smooth stone and worked and kneaded until there remained no tiny stone or bit of stick or grass to mar its smoothness. When it was flawless it was piled lightly on a slab of wood and carried outside where the wind and sun would dry it."[22] The passive constructions—the clay "was placed," "was transferred," was "worked and kneaded," and so on—both echo and borrow from the pervasive realist discourse of academic anthropology.[23]

Reviewers of ethnographic novels in scholarly journals and popular periodicals further emphasize and reinforce the knowledge-making quality of these texts. Many echo the sentiments of a reviewer of Parsons's *American Indian Life* in asserting that, in ethnographic fiction, "the artistry here cannot be dissociated from the science. The two support and justify each other."[24] Reviewing *Laughing Boy* for the *Journal of American Folklore,* Reichard reassures La Farge's readers that the book is full of "first rate ethnological observations," remarks approvingly that "not only are the ethnological observations accurate, but they are portrayed for the most part with a feeling which approximates the attitude of the Navajo," and singles out La Farge's portrayals of Navajo silver working and funeral ceremonies as especially valuable.[25] The *American Anthropologist* review of *Dezba, Woman of the Desert* calls Reichard's novel "a book which is both readable and accurate," praising Reichard for "conveying to the reader the flavor of the life of the Navaho, not by impressionistic sketches of the tribe and its environment, but by descriptions of the daily activities of a particular family."[26] Similarly, a *New York Times* review praises Reichard's novel for revealing to readers Navajo "work and play, their sports and dances, the training of their children and the exercise of their religious faith" within a "narrative mold" that is "alive and appealing."[27] In these and other reviews, the capacity of ethnographic novels to instruct readers by providing accurate ethnographic information is highlighted as a distinguishing feature of these fictional narratives.

In addition to techniques borrowed from professional anthropological discourse, ethnographic novels also use rhetorical resources drawn from fictional narratives. Compared with more typical academic forms such as research articles and monographs, fictional narratives offer greater resources for describing interior states, ascribing motivations to individuals, and narrating change over time. These resources helped ethnographic novelists counter the abstraction of professional science and the unfeeling institutionalization for which federal Indian education policy was specifically criticized. Fiction also proceeds through specificity rather than abstraction; in fiction, characters are named and identified, given motivations that prompt their actions, and rendered as individuals rather than abstracted as data points or symbols in a kinship structure. Ethnographic novels, then, are shaped by the combination of resources the genre draws from monographs and from fiction, combining the monograph's commitment to realism with the resources of the novel for narrating vividly how individual protagonists change over time.[28]

Reviewers and writers emphasized the opportunities the ethnographic novel offered for portraying individuality, interiority, and pathos, in contrast to the monograph, which was limited by the detached perspective required by objective science. For example, one reviewer critiques Robert Gessner's 1933 ethnographic novel, *Broken Arrow,* for merely "record[ing] events" without "conveying any deep understanding" of his protagonists' thoughts and feelings, highlighting the extent to which "intimate or individual revelation" was an expectation shared by readers of ethnographic fiction. Nelson's 1937 *Rhythm for Rain,* on the other hand, is praised for providing access to "Indian psychology."[29] Unlike monographs, which demand that the ethnographer merely observe behaviors and interpret cultural meaning, ethnographic novels license writers to construct psychological states for their characters, and thus offer readers imaginative access to protagonists' interiority—the motivations and emotional attachments that make the behaviors of both Native and white characters believable.

Focusing on a single individual offered ethnographic novelists a way to bring the humanity of Indian protagonists into view, a function that reviewers cited as crucial to the genre. Oliver La Farge, for instance, praises Ruth Underhill's ethnographic novel *Hawk Over Whirlpools* as "intensively the story of an individual," and finds John Joseph Mathews's *Sundown* successful because the book is "a well-written, well-planned, sensitive study of a young man," capable of compelling readers' interest because it is *not* an academic abstraction.[30] As Margaret Smith explains in the introduction to her ethnographic novel *Hopi Girl,* "Indians are human beings, even as you and I, and not biological specimens on the ends of hatpins to be examined under a microscope." "Learned dissertations," Smith argues, cannot offer such convincing evidence of shared humanity as the account of a single Indian individual's triumphs and tragedies.[31] Forecasting feminist critiques of scientific writing that would emerge decades later, ethnographic novelists eschewed abstraction as a *denial* of shared humanity, a textual strategy akin to treating humans as mere specimens for study. While writers of monographs abstracted the experiences of individual informants, Smith and other writers of ethnographic novels crafted individual protagonists to prompt audiences' sympathetic and active responses.

Ethnographic novelists used this genre to ground arguments targeting a variety of federal government policies. John Joseph Mathews's novel *Sundown,* for instance, portrays the competing desires that prompt his protagonist, Chal Windzer, to join the military against the backdrop of the Oklahoma oil boom in the early twentieth century. As Mathews depicts Chal's ambivalence toward the constraints and opportunities that confront his generation of Osage young adults, he also critiques allotment policies and exposes the exploitation of oil-generated wealth in the Osage nation that these policies enabled. Reichard's novel *Dezba* uses ethnographic detail to underscore the validity of Navajo shepherding practices despite federal programs, like the Soil Erosion Control project, that insisted those practices be changed. For instance, Reichard describes a frustrating encounter between Dezba's family and a white stockman employed by the Soil Erosion division, then uses the novel's resources for describing interior states to recount how Dezba processes this encounter, which she "could not help reviewing . . . in her mind" afterward.[32] Dezba understands that the "rangers did not like goats. They said they ruined the range, but Dezba and her people liked them because they lived on less and coarser forage than the sheep, and because they were good leaders of the herd."[33] As Dezba reflects on the qualities that make goats valuable for shepherding, eating, and weaving, Reichard underscores the validity of Dezba's *own* understanding of the role of goats within her family's economy, in contrast to the simplistic antagonism of the Soil Erosion Control official. Resources in fiction for portraying a character's interiority here allow Reichard to lodge a counterposition that speaks back to bureaucratic discourse.

Though writers use this genre to ground a range of arguments related to public policy, their most typical target of critique is the federal system of off-reservation boarding schools. Many writers use the genre's resources for describing spaces and cultural practices *and* narrating characters' interiority to articulate critiques of federal Indian education policies, critiques designed to move readers more successfully than dry statistical arguments for reform found in texts like the Meriam Report. Ethnographic novelists frequently embed critiques in narratives in which Native protagonists are forced to leave their homes to attend federal schools, where curricula are severely limited, discipline is strict and regimented, staff are insensitive and untrained, and students struggle to find sufficient food.

This genre enables writers to generate a vivid contrast between students' experiences in home and school spaces. Several novelists, for instance, critique the practice of BIA agents and boarding school officials forcibly removing students from their homes. Levi Horse-Afraid, the protagonist in Gessner's *Broken Arrow,* is handcuffed by a policeman and dragged from his parents' home by a school official, while his siblings and parents watch helplessly.[34] Oliver La Farge's ethnographic novel *The Enemy Gods* depicts parents who repeatedly demand that their children be allowed to leave a federal boarding school over the summer, while school officials use their captive student populations to maneuver against each other for power within the educational bureaucracy. Still other novels, such as Gillmor's *Windsinger* and Reichard's *Dezba,* portray the efforts of families to keep children out of sight of "recruiters" who will remove to federal schools any school-aged Native children they see, regardless of family wishes.[35] In their portrayals of the efforts of Native families to keep their children out of boarding schools and in their own communities, ethnographic novelists vividly countered racist notions that Native people lacked interest in their children and thus were eager to have the federal government house and feed them. These writers also suggest that Native efforts to contest the forcible removal of their children are, in part, spatial struggles, in which Native families insist upon their authority to educate their children in their own community.

Ethnographic novels include highly critical portrayals of the people who inhabit the spaces of boarding school education. Writers characterize school officials as, at worst, racist bullies, and at best, well-meaning but ineffectual participants in an inhumane system. Gessner, for example, depicts a brutish official who barks military-style orders at a new group of young students, shouting, "Hey, you fellers, stop talkin' there! . . . You fellers cut out that talkin' in Sioux. You s'posed to be 'mericans now. It's 'gin th' reg'lations fur you to talk in Sioux."[36] The dropped vowels and strongly emphasized dialect used by a character who demands that students stop speaking their native language to become "'mericans" registers Gessner's critique of ill-educated white people who were charged with educating Native students—and who rely only on "reg'lations" to guide their practices.

The inhumane practices that routinely occur within school spaces are targeted by novelists who depict the school experience as one of trauma for many students. D'Arcy McNickle, a Salish man who worked for the BIA and had some anthropological training, depicts in his 1936 ethnographic novel, *The Surrounded,* the change that overtakes the two young cousins of the protagonist, Archilde Leon, after their first experiences in a mission boarding school. Mike and Narcisse, both bright, high-spirited, and happy through the first half of the novel, must be tricked by their grandfather to be taken to the mission school; when they return, McNickle notes, "something was wrong. Mike was quieter. He showed no desire to clip a horse and ride break-neck across the meadow, he had given up shouting and blustering. The change showed itself in another way. Mike was afraid of the dark. He couldn't be dragged from the house once night had fallen." After Mike wakes up screaming in the middle of the night, Archilde learns that his cousin had been punished for his high spirits by being locked overnight in "a small room of unpleasant reputation." Following this experience, Mike worries that the priests are right—that he is evil and will be visited by evil. As a consequence of this trauma, McNickle suggests, Mike's sense of place and the pleasure he takes in participating in activities within his community and family are diminished even after he returns to his home.[37] McNickle's narrative critiques the long-lasting effects of such school experiences and furthermore argues that grief for these losses are shared communally, as not only Mike but the members of his family wrestle with the changes that his traumatic time at school have wrought.

The resources for characterization available in fiction are used by ethnographic novelists to extend their critiques to the broader system of schooling. They do this by suggesting that some characters, though specific, are also typical: the bureaucrat only concerned with his own career, for instance, or the bully cop who cherishes his power over Native people. Ethnographic novelists also portray a range of characters to argue that the inhumanity of federal Indian education is systemic. Even well-meaning characters are depicted as too deeply implicated in this system to successfully counteract its effects. In Gessner's novel, a German cook and a young doctor who work at the school both try to help Levi, the novel's young protagonist, by providing him with additional food and arguing for his medical care, but their efforts are forestalled by administrators who are primarily concerned with promoting the school publicly and strategizing about their own career advancement. The rhetorical resources of fiction allow ethnographic novelists to argue for systemic—not merely local—change to boarding school policy and practice.

In addition, the novel's resources for narrating interiority allow writers to contrast Native characters' educational desires with the kind of instruction provided in boarding schools. McNickle, for instance, portrays Catharine Wolf's reflections on her instruction in white domestic arts to narrate the significant gap between the desires that motivate Catharine and those her instructors hope to instill. Catharine reflects that the nuns who ran a mission school near her home "had taught her many arts but they had not quite taught her to be interested in using them. . . . It was nice to do those things just to find out what they were like; but as for doing them every day until she died, that was just a nuisance."[38] Although Catharine wants to learn for its own sake, to "find out what [these new practices] were like," she has no plans to refashion her life entirely in order to adopt the practices taught in the school—a distinction omitted from the Meriam Report, but that McNickle, as ethnographic novelist, can emphasize through his depictions of Catharine's inner dialogue. La Farge's *Enemy Gods,* Reichard's *Dezba,* and other ethnographic novels likewise characterize the bulk of instruction in boarding schools as misguided, charging school officials with attempting to instill adherence to white norms of domesticity rather than offering either intellectual or practical instruction in the subjects that students sought to learn.

These contrasts are made especially compelling through spatial portrayals that make these conflicting intentions concrete. For instance, Underhill's novel narrates the educational hopes that the protagonist Hawk Over Whirlpools (later Rafael) cherishes and must repeatedly relinquish throughout his several years at a federal boarding school, hopes that are rendered emblematically through Underhill's depiction of his movement through school spaces. Underhill's protagonist knows as a child that his grandfather, a Papago (Tohono O'odham) spiritual leader, will initiate him into secret knowledge when he comes of age. But when a recruiter from a federal boarding school comes to the village, Hawk Over Whirlpools is drawn by the possibility that he could also learn the secrets of white knowledge, asserting that he "want[s] both" when his grandfather asks him to choose his form of education.[39] When he arrives at school, he believes he will be taught how to create such formidable buildings in his own village; he moves through the school, touching the walls, imagining how such a structure will look in Lizard-on-the-Rocks. But he learns quickly that this is not knowledge that white educators are willing to let him access. His "frequent experiences of being pushed away and ordered about, brought it home for him. These buildings were not for Indians. These were white men's property which Indians might inhabit on sufferance, never possess."[40] As the narrative proceeds, he perpetually lowers his educational goals and still finds, repeatedly, that his teachers are unwilling to provide the instruction he seeks. Here Underhill capitalizes on the rhetorical resources of fiction to cast the entire physical structure of the boarding school as a symbol of educators' determination to maintain their power by *not* providing the forms of instruction Native students might desire. Through the contrast between the spaces that characters move through and the interiority that novelists ascribe to their protagonists, Underhill and other ethnographic novelists use the resources of this genre to emphasize a pervasive and profound mismatch between institutional and individual motivations.

Spatial resources of the ethnographic novel also allow writers to contrast the individuality of specific characters with the domination enacted in school spaces through relentless enforcement of uniformity and regimentation. The routine practices of stripping students of their names, forbidding them to speak their native languages, and forcing them to cut their hair—all practices designed to alienate students from their communities, their languages, and their bodies —are repeatedly critiqued in ethnographic novels. For instance, Underhill traces the trajectory of her protagonist in *Hawk Over Whirlpools* from his early family life through his education at an off-reservation boarding school, his later employment in a cannery, and his eventual return to his village. Through these moves, the boy is named successively Hawk Over Whirlpools, Rafael La Cruz, and Ralph Norcross; his forcible renaming mirrors his enforced alienation from his community. Several authors depict the trauma students feel after enforced haircuts; Gillmor's protagonist, Windsinger, evades school officials because he "knew that they would cut off his hair if they took him to school, and would forbid him to speak the language of the People."[41]

Other attacks on students' identities and affiliations are critiqued as well, such as the efforts of school officials to force Native students to wear uniforms and follow utterly routinized schedules. Levi Horse-Afraid, in *Broken Arrow,* is forced to stand in formation in the cold with other students, surrounded by "barrack-like buildings in strict regulation" facing a "drill field." In Underhill's novel, students at Rafael's school "all dressed in blue shirts and blue jean trousers. In winter they had dark-red sweaters. A bell rang in the morning and they rose; another, and they went to breakfast; another, and they marched out, piling their tin dishes at the kitchen window."[42] Underhill links uniform clothing with the extreme regimentation of school life, as two complementary practices that efface differences among students who come from dozens of tribes and speak diverse languages. Enforced uniformity of dress is paired with enforced uniformity of behavior, enabling teachers and administrators to see students as merely abstractions—as instantiations of the encompassing category "Indian," indistinguishable from one another but, as a race, essentially Other. The genre's resources for narrating interiority and individuality permit these texts to counteract practices that efface students' specificity, insisting instead upon the particularity of their protagonists.

Collectively, ethnographic novelists launch a critique of federal Indian education, charging that students are forcibly removed to schools where they are subjected to a host of practices that undermine their health and their connection to their home communities without offering meaningful instruction in recompense for this dislocation. Although the Meriam Report crystalized these widespread critiques in 1928, writers of ethnographic novels combined anthropological knowledge claims with vivid, individualized stories in order to humanize the "problem of Indian administration" the report so carefully outlined. Gessner's harrowing account of Levi Horse-Afraid's capture and removal to school or his description of the night Levi sneaks out of the dormitory with other boys not to make mischief, but to silently raid the garbage cans outside the kitchen in a perpetual struggle to evade starvation addresses readers who might not be moved by official reports that note the prevalence of compulsory education or the insufficiency of funds for students' nutritional needs.[43] Through fictional narratives, these rhetors sought to make both real and moving a situation that, in other genres, remained abstract or out of sight. In making these arguments to public audiences, writers of ethnographic novels engage in scientific popularizations that reveal the unsettled quality of professional anthropological discourse, in which disciplinary insularity is confronted by arguments that seek public audiences and public ends for anthropological knowledge.

Plotting Native Tragedy

The rhetorical resources of ethnographic novels offered writers opportunities to launch vivid and moving critiques of the practices of off-reservation boarding schools, yet the narrative trajectories plotted in some cases also reveal a troubling effect of such genre-blending: the attachment of scientific authority to sentimental texts that plot trajectories toward Native death. Indeed, the focus of reviewers and writers on the capacity of ethnographic novels to prompt emotional responses reveals a persistent link between the research-based portrayals found in ethnographic novels and the "legends of Fenimore Cooper."[44] Ethnographic novels such as *Laughing Boy, Hopi Girl,* and *Rhythm for Rain,* for instance, conform to narrative patterns that include romanticized portrayals of an idealized Native life and that eulogize the tragic death of the "noble savage" in ways that would be familiar to readers of sentimental fiction such as Catherine Maria Sedgwick's *Hope Leslie* and Lydia Maria Child's *Hobomok*.[45] Consequently, the critiques of federal Indian policy embedded in several ethnographic novels are undermined by narrative trajectories that move predictably toward tragic ends for Native people.

I refer to narrative trajectories to emphasize the capacity of this genre to combine richly detailed cultural contexts with the movement of individual characters over space and time. Narrative trajectories in ethnographic novels link individual change with movement through richly rendered cultural contexts, allowing rhetors to describe individual choices within material and historical circumstances. Although fictional plots in non-ethnographic texts likewise describe change over time, the concept of trajectory depends upon the tension present in this genre between depictions of individual protagonists' interiority and the extensive use of realist ethnographic detail to convey accurate observations of cultural practices. This tension generates spatial strategies for portraying the power of spaces to provoke and to limit individual and cultural change. Ethnographic novels create social and cultural spaces for their characters to move through and simultaneously grant their narrative trajectories greater epistemic authority than fictional texts typically claim. Although these spatial strategies are not, of course, unique to the ethnographic novel, the contrast between habitation and movement gains rhetorical power through the deep discontinuity in this genre between unique individual protagonists and the richly detailed, coherent cultural contexts rendered through ethnographic realism and holism.

The genre's rhetorical resources allow some writers to craft narrative trajectories that proceed inexorably toward Native death. In *Laughing Boy*, La Farge includes detailed ethnographic descriptions of artisanal practices of weaving and jewelry making, careful accounts of Navajo ceremonials and games, and precise depictions of Navajo religious beliefs and taboos. For instance, La Farge describes Navajo funerary rites by depicting Laughing Boy "walk[ing] carefully, avoiding bushes, observing all the requirements. . . . Over [the body] he put her blankets, at her head, food, by her hands, her weaving tools, cooking implements at her feet. He covered her form with silver and turquoise and coral and coins. As he arranged her, he prayed."[46] These ethnographic details lend the narrative significant authority. Against this backdrop of ethnographic detail, La Farge charts a narrative trajectory that articulates the impossibility of Native survival. The title character, Laughing Boy, meets and falls in love with Slim Girl, a Navajo woman who has lived near whites after attending an off-reservation boarding school, where she learned English and distanced herself from traditional practices. Slim Girl has also become a prostitute, which she continues in secret after marrying Laughing Boy. She and Laughing Boy begin saving money for their return to a place within the Navajo reservation, while Slim Girl undertakes to learn Navajo arts such as weaving. Laughing Boy discovers Slim Girl's secret sexual activities, forgives her, and sets off with her to the home they want to make on the reservation; during this journey, a rival for Slim Girl's affection, a character named "Red Man," shoots at Laughing Boy from a distance but strikes Slim Girl instead, who dies from the wound. After her death, Laughing Boy mourns for four days and then continues alone on his route deeper into the reservation.

The familiar elements within this narrative trajectory turn La Farge's characters into sentimental types: Slim Girl typifies the corruption that is seen as attending contact between Native and white characters, while Laughing Boy signifies a state of uncontaminated Native authenticity; their effort to integrate these symbolically separate states through their marriage is plotted in a heavily foreshadowed trajectory toward death. In contrast to historical accounts that suggest Native students who were subject to boarding school education nevertheless found inventive ways to *use* their experiences toward their own ends, La Farge plots a trajectory that discounts those potential uses as it proceeds inevitably from Slim Girl's contamination to her evocative and romantic death.

Not only individual protagonists, but also large numbers of Native characters are sometimes plotted similarly in ethnographic novels. Nelson's *Rhythm for Rain,* for instance, narrates the death of scores of inhabitants of a small Hopi settlement after a protracted, naturally occurring drought. Nelson represents Native death in this trajectory as inevitable, caused by natural processes that cannot be forestalled. Shaping such a narrative within an ethnographic novel is especially problematic, insofar as the writer claims greater authority because of his or her use of epistemic and rhetorical practices developed within professional anthropology. Nelson's book begins with the birth of the protagonist, a Hopi boy named 'Yeshva, establishing a narrative pattern of growth and maturation that allows Nelson to depict, as 'Yeshva matures, the community rites and ceremonial practices that take place over the course of a child's life; this narrative structure tends to suggest that 'Yeshva, while an individual protagonist, is also at the same time a *typical* Hopi, moving through rites and routines that all young Hopi males experience as they mature. This progression is interrupted by the central crisis of the novel: a historic two-year drought that profoundly affects the inhabitants of two neighboring villages. People in both villages guard their food and water supplies and carefully complete the year-round routine of dances meant to honor the Katchinas and bring rain, but no rain falls. Nelson's narrative describes an escalating series of horrors visited upon the villagers because of the lack of rain, culminating in cannibalism and the selling of young girls into "slavery" among Mexicans in exchange for corn and water to stay alive. At the very end of the book, a storm finally visits the desert again and the people who are still alive regain their strength and, finally, look forward to 'Yeshva's marriage to his love interest, Polimana.

If the plot structure of *Rhythm for Rain* is tragic, its use of the epistemic resources of anthropology, including oral history and participant observation, supports claims to accuracy that make this narrative particularly insidious. In particular, Nelson's narrator grants no credence to Hopi explanations for the drought or to their practices designed to alleviate it; as they complete their dances for bringing rain, Nelson portrays these dances as ineffectual efforts targeting natural forces beyond the control or even understanding of his Hopi characters. In this way, Nelson suggests both the limited agency of the Hopi over their existence and the inadequacy of their resources for understanding or responding to the world around them. He calls the rhetorical and epistemic resources available in the ethnographic novel into the service of an unsettling ideological position, namely, the naturalness and inevitability of the enormous number of Native deaths recorded in the novel.

The anthropologist's rhetorical resources for generating epistemic authority through participant observation are explicitly called into service in Nelson's novel as well. Nelson claims that *Rhythm for Rain* is based on ethnographic observations that uncover an otherwise hidden Native interiority, revealing "the Indian as he lives most richly: in the guarded, venerated faith of his fathers."[47] Echoing reviewers who critiqued ethnographic novels that failed to provide imaginative access to Native interiority, Nelson argues that readers "who have known only the outer Indian have never known him at all, for his real life and nature lie in the subconscious, intuitive realm that comes to the surface in his faith, in his art, and in his philosophy of life."[48] The practices of observation and realist ethnographic description developed within professional anthropology are crucial for the claims to accuracy and authority this fictional work insists upon. By observing, reading, and interpreting the "surface" realities of Native religious, creative, and ceremonial practices, Nelson posits and depicts a "subconscious, intuitive realm" of Native life that he contends is usually obscured rather than revealed in ethnographic accounts. The method Nelson has adopted in order to arrive at his purportedly deep understanding of Hopi life is explicitly the practice of participant observation, undertaken over the course of "ten years" during which, Nelson writes, "I let this ancient life and faith flow into my own being and then, gradually, I began to sense inner impulses that clamored for release. . . . So writing began; first as detailed accounts of ritual and legend until, unexpectedly, from the last survivor of the drought of eighty years ago I heard the stripped horror of that time."[49] Evoking the professional knowledge-making practice of participant observation within the frame of his fictional narrative permits Nelson to claim epistemic status for a text that deploys a practice of imaginative projection not fundamentally different from that of earlier novelists.

In short, using ethnographic realism and holism within fictional plots permitted certain kinds of genre work to take place in ethnographic novels. In particular, this genre located critiques of schooling practices in narratives designed to move readers to sympathy or outrage more effectively than official discourse. But the narrative trajectories plotted in some ethnographic novels also reveal the capacity of genre work to attach epistemic authority to narratives that represent Native death as natural and inevitable rather than a historical project of settler colonialism, a project against which Native people have successfully contended. Such trajectories, in texts that represent their cultural accounts as scientific knowledge, reinforce the broad discursive patterns that underwrote the brutal boarding school practices so many ethnographic novelists targeted through their popular texts.

Challenging Public and Professional Knowledge

The range of uses writers devised for the ethnographic novel highlights the underdetermined impact of genre work, a strategic blending of generic elements that could have both progressive and conservative effects. The ethnographic novels analyzed above primarily *use* anthropological discourse to target nonanthropological audiences, undertaking the work of popularization that Elsie Clews Parsons outlined. These authors use disciplinary forms of expertise to create engaging portrayals of Native life for the edification of a public that avidly consumed representations of Native peoples. Yet ethnographic fiction could be employed to pressure professional anthropological discourse as well. In particular, Gladys Reichard's ethnographic novel *Dezba, Woman of the Desert* demonstrates how the spatial resources available in ethnographic fiction could be used to complicate the simplified models of Indian education circulating in popular discourse and to challenge the univocal authority anthropologists enacted in their official genres at the same time.

Reichard composed this ethnographic novel following her involvement in the 1930s in an experimental school for Navajo adults. The widespread dissatisfaction with federal Indian policy voiced in the Meriam Report and elsewhere in the late 1920s was the impetus behind this school. Early in 1934, Reichard was invited to Washington to meet with the new head of the Bureau of Indian Affairs, John Collier, who had been appointed Commissioner by Franklin Roosevelt in 1933 and who initiated a large-scale revision to federal Indian policy, most notably through promoting the Wheeler-Howard Act (also known as the Indian Reorganization Act), which reversed nineteenth-century allotment policies. Reichard was initially skeptical about the new commissioner's plans, speculating in her letters to Boas that even if Collier's intentions were sincere, he would be incapable of counteracting the entrenched nepotism that governed the BIA. Nevertheless, Reichard returned from the meeting in Washington newly convinced that Collier's administration could improve the situation of Native people.[50] With Collier's personal support and financial backing from the BIA, that summer Reichard organized and taught in the experimental school, which she and Collier hoped would become a model for small-scale, community-based adult education that could replace the large-scale federal boarding schools that the Meriam Report had found so ineffective.

Instruction in the school centered on Navajo language, as Reichard taught written forms of Navajo to native and second-language Navajo speakers. This linguistic focus extended the impact of the school beyond the adult learners for whom it was designed. For instance, the students in the school practiced written Navajo by designing and writing copy for a newsletter, the White Sands News, which they mimeographed for distribution among Navajo speakers in the White Sands region; the newsletter included a short history of the school, written in Navajo, as well as a summary of phonetics written by Reichard in English, providing basic linguistic instruction for anyone who received a copy. Reichard's students included "a sophomore from the U. of N. Mex. & a little boy of 10, [with] everything else in between."[51] Reichard found that this range in student age linked school instruction with the broader Navajo community at White Sands, as students and nonstudents alike, the "whole neighborhood," walked "around spelling Nav. and practicing t'l, k,' t,' etc."[52] By the end of the first month, Reichard reported to Boas that "the Navajo and even some Whites go around saying 'How would you spell that?' And I answer, 'How do you think?'"[53] In these ways, the school maintained connections between the students who studied there and their broader community, which was also involved in literacy instruction.

The form of instruction Reichard adopted at the White Sands school linked language study with Navajo cultural traits, in sharp contrast to pedagogical practices that typified federal boarding schools. More precisely, the instruction at the White Sands school developed in tandem with the qualities of the students who studied there, because there is no evidence Reichard designed the school with specific pedagogical strategies in mind apart from a willingness to learn *how* the students who attended wanted to study. Her reports to Boas and Parsons at the end of the summer suggest her surprise at finding a number of "carryovers from [Navajo] culture" that influenced the kind and quality of students' learning. Specifically, Reichard noted that students' highly developed capacities for concentration and awareness of form helped them engage deeply with linguistic material and make significant strides over the short duration of the summer school. Reporting on the school's progress to Parsons, Reichard noted that "as they stay with a sing for 9 nights, so they stay with a verb for 4 hr. They get bawled up, they argue, they write, they murmur, they struggle, it is dinnertime, nevertheless they persist and at last they have it." The students' commitment to learning also reflects what Reichard sees as the students' "individualism," that is, the willingness of each student to "argue for 3 hr. about one word . . . [with] quiet talk and laughter and razzing and at the end of the 3 hr. each writes his word as *he* says it!"[54] In stark contrast to federal boarding schools' enforcement of uniformity, regimentation, and English-only instruction, educational practices at the White Sands school sought to integrate specific shared cultural traits with individualized attention to Navajo-language learning.

Furthermore, the space of the White Sands school was *not* sacrosanct or inviolable, nor subjected to the extremely regimented schedules common in federal boarding schools. Reichard found that her students showed up at all times of day, arriving when they were inclined to and remaining to continue working on a problem until they were satisfied they had solved it. In a letter to Boas, Reichard remarked with evident pleasure that "One student arrived on horseback at 5:45 A.M. of a Sat! I take them whenever they can do it." The space of the school, which was located in an unused hogan, was physically open to the outdoors, permitting community members to visit the school at their discretion. This openness to the broader environment brought occasional disruption, as when a goat wandered into the school through the open door frame. This provoked laughter from Reichard's students, who, Reichard recounted to Boas, welcomed the goat and then, after the goat left, said in Navajo, "'See him scram' . . . and proceed[ed] to add a glottal stop."[55]

The physical arrangement of the school becomes symbolic as well as material when the students include a drawing of their school on the cover of the White Sands News. This drawing depicts the school from the perspective of someone standing outside, looking at the school head-on, revealing a goat peeking out from inside the school through its open door. Above the school, Navajo-language inscriptions frame the drawing, and text in Navajo also occupies school space, placed in the window frame within the drawing. These visual portrayals announce a degree of Navajo ownership *over* this school that contrasts strongly with, for instance, the alienation from physical school spaces experienced by boarding school students in novels by Underhill, McNickle, and others. Simultaneously playful and symbolic, this drawing represents the White Sands school as significantly different from the regimented military spaces characteristic of federal Indian education.

Reichard suggested that the differences from federal schools that characterized the White Sands experimental school enabled its success. Reichard wrote to Boas that she would be "spoiled to death for Barnard students" after spending weeks teaching students who "are here because they *want* to learn." To Parsons, Reichard reported that if her students "liked the school a quarter as well as I did—& I think they did—they liked it a lot. Never have I had such satisfactory students." As an educational experiment focused on Navajo-language instruction and designed to accommodate students' varied lives, the school also had pragmatic success, Reichard argued, noting that "we finished the month with Day School jobs offered [to] four new ones [adult students], two are already employed by the Educational Service, and these writing Navajo far from perfectly but nevertheless intelligently, and reading well. The others will overlap into August and will teach their own children and families and are able to read."[56] In the terms that she valued as a faculty member, including student engagement and motivation, Reichard found the White Sands school extremely satisfying. In addition, in terms valued by the BIA—jobs secured for its students—Reichard argued that the school's flexibility and connection to the Navajo community made it more effective than boarding school education.

This educational experiment significantly shaped Reichard's rhetorical purposes and practices as she returned yet again to the ethnographic material she had drawn on for her monograph and field autobiography. The knowledge that Reichard constructs through her ethnographic novel, *Dezba, Woman of the Desert,* differs in key ways from those earlier texts and from the characteristic qualities of other ethnographic novels. For instance, although Reichard's monograph and field autobiography both primarily examined Navajo shepherding and weaving practices, Reichard's novel includes extensive discussions of a range of educational practices, taking up this genre's widely shared concern for Indian education. At the same time, the narrative in *Dezba* proceeds in a far less linear fashion than is found in other ethnographic novels such as *Laughing Boy, Broken Arrow,* or *The Surrounded.* The *New York Times* review of *Dezba,* for instance, calls the book a "crystallization in story form" of Reichard's anthropological research, yet also warns the reader that "the word 'story' must be given a loose interpretation, to be sure, for this book has no plot and cannot be described as fiction; it is, rather, a collection of character sketches and word pictures, cast in one general narrative mold."[57] The narrative in *Dezba* is a dispersed one, as the novel follows the daily activities of a large collection of characters, fictionalized composites of specific people, all of whom are at least loosely connected to the central figure, Dezba, the matriarch of a large and complex family. This narrative structure enables Reichard not only to respond to broad public concern over Indian education, but also to devise an innovative multivocal form of anthropological knowledge.

Rhetorical Trajectories

The rhetorical trajectories Reichard crafts for her array of characters allow her to address the broad public readership that repeatedly debated "the problem" of Indian education during the interwar period. The spatial-rhetorical resources of the ethnographic novel provide Reichard an opportunity to narrate the tension between agency and structure, a tension that Reichard employs to characterize individuals as neither wholly free agents nor mere expressions of broad cultural abstractions. Reichard charts characters' movements in *Dezba* through space and over time across a series of trajectories that portray education as a process with deeply spatial and affective dimensions. This strategy allows Reichard to describe individual choices within constrained material and historical circumstances. That is, movement is directed by individual agents, but shaped by a network of contextual factors, including family histories, physical barriers, social prohibitions, and ideological and emotional attachments that limit the range of individual possibility in patterned ways.

Reichard lends educational trajectories a spatial dimension through the paired concepts of fit/lack of fit and familiar/strange. Reichard suggests that places become familiar through long habitation while new spaces are strange; long habitation permits individuals to fit into their spatial and social environments, while movement and relocation often generate an initial lack of fit between individuals and their new environments. These spatial topoi enable Reichard to put characters in motion, through space, over time, changing the characters and the attachments that link those characters to specific places. In these ways, Reichard represents education as something inseparable from spatial considerations. For instance, in Reichard's depictions, inhabiting a particular space, such as a school, prompts changes to individuals who then no longer fit comfortably into spaces they occupied earlier. These changes set individual characters on different paths through additional spaces and contexts. Reichard thus underscores the affective investments that give particular spaces such power. Tracing movement and habitation across multiple spaces over time, Reichard inscribes trajectories that portray Native education in terms far more complex than official policies recognized during the period, counteracting the tendency of contemporary debates to reduce "Indian education" to the choice between wholesale assimilation or mere accommodation to white norms.[58]

The first trajectory Reichard traces is one most familiar from other ethnographic novels critical of the project of off-reservation boarding schools. This is the trajectory of *mis-fit*, in which removal from one's home environment renders a student incapable of returning in a satisfying way to the place she or he was originally from. In *Dezba,* Mary, the daughter of Dezba's friend, faces the typical difficulties encountered by students who must rehabituate themselves to their homes after years spent living in other spaces. Although Mary did well at her boarding school, she is like most female graduates of boarding schools in being unable to find work even in domestic service after her education, and so returns to her mother's home. Mary fails to "fit in with her mother's surroundings" after her years at school, and Reichard suggests that this lack of fit results from Mary's inability to achieve domestic comforts and feminine adornments that her schooling has taught her to desire. Dezba reflects that returned students like Mary "needed so many things that the Navajo could not get to carry out their new ideas." For instance, noticing that returned students "liked to bathe every day under a shower or in a bathtub," Dezba reflects that other "Navajo on the Reservation also liked to bathe, but Dezba, who was more fortunate than most of her friends, had to haul every drop of water she used at least two miles." She also reflects that she likes the way manicured nails look—another adornment Mary desires—but Dezba finds that "chopping splintery cedar wood, dyeing yarn, butchering sheep, and washing clothes in hard water made a manicure seem futile."[59] Through Dezba's reflections, Reichard critiques educational practices that fail to prepare female students for the labor realities that face them after school. Mary's desires are not portrayed as unreasonable in themselves, but only impracticable in the location where Mary has to make her life, shaped as her mobility is by such factors as a domestic labor market saturated with female boarding school graduates who share similar educations. Mary's education has been fundamentally inattentive to the varieties of environments where people live, teaching desires without attending to the relations of these learned preferences to the context of Mary's life. Reichard suggests that while habitation in school spaces alters students' desires in many ways, it is both insensitive and destructive to demand that students from diverse home environments adopt behaviors and desires identical to those of whites.

Habitation as a spatial strategy is often intertwined with representations of movement. Movement between competing spaces can create the trajectory of mis-fit Reichard demonstrates through the character of Mary, when failure to fit one's environment generates further mobility, as an individual's reordered desires and emotions direct her future movement. In this way, Reichard portrays both movement and habitation as deeply affective processes, intimately linked through the emotional attachments that tie individuals to specific people and places. A protagonist's movement, for example, is often directed toward places where the protagonist has emotional investments, and movement itself is capable of reorienting an individual's emotional attachments, forging connections to new places or increasing the range of spaces to which one feels attached.

Reichard exploits these genre-based resources to explore beyond the familiar trajectory of mis-fit that Mary represents. By tracing several educational trajectories in *Dezba*, Reichard argues that one cannot characterize the relationships among space, emotion, and education as a straightforward progression in which one begins feeling perfectly fitted to one's home, loses that fit through education elsewhere, and then generates narrative tension through one's inability to fit in any place. Instead, Reichard maps three additional stories of Indian education that together suggest that movement and education are gendered, that emotional investments in particular spaces can override the influence of physical mobility, and that even loose affiliations with one's home community can still shape educational outcomes. To advance these arguments, Reichard inscribes not only Mary's trajectory of mis-fit, but also a trajectory of *indigenous instruction* in the form of education that Dezba's own daughter, Gray Girl, has been subjected to since her childhood, and two contrasting trajectories of *repeated integration* and *roving relation* that characterize the movement of Dezba's two sons.

By contrasting these four trajectories, Reichard registers the gendered nature of educational practices that were designed to shape male and female students for different kinds of spaces. After seeing what boarding school education has made possible for her own two sons and for her friend's daughter, Mary, Dezba recognizes that the possibilities that off-reservation education opens up for female students are significantly narrower than those made available to male students. Dezba sees several reasons for boys' education away from their homes, where male students might learn "building, carpentering, and machinery, and all of these could be useful to him"; furthermore, male students sometimes "became interpreters, and there were more jobs for Navajo men who could speak English than for those who could not."[60] In contrast, Dezba reflects that female students are likely to follow a trajectory like Mary's, in which they receive no practical or technical training and instead are taught only to desire comforts difficult to reproduce in their own homes.

Through tracing the trajectory of indigenous instruction that Dezba adopts for her own daughter, Gray Girl, Reichard insists that Navajo education has its own meaningful shape and purpose. Prompted by her attention to these gendered differences in educational opportunities, Dezba undertakes Gray Girl's education entirely within her Navajo community. Gray Girl represents, to her mother, the ideal of Navajo domestic achievement; she creates orderly space even in the disorder of the sheep dip, finds numerous areas within the community in which to be productive and learn new skills, and contributes those skills in turn to ever-widening circles of influence within her community. Gray Girl's indigenous instruction has been "constant, informal, and persistent," following a trajectory that keeps her close to her family and deeply involved in the spaces where she is attached.[61] This, of course, is also a gendered form of education, but Gray Girl's education is one fitted to her desires, her material reality, and her trajectory into Navajo womanhood. In contrast, both Dezba's sons go away to boarding school, and by tracing where their trajectories converge and diverge, Reichard explores the possibilities that boarding school education affords male students yet denies to female students.

For Dezba's oldest son, Tuli, Reichard inscribes a trajectory of repeated integration. Tuli's habitation in and movement through boarding school is unsatisfying in many of the same ways that characterize the student protagonists of other ethnographic novels, such as Rafael La Cruz and Levi Horse-Afraid. Nevertheless, Reichard charts a trajectory for Tuli that does not lead either to the sanatorium or to social isolation back at home. Tuli, like other student protagonists, is always hungry at school, but his physical deprivations are less severe than the intellectual deprivations he suffers. His education at school consists of endless rounds of labor: washing dishes, working in the laundry, planting and watering decorative flowers, and so on.[62] As contemporary historians of Native educational history have pointed out, even the term "vocational training" hardly justifies the enormous amounts of labor most students in Indian boarding schools were required to perform—labor that kept schools running.[63] But Reichard portrays Tuli as determined to learn despite his teachers' determination to exclude him from the forms of education he desires. He wants badly to study in the machine shop, for instance, but is not permitted to do so. Nevertheless, he watches what takes place in the machine shop to glean ideas "which he put into practice for the convenience of all" when he returns to his community, where he "devised an efficient hay-baler, made of boards and an automobile jack. Whenever anyone about the place needed construction of any kind he called on Tuli who found a way to accomplish it even with crude and scanty materials."[64] Tuli's determination to garner useful knowledge from his time at boarding school thwarts the intentions of the school officials, as he persists in making use of his knowledge to meet needs shared within his home community. Using rhetorical resources drawn from fiction and ethnographic description, Reichard emphasizes this link between Tuli's desires and his community's needs.

Moreover, Reichard describes Tuli's trajectory as one of repeated integration to interrogate the ways that movement into new spaces can revise yet not supplant attachments to former spaces. Despite Tuli's time away at school, Reichard notes, many of his affections and desires remain unchanged. Although his mother "steeled herself" every summer "to meet the change in him which she feared," he remains each year "the smiling son she had sent away, anxious to get home, eager to herd sheep or ride the range. He had not forgotten his horsemanship. . . . He was always willing to hoe corn or haul wood or water, even as in the old days."[65] Against Dezba's fears, Tuli's education in boarding schools fails to erode his emotional attachments to his family, undermine his religious beliefs, or disrupt his integration into his home. Echoing the positive possibilities for Native survival that contemporary scholars such as Lomawaima and Child outline, and in spite of the genocidal aims of federal boarding schools, Tuli's boarding school education "had not changed Tuli's attitude toward his work or his own people."[66] He exemplifies many students' determination to use their educational experiences to maintain the communities where their affection is still invested. These emotional investments have spatial dimensions in Reichard's narrative, where Tuli's opportunity to return home each summer provides movement that keeps him connected to his family. This process of repeated reintegration serves as a curb on the other changes that Tuli's time in a different environment might effect. Reichard maps Tuli's movement—toward school, then home, repeatedly—to underscore this student's determination that his learning should take a particular direction, that is, back toward his home community.

Reichard pairs this narrative with a contrasting one to indicate the complexity of the ways in which place, emotion, and education intertwine. The trajectory of roving relation that Reichard inscribes for the character John Silversmith, Tuli's brother, depicts looser connections that permit a great range of movement while still orienting this student toward his home. John, Dezba's younger son, moves further from his home than his brother yet remains connected to his community in ongoing ways. Unlike Tuli, John is a favorite among his teachers, which results in his being kept at school over the summer; five years pass after he leaves for boarding school before he first returns to his family home. This longer habitation at school loosens John's link to his home community, and Reichard represents this alteration spatially: returning home, John "seemed to sit on the very edge of a sheepskin, hardly touching it. He drank gingerly from a cup, or even used one of his own which he carried with him and lent to no one."[67] These marks of physical separation which John's mother notes indicate the changes he has undergone through his long habitation elsewhere.

John also moves through the widest range of educational institutions: he attends a series of boarding schools and then a state university before eventually enrolling in the Hogan School, a fictionalized name for the school Reichard conducted at White Sands in 1934. John pursues an education significantly beyond what boarding school educators traditionally provide. If he had been a "docile or phlegmatic pupil," Reichard writes, he would merely have "continued as far as that school would take him. But John was neither phlegmatic nor docile." Instead, Reichard narrates the sequence of school spaces he has inhabited, prompted by his dissatisfaction with his boarding school education and by his own ingrained desire for knowledge: "After three years at the school nearest his home, he made up his mind to try another and managed to get to it. Having arrived from a long distance, he was allowed to stay. His first move was typical of all his schooling. . . . There was hardly an Indian boarding-school which he had not attended. He was always sure that the one he heard about would be more suitable for him than the one where he was." Across these various educational spaces, John has studied "geology, archaeology and anthropology . . . [and] philosophy," as well as Navajo-language literacy, because "he wanted to work intensively on Indian languages."[68] John's education is prompted by intellectual interests as well as practical goals, including his desire to become a teacher to provide adult education among the members of his immediate community at White Sands. At the end of his trajectory, his education includes learning indigenous history, conducting research among religious figures on the reservation, and teaching medicine and other adult courses among his peers. Although he is not so integrated into his family's life as his brother, he still maintains a comfortable—if looser—relationship, one that he continually renegotiates as an adult.

In both of these trajectories, Reichard represents John and Tuli's original movements toward boarding school not as actions imported from elsewhere, but as emerging from desires rooted in their home communities. Although John desires to pursue scholarship and Tuli seeks useful, practical skills, Reichard insists that both of these desires are thoroughly and already part of the Navajo world, not a white importation. John, for instance, attends a boarding school off-reservation because "he was not satisfied with the answers to the many questions in his mind, and he was sure school would help with them. Besides, there must be many wonderful sights and experiences at the far places to which the children were taken and on the way as well."[69] The desires that lead John away from the reservation—for knowledge, broader access to the world, and opportunities for travel—are all familiar within the Navajo community. Reichard writes John and Tuli's movement toward boarding schools neither as a desire for white culture nor as a chafing against traditional restraints, but rather as desires rooted in Navajo community life.

Through these four contrasting educational trajectories, Reichard uses the resources of the ethnographic novel to address the complex relationship between individual choice and structuring social forces. As she inscribes these trajectories, tracing Mary's, Gray Girl's, John's, and Tuli's movements as they are shaped by emotional attachments that are modified over time, Reichard constructs a version of Indian education that attends closely both to individual differences and to cultural contexts. In this way, Reichard's novel does not only create knowledge of the Navajo in a form that popular audiences would find readable—the goal of ethnographic fiction outlined by Elsie Clews Parsons in 1922—but also explores interactions among attachments, desires, and the spaces that shape one's education. Using the resources of the genre to construct detailed cultural environments, to propel individual protagonists through such environments, and to demonstrate to readers the multiple factors that motivate such movement, Reichard defines education as a negotiated process that takes place over time.

Ultimately, through these four distinct trajectories—alongside many other instances throughout the book that emphasize the learning that always takes place within a Navajo community and family—Reichard underscores the complexity of Indian education. She joins with other ethnographic novelists in critiquing poor curricula and racist teachers, yet locates the *desire* to learn as something emerging from *within* the Navajo community and posits neither *home* nor *away* as the best location for Native learning. Instead, her text emphasizes the *use* of education, something scholars in Native studies have also recently emphasized: that linguistic, literate, and pragmatic skills learned in boarding schools could be used by Native students in ways unanticipated by the institutional structure of federal Indian education.

Multivocality

These myriad trajectories respond to public discussions surrounding the aims and ends of Indian education, but Reichard also engages in a rhetorical practice in *Dezba* that disrupts the authority claimed by anthropologists over Native lives and representations. The multiple, competing voices that Reichard orchestrates in her ethnographic novel destabilize anthropological authority—

an authority asserted not only in monographs and folklore collections, as prior chapters have demonstrated, but also secured through the epistemic claims made in other works of ethnographic fiction, as well.

My examination of the multivocal qualities of Reichard's text builds on contemporary discussions in language theory and anthropological theory that emphasize the capacity of texts to either accommodate or circumscribe the presence of multiple speaking positions within a single utterance. Bakhtin argues that all language is "heteroglossic," composed of myriad voices; consequently, even a text authored entirely by one writer—such as the novels by Dickens that Bakhtin praises—can take multivocal form if distinct speakers populate and voice the text. In contrast to such openness to multiple voices, certain genres and discourses seek to minimize the sense that even one's own language is inhabited by other speakers and made possible by others' utterances. Such prohibitions against the irruptions of multivocality are especially prevalent in scientific discourses, wherein writers seek to control, rationalize, and unify language to portray knowledge production as an individual accomplishment. For instance, anthropologist James Clifford argues that all ethnographic writing emerges out of contexts that are fundamentally, inherently multivocal; that is, this writing is crafted by an ethnographer out of material that *other people say*. Yet complex processes of interaction, exchange, and textual inscription are rendered in traditional ethnographic texts as a univocal feat of knowledge production.[70]

Opening up a text to multiple voices is an act with epistemic as well as rhetorical implications. For this reason, contemporary anthropologists have argued that ethnographers *should* craft multivocal ethnographies to create more equitable relations for knowledge production. Joseph Tobin, for instance, argues that because multivocal ethnographies remain open to rather than assimilating the voices of speakers other than the anthropologist, such texts offer writers a way to "ameliorate . . . traditional power inequities" in anthropological scholarship.[71] A multivocal text challenges inequities of knowledge production by including numerous voices, which undermine the easy assumption of authority on the part of the author, limit the generalizability of the author's claims, and respond to and sometimes challenge the interpretations the author attempts.

Exploiting the capacity of the novel to include such a multiplicity of specific voices, Reichard creates in *Dezba* an ethnographic text that yields discursive space for a range of Native characters to speak at length about their own educational plans, efforts, and critiques. As she fictionalizes not only her fieldwork among Navajo weavers but also her experimental school at White Sands, Reichard shares control of the narrative with other speakers, disrupting through the resources of fiction the monologic quality of the knowledge produced in traditional monographs.

By handing over significant portions of *Dezba* to Native speakers who voice a range of arguments and attitudes concerning educational practices and policies, Reichard disrupts this univocal authority in numerous ways. For instance, Reichard reinforces the claim that the impulse toward education is neither white-owned nor government-owned. She notes, for example, that one Navajo woman in the experimental Hogan School "had organized and conducted a day school successfully for two years before the Government undertook its more ambitious new plan."[72] This teacher—and Hogan School student—discusses her experiences as a student and as an educator at length. She speaks eloquently of being taken to a school in Santa Fe far from her home because of the inability of the school officials to tell the difference between a Hopi and a Navajo. After four years spent without seeing her parents, she was finally returned to Gallup, where she had to convince a school official to let her look for her father in the town. This experience prompts the speaker to make "a vow that if ever I could do anything to keep a Navajo child from being taken from its parents I would do it. That is why I am in favor of day schools and that is why I have struggled to show they can be a success, even if it was hard."[73] This student's story mirrors the trajectory of trauma described by many ethnographic novels: taken from home without warning, subjected to dehumanizing stereotypes that represented all Native people as indistinguishable. Yet this speaker does not chart that traumatic story as an ultimate end; instead, she speaks with a future orientation toward her *use* of that experience to create further action, to galvanize her commitment to educational reform. She recounts this personal story to assert that her investments in the question of educational policy are political and that the stakes of these discussions are collective.

The multivocal quality of this text further underscores the significance of educational traditions within Navajo communities. The teacher in *Dezba* asks the Hogan School students to produce a "health talk" about germs, both as an exercise in Navajo language literacy and as a public health measure. The students begin by discussing their own understandings of germs and public health for "nearly two days." Reichard narrates the process by which the group moves forward with their writing through the involvement in the school of a community elder: "During this time Shooting Chanter, an old Navajo medicine-man, came in to visit the School and the pupils explained their difficulties to him. He who acknowledged nothing new under the sun told them a Navajo story."[74] Shooting Chanter then takes over the narrative to recount a time when Navajo singers first realized that the clay used to spot their bodies during a performance was leaving behind sores; this knowledge prompted the singers to make a rule against performing when not in perfect health so as not to pass the illness among themselves. Shooting Chanter leaves the school after concluding his story, a story that Reichard indicates enables the students to proceed with their writing after previously being stalled by the difficulty of explaining an unfamiliar concept to their Navajo-speaking audience.

Both the elder's narrative and the article the students generate in response to their teacher's assignment are reproduced at length within *Dezba,* revealing that the students' text draws from the discursive resources provided by Shooting Chanter's narrative:

> A hundred years ago our people lived so that they were able to endure many hardships, cold, for example, heat, hunger, thirst and poverty, and at that time they did not have much disease. Death did not take many because all were capable of withstanding much suffering. So it was that our (now) deceased grandmothers and grandfathers lived. Our old men tell us about it.
>
> About seventy-five years ago with the railroad the Whites came among us and seemed to pour into our midst all kinds of diseases: whooping-cough, rashes of all kinds, measles, and smallpox. Just as dangerous were what we call tuberculosis and eye troubles, especially the "one which makes the eyelids rough" (trachoma).
>
> Now they are trying to prevent epidemics, that is, something of a special kind which causes sickness and seems to start without a cause. The sicknesses seem to come from certain so-called wormlike objects which we do not understand because we cannot see them. . . . They have no Navajo name and for that reason are not easy to explain precisely. . . . We Navajo are generous with our possessions. We consider it stingy not to let our brother use the same cup and towel, but of course we never think about these worms since we are ignorant of their effects.
>
> It would be much better if we were careful not to transfer these worms which we cannot see. It may be true that facilities for washing are limited, but every day the sun traverses the sky. The doctors teach us that the sun can annihilate most of these germs. So if you would put your dishes, clothing, and bedding outside it would be a good thing, for the harmful worms would be tortured by his heat. As for us, we would all live more healthily.[75]

This article, included in its entirety in *Dezba,* offers readers a Navajo-produced educational text that draws on a shared cultural quality—respect for elders—as an exigence that shapes this particular performance of collective writing. This collaboratively produced student text significantly resituates "germs" as a concept requiring explanation to their Navajo-speaking readers. For instance, the article historicizes the presence of disease among Navajo people, redescribing "germs" not just as a white-owned scientific discovery but also as a phenomena tied to European-American violence against Native people. In this way, this narrative included within the ethnographic novels portrays Native death *not* as an inevitable consequence of progress, but as a specific historical phenomena brought about by colonialism. Reichard includes this range of texts—the narrative of educational trauma voiced by the woman who organized a Navajo day school, the narrative of Navajo forms of knowledge-making encoded in Shooting Chant's story, and the collaboratively written health article produced by Navajo students for a local Navajo audience—in a form that permits these texts to remain intact, juxtaposed against rather than smoothly incorporated into Reichard's own narrative voice. Opening up her knowledge-making practice to the presence of other voices constitutes a significant departure from more univocal presentations of research.

The effects of this multivocal form of ethnography are particularly striking in a long section that recounts discussions among Hogan School students regarding their beliefs about and desires related to education. For instance, an adult student named John Young talks about *demonstrating* the efficacy of new educational ideas, contrary to the imperative to simply tell their elders what to do that some students learned at boarding school:

> The old men do not like to be told what to do by the young ones. People at the Agency always blame us for not going back and teaching our people what we have learned at school. They do not understand that our elders tell us what to do, they do not ask us. Once in a while we might make a suggestion but if it is not taken up we cannot do anything more. If we insisted, we would seem disrespectful. Returned students often make that mistake, but it doesn't get them anywhere. I have often noticed that returned students are impatient and in a hurry when talking to the old men. The old men then become stubborn and nothing can budge them. If the Government would give us someone to show us how to conduct the community centers, I am sure we could bring about great changes, but they would have to come slowly. And showing the people would do more good than talking to them.[76]

This example is one of many instances throughout *Dezba* when Reichard hands over the narrative to speakers who take stances, respond to other interlocutors, and argue vigorously and creatively in support of their positions. Such conversations contradict representations of Native people as lacking investment in, understanding of, or attention to educational policies; furthermore, these conversations speak back to discourses of expertise that located authority over policy decisions exclusively among trained officials rather than distributing authority among members of the communities influenced by such policies.

In other extended conversations, students discuss their perspectives on issues such as irrigation, federal involvement in reservation affairs, and Navajo attachment to cultural practices. For instance, John Silversmith, who works for the Soil Erosion Control project, explains both the beliefs that animate the federal erosion project and the beliefs that ensure resistance to these projects among the Navajo. He recounts the government's theory,

> that more people can live on the same amount of land if they carry on more agriculture than they can by herding large flocks of sheep. This is of course apparent and it has been proved in the Shiprock region where many acres have been farmed for a long time with water from the San Juan. But it will mean a basic change in the entire Navajo economy if it is extended all over the Reservation. The Navajo are putting up a very strong resistance to the plan because they do not want to be tied down to a small area. They want to wander about as they do now. Besides, they do not think there is enough water available at many places on their 16,000,000 acres for such elaborate irrigation projects to keep them all. And some say, too, that after the white man gets the Navajo country all nicely fixed up so that the land is valuable, they will chase the Navajo off of it. We are up against all these things in trying to teach them to conserve the soil.[77]

This excerpt from John Silversmith's long deliberation reveals how complexly he articulates his own position on economic and ecological policies within the Navajo reservation. His argument reveals his shifting identifications—with Navajo people as a whole, with the immediate community around Shiprock, and with the federal bureaucracy employing him to counteract erosion in the region.

Ultimately, this genre affords Reichard an alternative set of rhetorical resources for making knowledge. As she crafts complex trajectories of Native education, Reichard takes up the distinct spatial-rhetorical resources this genre made available to intervene in broad public discussions. She also assembles a nuanced range of Navajo perspectives on pressing issues. By narrating conversations in which participants passionately defend a range of positions, rather than assimilating all voices into her own, Reichard counteracts the tendency of even popular genres like the ethnographic novel to extend and secure anthropologists' epistemic authority over indigenous peoples.

Narrating Critique

This chapter has investigated the promise that ethnographic fiction seemed to hold among writers who believed that their ethnographic research could influence public debates and public policy. These narratives demonstrate that the rhetorical resources available in this new genre *did* offer writers an avenue for both critique and creativity: critique of the insularity of professional genres as well as creativity in devising new forms that repurposed anthropological knowledge for public ends. But the use of these resources did not necessarily result in better knowledge or more effective policy. Instead, the ethnographic novel offers further evidence that the resources a genre makes available to writers *shape* but do not *determine* a genre's uses, as many ethnographic novelists drew upon sentimental narrative trajectories that undermined the force of their policy critiques.

Although functioning primarily as a public rather than professional genre, the ethnographic novel nevertheless initiated a range of arguments with both professional and public implications. For instance, in relying upon ethnographic research and writing techniques to ground their authority and claims of expertise, writers who used this genre also participated in discursive practices that shored up anthropologists' authority over Native people. Deploying ethnographic realism and holism as portable tools for knowledge-making in new generic sites, these writers helped to solidify the epistemic status of these ethnographic techniques.

Yet my analyses of ethnographic novels also underscore the capacity of texts that are oriented toward public audiences to exert pressure on professional practices as well. For instance, by using anthropological knowledge to target *policy,* many ethnographic novelists implicitly disrupt the value of insularity in professional anthropological discourse. In this way, the emergence of ethnographic novels in the decades following the solidification of rhetorical norms in the monograph and the achievement of professionalization speaks to the ongoing presence of a range of aims and ends even within this ostensibly *disciplined* professional community. These public-oriented texts reveal significant tensions still underlying professional practice, including questions regarding the role of professional expertise and anthropologists' responsibility toward policy discussions. The multivocal quality of Reichard's narrative counters anthropologists' disciplinary claims to speak for as well as about Native people. Fictionalizing her own involvement in an educational experiment leads Reichard to fashion knowledge in a way not already present—nor permitted—within the monograph genre.

Ultimately, this chapter underscores the extent to which the outcomes of "genre work" are not predetermined. In drawing discursive techniques from genres that typically operate very differently, the writers who blended ethnographic knowledge and fictional plots in ethnographic novels used this genre to pursue sometimes contradictory ends. Studying momentary, short-lived genres like the ethnographic novel offers us access to historical traces of epistemic and community change, revealing that even after the monograph solidified disciplinary boundaries, the methods and aims of anthropological knowledge-making were still under negotiation.

Conclusion

Rhetorical Archaeology

From a historical perspective on the rise of the professions, written genres, like
pottery shards, bones, and rock strata, are material artifacts providing valuable
information on how disciplines/professions that were initially undifferentiated
established themselves as discrete knowledge-producing communities.

—Carol Berkenkotter, *Patient Tales*

IN HER investigation of narrative in the knowledge-making practices of
the field of psychiatry, Carol Berkenkotter's portrayal of genres as "pottery
shards, bones, and rock strata" evokes a provocative image of historical genre
study. I take up this metaphor of genres as artifacts—specifically, artifacts that
are incomplete, foundational, and sequenced—to develop here a vision of historical genre study as a practice of *rhetorical archaeology*. This research practice
understands genres as material instantiations of a community's norms, values,
and priorities and investigates genre change to unearth and envision the prior
life of a community. Like pottery shards, genres are only partial fragments of
the rhetorical life they enable. Like bones, however, genres are also foundational fragments, structures upon which a host of more fleeting, less easily preserved
rhetorical practices are built. And like rock strata, genres and individual texts
can be read sequentially, revealing in their spatial and temporal relations the
operation of incremental or abrupt processes of change. Furthermore, each of
these metaphors depends upon the status of genres and texts as material traces,

forms of evidence that are available to researchers even when more ephemeral dimensions of a community's life have passed out of view.

Combining methodological practices from historians and genre scholars, rhetorical archaeology unearths material traces of a community's epistemic and discursive negotiations, revealing alternatives that existed alongside the practices that ultimately won out. These traces consequently expose not only the *disciplining* of epistemic practices, but also the presence of competing textual forms in genres that revise or contest the outcomes of this disciplinary process. By investigating traces of discarded epistemic and rhetorical possibilities, scholars are able to historicize community practices in ways that challenge the naturalness of narratives of scientific progress and to argue instead that certain entrenched conceptual linkages—for instance, between objectivity, distance, and scientific rigor—have been forged and reinforced through repetition, but were not inevitable. For instance, this study has shown that some early anthropologists attempted to make rigorous knowledge out of relations of closeness, reciprocity, and responsibility, contesting their peers' claims that accurate knowledge emerged out of relations of distance and domination. By revealing that these associations among objectivity, distance, and scientific rigor emerged as historical choices among competing alternatives, we can see these connections as rhetorical accomplishments rather than axioms that are necessary for scientific discourse to function.

Treating genre investigation as an archaeological endeavor creates several affordances that lend this approach conceptual utility. In particular, rhetorical archaeology emphasizes the researcher's active role in assembling textual traces of a community's prior life, interpreting those traces through concepts of sequence and position, and building inferences into a careful reconstruction of practices that have otherwise passed out of view. An archaeological metaphor lends particular stress upon the spatial concept of *position* as a key mechanism for interpreting the social relations and routines that historical investigations uncover. Previous chapters have attended closely to differences among the positions of specific writers and the texts they produced in order to reflect the ways that widespread gender and race-based inequities, often materialized in a writer's institutional location, influenced the kind of knowledge these writers generated and the ways in which that knowledge was integrated into or isolated from mainstream disciplinary practice. This archaeological model also grounds my claim that anthropologists' disciplinary histories do not provide the full story of their field's transformation into a professional science. My own field's textual tools, particularly genre theory and rhetorical analysis, can be used to shed new light on the prior practices of anthropology's professional community.

Rhetorical archaeology builds upon the historiographic projects of rhetorical scholars such as Jacqueline Jones Royster, Richard Enos, and others who have called for expanding the methodological paradigms employed by rhetorical scholars to conduct fuller investigations into histories of rhetorical practice. These scholars draw upon spatial metaphors with particular significance for anthropological discourse, such as *excavation* and *ethnographic stance,* to define new historiographic undertakings for the field of rhetoric. Enos, for instance, calls for increased use of field methods to literally and figuratively excavate new primary sources, such as inscriptions on stone monuments and other "small bits of archaeological evidence," that might enable fuller and more inclusive rhetorical histories.[1] Royster identifies her method as "historical ethnography" because it emphasizes the stance, location, and orientation of the historiographer and her subjects of inquiry. Her work demonstrates the power of multiple viewpoints to "reduce distortion by positioning various views in kaleidoscopic relationships to each other," and calls upon scholars to examine a multiplicity of women's literate practices in order to gain "closeup views from different standpoints on the landscape."[2]

The practice of rhetorical archaeology, like Enos's project, calls upon scholars to make full interpretive use of the fragments that remain in order to envision and engage critically with a community's prior life—even when those fragments are idiosyncratic, difficult to locate, or found in genres that a community appears to have discarded. Like Royster's project, rhetorical archaeology emphasizes the interpretive work required to assemble material traces into historical accounts. Archaeology is an *-ology,* that is, a *study* of collective human activity, reminding us that the textual traces that remain—the genred forms of communication that have persisted in some record and been assembled by the researcher—do not come readily provided with functional explanations for their persistence or their disappearance. Instead, the researcher must attend to relations, sequences, and positions among these textual traces in order to reconstruct negotiations or tensions that have been erased.

Furthermore, rhetorical archaeology focuses on genres to generate its insights. Genres, which Amy Devitt, Anis Bawarshi, and Mary Jo Reiff argue are "as material as the people using them,"[3] often serve as sites where members of a specific community negotiate between polarities, such as structure and agency, convention and innovation, or collective and individual rhetorical action.[4] Traces of these negotiations remain, materialized in the genres a community has adopted, discarded, and transformed. Consequently, genres offer historians of rhetoric a rich site for recovering insights into community anxieties, needs, and priorities. Because genres provide traces of the "shared expectations . . . [that] help participants act together purposefully,"[5] studying even discarded and transmuted genres reveals possibilities for acting together *differently*, through forms available to—if not finally taken up by—a particular community. This study of anthropology's privileged and alternative genres has thus located moments early in that discipline's history when practitioners crafted new genres, using anthropology's discursive repertoire to challenge, revise, and re-articulate their community's epistemic practices.

Such an investigation reveals the extent to which professionalization masked deep, ongoing negotiations surrounding the methods, aims, and legitimate members of the anthropological community. Responding to Devitt's invitation for genre scholars to take up questions concerning "the nature of different groups and the roles genres play within them" as well as "who starts a new genre and how,"[6] this book suggests that genres served as sites for consolidation as well as contestation of discursive and epistemic norms. Even as changes in the ethnographic monograph enabled sharper distinctions between legitimate and illegitimate practices and participants, other genres that emerged subsequently reveal the ongoing presence of significant heterogeneity within the professional anthropological community. As people of color and white women were marginalized by anthropology's professionalization, these writers developed new genres such as the field autobiography and the ethnographic novel and revised standard genres such as the folklore collection in ways that carried significant—if implicit—challenges to professional practice. The writers in this study used these genres to inscribe themselves within the narrowed boundaries of a powerful intellectual community and simultaneously to question that community's norms and priorities.

Even as I argue that field autobiographies, folklore collections, and ethnographic novels generate knowledge through alternative epistemic practices and textual forms, this argument does not entail ascribing *intentional* acts of critique to the writers I have examined. In the absence of significant evidence of their motivations and composition practices, I cannot safely speculate on writers' intentions—what led them to write autobiographically about their field research, or why they chose to write folklore collections that deviated in particular ways from the collections of their colleagues. Nevertheless, their genre-based rhetorical choices persist in the texts they produced, as material evidence that professionalization failed to fully govern the textual products that disciplinary insiders generated out of their anthropological practice.

In this way, the practice of rhetorical archaeology takes advantage of the recalcitrant materiality of written texts to account for writers' agency without rendering the author as a rhetorical hero, dramatically altering her profession through her choices. Rhetorical agency in this account is distinct from both intentions and effects; it holds that in every instance of rhetorical production, in each spoken, written, and embodied performance, a rhetor exercises agency as she enacts certain possibilities and not others. Because these choices are inscribed into the world as material performances, they also repeat, subvert, establish, or destabilize rhetorical possibilities for other writers, shaping in myriad minor ways what other writers and speakers view as possible, effective, or powerful ways to act.[7] Though intention is not necessary for my analyses in this book, recognizing writers' agency is, for, as I discuss further below, an archaeological metaphor for genre study responds in particular to the tendency of evolutionary metaphors to circumscribe human agency and thus naturalize scientific and professional practice. Against that tendency, rhetorical archaeology views all textual inscriptions—even in genres that were marginal to mainstream disciplinary practice—as acts requiring human agency, and thus as acts that merit interpretive attention whether they secured repetition or not.

The focus of rhetorical archaeology on the relative positions of texts and writers within a community clarifies the significance of those textual features that were repeatedly taken up by professional anthropologists as well as those that were generated, published, available to professional practice and yet not taken up in ways that enabled them to accrete and stabilize as norms. This method adopts Anne Freadman's concept of uptake, which has focused the attention of genre scholars on the ways that texts interact in chains of response. Freadman argues that every text is "contrived to secure a certain class of uptakes," and uptakes, in turn, may confirm their own "status by conforming" to expectations established in prior texts, or may deny, subvert, or reframe expectations.[8] For instance, in the case of anthropological genres, one way that monographs confirm their status as monographs is through citational uptakes in subsequent texts; such uptakes verify and legitimate both the present and the prior text simultaneously, establishing the generic status of both the text that is *citing* and the one that is *cited*. Such chains of response are interpretable but not fully predictable; as Freadman explains, "No genre can do more than predict the kind of uptake that would make it happy, and no speaker or writer can completely secure an uptake," in part because "no discursive event is a pure example of any genre, and partly because of the unpredictable historical complexity of its moment and its ongoing action."[9] Following Freadman, rhetorical archaeology focuses not on writers' intentions but on uptakes—those accomplished as well as those "contrived" or invoked by anthropological texts. In this case, the rhetorical features of field autobiographies, folklore collections, and ethnographic novels solicit uptakes related to securing writers' professional identities, recruiting other women into the discipline, and positing revisions to ethnographic practice.

Historical reconstructions of community life cast up some evidence of these uptakes, as in reviews that represent Ann Axtell Morris as a legitimate professional archaeologist, and in newspaper stories that feature Morris's readers crediting her texts for their involvement in archaeology. We can also see gaps or omissions that may indicate uptakes that failed to materialize—for instance, in the long historical gap between Reichard's ethnographic experiments in *Dezba* and *Spider Woman* and the late-twentieth-century ethnographies that deploy autobiography and multivocality to reposition the ethnographer's authority. Such a gap suggests potential but unrealized uptakes of marginalized textual innovations, as anthropologists in the 1980s generated similar textual strategies in apparent unawareness of Reichard's long-out-of-print works. Furthermore, the attention paid in rhetorical archaeology to *position* helps to underscore the ways that relations of power shape the ability of a text to secure an uptake or of an innovation to gain status through repetition. For instance, Malinowski's textual choices helped to shape subsequent monographs not only because other anthropologists saw in his rhetorical strategies solutions to their own problems in representing fieldwork, but also because he occupied a position of influence that afforded him access to crucial material resources: in particular, to elite graduate students at the London School of Economics and Yale University who gave him crucial opportunities for influence. Other writers lacked the resources available from such powerful institutional positions, despite the potential problem-solving power of their own textual innovations.

In its attention to the influence of a writer's power and position on the uptakes her work secures or fails to secure, rhetorical archaeology is a method that works alongside recent research on gender in public memory. This scholarship, as Jessica Enoch and Jordynn Jack argue, investigates "what it means to remember and forget" women, as well as "how the rhetorical practice of remembering women can reshape ideas in the contemporary moment about who women have been and who they might become."[10] Similarly, my study argues that feminist scholars should create historical accounts that can help us resist viewing historical erasures as markers of merit, or as evidence confirming the limited roles women have played in rhetorical and scientific traditions. Instead, we might actively investigate such gaps and erasures, perhaps finding evidence instead of discriminatory memory practices that have systematically eclipsed the rhetorical, scientific, and public innovations of people of color, women, and others positioned disadvantageously relative to official memories.

Investigating historical gaps as erasures, scholars may reexamine the evolutionary model of genre change that has served as our most pervasive metaphor in recent years. Several early studies took up evolutionary language in their discussions of genre in ways that subsequent scholars have found enormously productive; for instance, Carolyn Miller remarked that "genres change, evolve, and decay" in her important 1984 article, "Genre as Social Action," and Kathleen Jamieson's influential 1975 article, "Antecedent Genre as Rhetorical Constraint," argues that texts "bear the chromosomal imprint of ancestral genres."[11] Subsequent scholars have adopted the language of evolution, making analytical use of terms such as "speciation," "fit," "adaptation," "niche," "selection pressures," "hybrid," and so on in their accounts of genre change over time.[12] In recent decades, evolutionary language has been used extensively in studies of the ways that genres change, emerge, recombine, or adapt to new technological contexts. This use reflects scholars' recent emphasis on, in Catherine Schryer's words, the fact that genres "have a complex set of relations with past texts and with other present texts: Genres come from somewhere and are transforming into something else."[13]

In recognition of this pervasive evolutionary metaphor, some scholars have worked to articulate more precisely the heuristic benefits that evolution as a model makes available to genre scholars. For instance, Carolyn Miller argues that adopting a minimal model of evolution as the differential survival of heritable traits provides genre scholars with a metaphor that accounts for both diachronic and synchronic variation—that is, change across time as well as variation at a given moment across instances, such as organisms or texts.[14] A further benefit is the emphasis evolutionary models place on *ordinary* variation as the key to long-term change; in genre studies, such an emphasis permits us to see most textual change as the cumulative effect of repeated, routine choices, sedimented into convention, rather than the result of lone acts of dramatic textual innovation. This focus on ordinary variation is significant in shaping the accounts of agency that evolutionary models of genre make available; as Miller argues, viewing genre change as evolution requires us to account for innovation within a context of replication and stabilization, a system within which "both recurrence and innovation have meaning and are judged."[15] Textual variations may be quickly eliminated, or they may acquire function and persist, and that persistence comes about through recurrence within a system that perpetuates or eliminates variations. In the realm of biology, a trait's persistence or disappearance is secured through natural selection, an algorithmic process that philosopher Daniel Dennett calls "mindless all the way down."[16] In the realm of human communication, Miller suggests, evolutionary models can help us attend to the systemic pressures that mitigate against innovation, and that shape those innovations that are taken up and those that are discarded.

There is, however, significant difficulty in accomplishing this careful translation across domains—the difficulty of *not* permitting the "mindless algorithm" at work in the genetic domain to override our understanding of the human agency involved in the realm of human choices, complex purposes, and power-saturated human environments. Because the evolutionary model of genre change borrows from the domain of biological evolution, it lends these qualities to the social domain of human communication. We can repeat caveats, reminding our readers and ourselves that evolution is merely a metaphor, that certainly cultural replication operates differently from genetic replication, and that "fitness" names a more complex concept in human cultural change than in the biological domain we draw it from. But by repeating such reminders one does not entirely forestall the naturalizing effects of this pervasive biological metaphor.

Such effects are particularly problematic in studies of scientific and professional communities. Professional science is already shot through with teleological ideas, with the sense that professionalization naturally follows a course toward greater exclusivity, greater rigor, and better science, and these terms—exclusivity, rigor, and science—are already bound up with each other in ways that are difficult to contest. I contend that one project of historical study of genres should be to contest narratives that naturalize the human-created associations between these terms, and to complicate the commonplace understanding of professionalization as progress. Because my aim as a scholar is to historicize professional science as a rhetorical accomplishment, using biological metaphors for the textual changes that accompany professionalization undermines that effort.

Furthermore, evolutionary explanations for the recurrence and survival of genres and textual features leave significant questions unanswered precisely because of the complexity of the human agency involved in maintaining a genre system. Because fitness in biological terms is confirmed through replication, we are susceptible, when translating "fitness" into the human realm of cultural production, to thinking that nonreplication indicates nonfitness, an innovation that failed to be functional, a textual feature that did not persist because it was ill suited to its rhetorical environment. I find this insufficient as an explanation for the textual features of the alternative anthropological genres analyzed in previous chapters, because of the extent to which it removes humans—their rhetorical agency, their bodies, their social and institutional positions, their relations to power—from the historical account. By naturalizing genre change, evolutionary models can inadvertently contribute to the ongoing marginalization of minor genres, alternative practices, and marginalized writers by suggesting implicitly that those left out were relics, quirks, or nonfunctional adaptations, insufficiently fitted to their changing environments.

Instead, I propose conceiving of historical genre study as an archaeological investigation into prior forms of community life. As an archaeological practice, studying genre change involves us in the excavation of genres and texts as traces of human activity—material traces that provide evidence of prior choices, commitments, practices, and priorities, but whose persistence into the present is not seen as the ultimate arbiter of their significance. As an archaeological practice, historical genre study can attend to the sequencing, multiplicity, conformity and variability of the traces that remain—Berkenkotter's pottery shards, bones, and rock strata—using metaphors that come to us already from within the world of human cultural productions. Understanding our studies of genre change as archaeological reconstructions persistently focuses our attention on human cultural activity as the matter under investigation, helping us to generate accounts in which members of a community respond creatively and in patterned, recurrent fashion to the exigencies of their environments and the complex purposes that characterize human effort. An archaeological model likewise examines both synchronic variation and diachronic change, yet relies on the spatial and temporal concepts of *sequence, position,* and *stance* rather than the biological concepts of *niche, speciation,* or *hybridization.* Rhetorical archaeology also resists a teleological rendering of cultural change as a direct path of progress toward the present, as it values not only what persisted but also the debris of human cultural activity that excavation and recovery return to our attention.

Ultimately, *Rhetoric in American Anthropology* calls for scholars to embrace the project of evaluating, not just describing, the functions of genres within their communities of use. Scholars in rhetorical genre studies have sometimes been reluctant to evaluate overtly the genres and practices that our analyses lay bare.[17] Yet, because genres are intimately connected to the workings of power, our accounts of how genres function should not only describe but also critique situations in which genres are configured so as to reinforce or enable domination, exclusion, and acts of epistemic and material violence.

Considerations of power are too easily sidelined in accounts of genre change that rely upon evolutionary metaphors. Such metaphors have led some scholars "to display the same respect for the intricacy and functionality of a social system as we have learned to show for a biological one."[18] This is seen, for instance, in Richard Coe's claim that just as "one explains the development of a species as an adaptation to a niche in an ecosystem, so one should explain a recurring text type as a functional response to a recurring rhetorical situation."[19] Although genre changes might be explained in part as functional adaptations to an evolutionary niche, such explanations also bear significant limitations: namely, if we adopt these terms, then the features we see in contemporary genres seem provided with a ready-made explanation for their emergence. Evolutionary explanations suggest that genre features exist because they emerged as successful adaptations that improved in some way the "fittedness" of a certain genre to the environment of its use. For instance, although Gross, Harmon, and Reidy note that "the scientific article has evolved, not in the sense of becoming better (or worse), but in the sense of changing to cope with the communicative and argumentative needs of an evolving set of disciplines," arguing that specific textual features emerged because of their fittedness for certain ends nevertheless naturalizes those features that "succeeded," rather than historicizing textual artifacts against configurations of social and institutional power.[20]

This study of anthropological genres reveals that evolutionary descriptions of genre change only partially explain how genres come to take their specific shape. Certainly the features anthropologists built into the monograph were functional, and in that sense can be understood as developing in response to specific institutional and historical pressures. For instance, the lack of consolidation of norms in early monographs served institutional ends by permitting anthropologists to perceive their extraordinarily varied discursive and epistemic practices as coordinated within a shared intellectual project. Yet to say that a more constrained form of fieldwork evolved as anthropology professionalized would be to mask the human effort that was necessary as anthropologists *built* this constraint into their privileged genre. Evolutionary explanations also forestall investigation into other explanations of the emergence of genre characteristics: for instance, that other textual features might have appeared "more fit" to some members of a community, but those members were not in positions of institutional power to achieve their adoption. I argue, as does Dylan Dryer, that accepting such ready-made explanations for genre change and genre stability "constrain[s] our understanding of—and thus our ability to intervene effectively in—the injustices that some genre systems reflect and produce."[21]

An archaeological metaphor is particularly useful to scholars who aim to denaturalize the textual shape of professional discourse. This metaphor suggests that, although a professional community worked out its practice in the way that it did, that working out took its particular shape not through the inherent, necessary *fittedness* of certain kinds of texts to professional practice, but through a more complex reckoning in which alternate textual forms were generated but not incorporated, posited by professional writers as responses to recurrent professional situations but not taken up by sufficient numbers of their more powerful colleagues. This alternative to evolutionary models enables further examination of the possible effects, the implicit consequences, the agency if not the accomplished action still retained by textual performances that fell away from mainstream community practice. Rhetorical archaeology prompts historical researchers to consider what we must show, what we must be able to access as material evidence in order to claim that prior writers were agentive. If their practices have not persisted, what conclusions must we draw from that apparent failure? An archaeological metaphor offers a way to look to the past not for explanations that demonstrate the present fittedness of persistent traits, but for vanished or diminished or idiosyncratic responses from human communities to persistent problems—of communication, of artistic creation, of social organization, and so on.

The project of rhetorical archaeology outlined in these pages offers, then, a metaphor and a related vocabulary to help genre scholars generate enriched accounts of rhetorical practices through further studies of nondominant and ephemeral genres. Even as genre studies proliferate, our attention—particularly in historical work—has often remained focused on genres that have been privileged, stable, and longstanding, such as the research article or the lab report. Studies such as Dorothy Winsor's *Writing Power* and Clay Spinuzzi's *Tracing Genres through Organizations* focus new attention on the momentary, ephemeral genres that emerge as writers negotiate between more permanent generic sites in the course of their collective work. Yet such gaps between stable genres can be difficult to fill in historical research. Rhetorical archaeology offers a way to view even minor or short-lived genres as traces that materialized broader relations and practices, traces that can both enrich and complicate our accounts of disciplinary change.

Rhetoric in American Anthropology has attempted to demonstrate the many ways in which historical studies of genre change can press beyond evolutionary models in order to denaturalize textual features that seem inevitable when viewed in evolutionary terms. Although anthropologists responded to a felt need for rigor by creating constraints that made the monograph genre more exclusive and less widely available, this connection between rigor and exclusivity is historical, not inevitable. Using fitness or effectiveness as primary criteria leads one to a functional view of genre that implicitly argues that persistent textual features must have worked better than other alternatives—a suggestion that this study contests. Instead, this book underscores the ways in which writers work actively to *fit* genres and professional discourse for varied, sometimes contradictory ends. The practice of rhetorical archaeology counteracts evolutionary models of genre change by promoting careful investigations into discarded genres as textual traces that remain to speak eloquently of other possibilities, other relations, and other grounds for knowledge.

Notes

Introduction: Gender, Genre, and Knowledge in the Welcoming Science

1. Preference varies among indigenous people and scholars for the terms "Native American," "American Indian," "First Nations," and for specific tribal and clan designations. Some writers, such as Louis Owens, *Other Destinies: Understanding the American Indian Novel* (Norman, OK: University of Oklahoma Press, 1994), 3, prefer the term "Indian" as that most commonly used for self-identification within many North American indigenous communities. In contrast, Gerald Vizenor, *Manifest Manners: Postindian Warriors of Survivance* (Hanover, CT: University Press of New England, 1994), 10, calls the term "Indian" a "colonial enactment"; and Hilary N. Weaver, "Indigenous Identity: What Is It, and Who *Really* Has It?," *American Indian Quarterly* 25, no. 2 (2001): 243, finds the term "Indian" so thoroughly linked to romanticized colonial images that it serves as "a label for people who are fundamentally unknown and misrecognized by nonindigenous people." I follow the practice of scholars Malea Powell and Jessica Enoch in using "Native" primarily, and specific tribal affiliations when possible to resist characterizing indigenous peoples as monolithic. For the sake of clarity, I also use "Indian" and "Native American" when echoing the language used in the early twentieth century texts I refer to in specific chapters, and generally I adopt the tribal designations employed by the writers whose texts I am analyzing—using, for instance, the term "Navajo" instead of "Diné" to maintain clarity when discussing Gladys Reichard's research.

2. Margaret Mead, introduction to *The Golden Age of Anthropology,* ed. Margaret Mead and Ruth Bunzel, 1–12 (New York: George Braziller, 1960), 5.

3. Both Visweswaran and Parezo suggest that the public careers of these nineteenth-century women anthropologists encouraged many women to pursue this new science in the early twentieth century. See Kamala Visweswaran, "'Wild West' Anthropology and the Disciplining of Gender," in *Gender and American Social Science: The Formative Years,* ed. Helene Silverberg, 86–123 (Princeton, NJ: Princeton University Press, 1998); and Nancy J. Parezo, "Anthropology: The Welcoming

Science," in *Hidden Scholars: Women Anthropologists and the Native American Southwest,* ed. Nancy J. Parezo, 3–37 (Albuquerque: University of New Mexico Press, 1993).

4. Feminist scholarship in anthropology has recovered many marginalized or forgotten women anthropologists and has challenged misrepresentations of Margaret Mead and Ruth Benedict as exceptions or as "daughters of Boas." See Lois W. Banner, *Intertwined Lives: Margaret Mead, Ruth Benedict, and Their Circle* (New York: Knopf, 2003); Sally Cole, introduction to *The City of Women,* by Ruth Landes (Albuquerque: University of New Mexico Press, 1994); Sally Cole, *Ruth Landes: A Life in Anthropology* (Lincoln: University of Nebraska Press, 2003); Desley Deacon, *Elsie Clews Parsons: Inventing Modern Life* (Chicago: University of Chicago Press, 1997); Ute Gacs, Aisha Khan, Jerrie McIntyre, and Ruth Weinberg, eds., *Women Anthropologists: A Biographical Dictionary* (New York: Greenwood Press, 1988); Deborah Gordon, "Among Women: Gender and Ethnographic Authority of the Southwest, 1930–1960," in *Hidden Scholars: Women Anthropologists and the Native American Southwest,* ed. Nancy J. Parezo, 129–45 (Albuquerque: University of New Mexico Press, 1993); Roseanne Hoefel, "'Different by Degree': Ella Cara Deloria, Zora Neale Hurston, and Franz Boas Contend with Race and Ethnicity," *American Indian Quarterly* 25, no. 2 (2001): 181–202; Cynthia Irwin-Williams, "Women in the Field: The Role of Women in Archaeology before 1960," in *Women of Science: Righting the Record,* ed. Gabriela Kass-Simon, Patricia Farnes, and Deborah Nash, 1–41 (Bloomington: Indiana University Press, 1990); Louise Lamphere, "Feminist Anthropology: The Legacy of Elsie Clews Parsons," *American Ethnologist* 16, no. 3 (1989): 518–33; Lamphere, "Gladys Reichard among the Navajo," *Frontiers: A Journal of Women's Studies* 12, no. 3 (1992): 79–115; Catherine J. Lavender, *Scientists and Storytellers: Feminist Anthropologists and the Construction of the American Southwest* (Albuquerque: University of New Mexico Press, 2006); Maria Lepowsky, "Charlotte Gower and the Subterranean History of Anthropology," in *Excluded Ancestors, Inventible Traditions: Essays toward a More Inclusive History of Anthropology,* ed. Richard Handler, 123–70 (Madison: University of Wisconsin Press, 2000); Nancy O. Lurie, "Women in Early Anthropology," in *Pioneers of American Anthropology,* ed. June Helm, 29–81 (Seattle: University of Washington Press, 1966); Parezo, *Hidden Scholars;* Rosemary Lévy Zumwalt, *Wealth and Rebellion: Elsie Clews Parsons, Anthropologist and Folklorist* (Urbana: University of Illinois Press, 1992).

5. Thirteen African American anthropologists who completed some graduate education before World War II have been identified by the recovery work of Faye Harrison and Ira Harrison; that list includes Caroline Bond Day, who received her master's in anthropology from Harvard in 1930; Mark Hanna Watkins (PhD, Chicago, 1933); Zora Neale Hurston, who studied anthropology at Columbia with Franz Boas but did not earn a PhD; Louis Eugene King, who completed his fieldwork between 1926 and 1931, but wasn't awarded his PhD from Columbia until 1966, when his dissertation was finally published; Laurence Foster (PhD,

Pennsylvania, 1931); W. Montague Cobb (PhD, Western Reserve, 1932); Katherine Dunham (PhD, Chicago, 1936); Ellen Irene Diggs (MA, Atlanta University, 1933; Roosevelt Fellowship, University of Havana, 1943–45); William Allison Davis (PhD, Chicago, 1942); Arthur Huff Fauset (PhD, Pennsylvania, 1942); Manet Fowler (PhD, Columbia, 1952); St. Clair Drake (PhD, Chicago, 1954); and Hugh Smythe (PhD, Northwestern, 1946). See Ira E. Harrison and Faye V. Harrison, eds., *African-American Pioneers in Anthropology* (Urbana: University of Illinois Press, 1999). Identifying Native American anthropologists is complicated by the longstanding practice of white researchers collaborating closely with indigenous people as "informants," but resisting identifying those informants as colleagues conducting anthropological work in their own right; this describes the extensive anthropological writing, translating, and collecting work completed by George Hunt over several decades of collaboration with Franz Boas, for instance. See Judith Berman, "George Hunt and the Kwak'wala Texts," *Anthropological Linguistics* 36, no. 4 (1994): 482–514; Richard Rohner, ed., *The Ethnography of Franz Boas* (Chicago: University of Chicago Press, 1969). In minor ways, Boas acknowledged Hunt's role in his work, as in, for instance, his *Social Organization and Secret Societies of the Kwakiutl Indians* (Washington, DC: Government Printing Office, 1897), where he writes that his research is "based on personal observations and on notes made by Mr. George Hunt." Native anthropologists known to have completed some formal study of anthropology before 1945 include William Jones (Fox; PhD, Columbia, 1904), Henry Roe Cloud (Winnebago; MA, Yale, 1914); Edward Dozier (Tewa Pueblo; PhD, UCLA, 1952), Francis La Flesche (Omaha), Arthur C. Parker (Seneca), Louis Shotridge (Tlingit), and Gladys Tantaquidgeon (Mohegan). See Hartley Alexander, "Francis La Flesche," *American Anthropologist* 35, no. 2 (1933): 328–31; Franz Boas, "Anthropologic Miscellanea," *American Anthropologist* 11, no. 1 (1909): 137–39; Melissa Jayne Fawcett, *Medicine Trail: The Life and Lessons of Gladys Tantaquidgeon* (Tucson: University of Arizona Press, 2000); Hazel Hertzberg, "Nationality, Anthropology, and Pan-Indianism in the Life of Arthur C. Parker," *Proceedings of the American Philosophical Society* 123, no. 1 (1979): 47–72; Joan Mark, "Francis La Flesche: The American Indian as Anthropologist," *Isis* 73, no. 4 (1982): 497–510; Maureen Milburn, "The Politics of Possession: Louis Shotridge and the Tlingit Collections of the University of Pennsylvania Museum" (PhD diss., University of British Columbia, 1997); Marilyn Norcini, *Edward Dozier: The Paradox of the American Indian Anthropologist* (Tucson: University of Arizona Press, 2007); Joel Pfister, *The Yale Indian: The Education of Henry Roe Cloud* (Durham, NC: Duke University Press, 2009); Joy Porter, *To Be Indian: The Life of Iroquois-Seneca Arthur Caswell Parker* (Norman: University of Oklahoma Press, 2001); Henry Milner Rideout, *William Jones: Indian, Cowboy, American Scholar, and Anthropologist in the Field* (New York: Stokes, 1912).

6. Burton Bledstein, *The Culture of Professionalism: The Middle Class and the Development of Higher Education in America* (New York: Norton, 1978), 327–28.

7. Philippa Levine, *The Amateur and the Professional: Antiquarians, Historians and Archaeologists in Victorian England, 1838–1886* (Cambridge: Cambridge University Press, 1986), 6.

8. Ibid., 6.

9. Thomas F. Gieryn, *Cultural Boundaries of Science: Credibility on the Line* (Chicago: University of Chicago Press, 1999), 5, 30.

10. Levine, *The Amateur and the Professional;* Charles Alan Taylor, *Defining Science: A Rhetoric of Demarcation* (Madison: University of Wisconsin Press, 1996); Marc Rothenberg, "Organization and Control: Professionals and Amateurs in American Astronomy, 1899–1918," *Social Studies of Science* 11, no. 3 (1981): 305–25; George W. Stocking Jr., "Franz Boas and the Founding of the American Anthropological Association," *American Anthropologist* 62, no. 1 (1960): 1–17.

11. Rothenberg, "Organization and Control," 306.

12. Alfred Kroeber to Elsie Clews Parsons, 13 April 1929, Elsie Clews Parsons Papers, American Philosophical Society, Philadelphia.

13. Margaret W. Rossiter, *Women Scientists in America: Struggles and Strategies to 1940* (Baltimore: Johns Hopkins University Press, 1982), 272.

14. For instance, arrangements for printing (including determining who would pay for printing costs) were often the primary subject under discussion during negotiations to secure publication of dissertations and other pieces of research. Ruth Benedict, for instance, asked Boas whether funds could be set aside to pay for the publication of Ruth Bunzel's recent work on Zuni economics (Ruth Benedict to Franz Boas, 20 Aug. 1932, Franz Boas Papers, American Philosophical Society, Philadelphia). Many petitions for funding were directed to the Southwest Society, the organization that Elsie Clews Parsons founded expressly to pay for field research and publication out of her personal finances. Such letters occur routinely in the correspondence of powerful anthropologists who allocated funding to ensure the publication of their students' and friends' manuscripts. Being connected to and endorsed by powerful people aided the likelihood that one's research could find publication in one of the anthropological series funded by universities, government agencies, or private persons. Contrast the difficulty Louis Eugene King experienced earning his PhD even after completing his dissertation work with that of Frank Speck, who was hired by the Museum of the University of Pennsylvania in 1908, at which point the university then conferred Speck's PhD and published his dissertation as a monograph—even though his research had been undertaken at Columbia with Boas.

15. A great deal of scholarship reveals anthropologists' concern with identifying, acknowledging, and overcoming their discipline's historical and ongoing entan-

glements with colonialism. See Talal Asad, *Anthropology and the Colonial Encounter* (New York: Ithaca Press, 1973); Thomas Biolsi, "Bringing the Law Back In: Legal Rights and the Regulation of Indian-White Relations on Rosebud Reservation," *Current Anthropology* 36, no. 4 (1995): 543–71; Thomas Biolsi and Larry J. Zimmerman, *Indians and Anthropologists: Vine Deloria, Jr. and the Critique of Anthropology* (Tucson: University of Arizona Press, 1997); Alice Kehoe, "Revisionist Anthropology: Aboriginal North America," *Current Anthropology* 22, no. 5 (1981): 503–17; Nancy O. Lurie, epilogue to *Irredeemable America: The Indians' Estate and Land Claims,* ed. Imre Sutton, 363–82 (Albuquerque: University of New Mexico Press, 1985); Marc Pinkoski, "Julian Steward, American Anthropology, and Colonialism," *Histories of Anthropology Annual* 4 (2008): 172–204; Merrill Singer, "Applied Anthropology," in *A New History of Anthropology,* ed. Henrika Kuklick (Malden, MA: Blackwell, 2008), 327–29; William S. Willis Jr., "Skeletons in the Anthropological Closet," in *Reinventing Anthropology,* ed. Dell Hymes, 121–52 (New York: Pantheon, 1972); Patrick Wolfe, *Settler Colonialism and the Transformation of Anthropology: The Politics and Poetics of an Ethnographic Event* (London: Cassell, 1999).

16. See Henrika Kuklick, "The British Tradition," in Kuklick, *A New History of Anthropology,* 52–78; Kuklick, *The Savage Within: The Social History of British Anthropology, 1885–1945* (Cambridge: Cambridge University Press, 1992); H. Glenn Penny and Matti Bunzl, eds., *Worldly Provincialism: German Anthropology in the Age of Empire* (Ann Arbor: University of Michigan Press, 2003); H. Glenn Penny, "Traditions in the German Language," in Kuklick, *A New History of Anthropology,* 79–95; Penny, *Objects of Culture: Ethnology and Ethnographic Museums in Imperial Germany* (Chapel Hill: University of North Carolina Press, 2002); Emmanuelle Sibeud, "The Metamorphosis of Ethnology in France, 1839–1930," in Kuklick, *A New History of Anthropology,* 96–110; Fredrik Barth, Andre Gingrich, Robert Parkin, and Sydel Silverman, *One Discipline, Four Ways: British, German, French, and American Anthropology* (Chicago: University of Chicago Press, 2005); Adam Kuper, *Anthropology and Anthropologists: The Modern British School* 3rd ed. (London: Routledge, 1996).

17. Robert Parkin, "The French Speaking Countries," in Barth et al., *One Discipline, Four Ways,* 157–256. See also Sibeud, "The Metamorphosis of Ethnology."

18. Penny, "Traditions in the German Language," 80.

19. See A. I. Hallowell, "The Beginnings of American Anthropology," in *Selected Papers from the American Anthropologist, 1888–1920,* ed. Frederica de Laguna, for the Publications Committee of the American Anthropological Association, 1–90 (Evanston, IL: Row, Peterson/American Anthropological Association, 1960); Sydel Silverman, "The United States," in Barth et al., *One Discipline, Four Ways,* 345; Regna Darnell, "North American Traditions in Anthropology: The Historiographic Baseline," in Kuklick, *A New History of Anthropology,* 35–36. Balance between the four fields shifted in the United States over time, in particular as phys-

ical anthropology grew less significant and cultural anthropology became more dominant, but the four-field structure remains a trademark of many institutions of American anthropology even today.

20. Robert Thornton, "Narrative Ethnography in Africa, 1850–1920: The Creation and Capture of an Appropriate Domain for Anthropology," *Man* 18, no. 3 (1983): 513–14.

21. Kuklick, "The British Tradition," 61.

22. Singer, "Applied Anthropology," 329.

23. Sibeud, "The Metamorphosis of Ethnology," 107–9.

24. Kuklick, "The British Tradition," 63–66.

25. William Halse Rivers, Albert Jenks, and Sylvanus Morley, *Reports upon the Present Condition and Future Needs of the Science of Anthropology* (Washington, DC: Carnegie Institution of Washington, 1913), 7.

26. See Curtis Hinsley, *Savages and Scientists: The Smithsonian Institution and the Development of American Anthropology, 1846–1910* (Washington, DC: Smithsonian Institution, 1981); Don D. Fowler, *A Laboratory for Anthropology: Science and Romanticism in the American Southwest, 1846–1930* (Albuquerque: University of New Mexico Press, 2000). British-Polish anthropologist Bronislaw Malinowski noted in *Argonauts of the Western Pacific,* his famous 1922 monograph, that it "may be interesting for intending field-workers" to learn that merely £250 per year was sufficient not only for "all the expenses of travel and research," but these funds also enabled him to purchase artifacts and "ethnographic specimens" to provide materials for museum collections. See Bronislaw Malinoski, *Argonauts of the Western Pacific: An Account of Native Enterprise and Adventure in the Archipelagoes of Melanesian New Guinea* (1922; repr., Prospect Heights, IL: Waveland Press, 1984), xix.

27. H. Glenn Penny, "Bastian's Museum: On the Limits of Empiricism and the Transformation of German Ethnology," in *Worldly Provincialism: German Anthropology in the Age of Empire,* ed. H. Glenn Penny and Matti Bunzl, 86–126 (Ann Arbor: University of Michigan Press, 2003), 101. See also Donna C. Mehos, "Colonial Commerce and Anthropological Knowledge: Dutch Ethnographic Museums in the European Context," in Kuklick, *A New History of Anthropology,* 173–90.

28. James Urry, "'Notes and Queries on Anthropology' and the Development of Field Methods in British Anthropology, 1870–1920," *Proceedings of the Royal Anthropological Institute of Great Britain and Ireland* (1972): 49.

29. Talal Asad, "From the History of Colonial Anthropology to the Anthropology of Western Hegemony," in *Colonial Situations: Essays on the Contextualization of Ethnographic Knowledge,* ed. George W. Stocking Jr., 314–24 (Madison: University of Wisconsin Press, 1991), 314.

30. Johannes Fabian, *Time and the Other: How Anthropology Makes Its Object* (New York: Columbia University Press, 1983), 143.

31. Peter Pels, "The Anthropology of Colonialism: Culture, History, and the Emergence of Western Governmentality," *Annual Review of Anthropology* 26 (1997): 164.

32. Vine Deloria Jr., *Custer Died for Your Sins* (1969; repr., Norman: University of Oklahoma Press, 1988), 82.

33. Anthropologists have responded to these sovereignty efforts and increasingly recognized community ownership over cultural materials, including materials collected by earlier generations of anthropologists. See Fergus Bordewich, *Killing the White Man's Indian: Reinventing Native Americans at the End of the Twentieth Century* (New York: Doubleday, 1996); Kathleen S. Fine-Dare, *Grave Injustice: The American Indian Repatriation Movement and NAGPRA* (Lincoln: University of Nebraska Press, 2002); Devon A. Mihesuah, ed., *The Repatriation Reader: Who Owns American Indian Remains?* (Lincoln: University of Nebraska Press, 2000).

34. Kate Vieira, "Undocumented in a Documentary Society: Textual Borders and Transnational Religious Literacies," *Written Communication* 28, no. 4 (2011): 436–61; Amy Burgess, "Doing Time: An Exploration of Timescapes in Literacy Learning and Research," *Language and Education* 24, no. 5 (2010): 353–65; Angeles Clemente, Michael James Higgins, and William Michael Sughrua, "'I Don't Find Any Privacy around Here': Ethnographic Encounters with Local Practices of Literacy in the State Prison of Oaxaca," *Language and Education* 25, no. 6 (2011): 491–513; Tom Van Hout and Felicitas MacGilchrist, "Framing the News: An Ethnographic View of Business Newswriting," *Text & Talk* 30, no. 2 (2010): 169–91; David Hutto, "When Professional Biologists Write: An Ethnographic Study with Pedagogical Implications," *Technical Communication Quarterly* 12, no. 2 (2003): 207–23; Michelle LaFrance and Melissa Nichols, "Institutional Ethnography as Materialist Framework for Writing Program Research and the Faculty-Staff Work Standpoints Project," *College Composition and Communication* 64, no. 1 (2012): 130–50; Ellen Grote, "Challenging the Boundaries between School-Sponsored and Vernacular Literacies: Urban Indigenous Teenage Girls Writing in an 'at Risk' Program," *Language and Education* 20, no. 6 (2006): 478–92; Theresa Lillis, "Ethnography as Method, Methodology, and 'Deep Theorizing': Closing the Gap between Text and Context in Academic Writing Research," *Written Communication* 25, no. 3 (2008): 353–88; Jacqueline Preston, "The Fertile Commonplace: Collective Persuasions, Interpretive Acts, and Dialectical Spaces" (PhD diss., University of Wisconsin, 2011); Amber Lauren Johnson, "'We Don't Write Just to Write, We Write to Be Free': A Rhetorical Ethnography of Spoken Word in Los Angeles" (PhD diss., The Pennsylvania State University, 2006); Timothy Laquintano, "Sustained Authorship: Digital Writing, Self-Publishing, and the eBook" (PhD diss., University of Wisconsin, 2010); Stacey Pigg, "Embodied Rhetoric in Scenes of Production: The Case of the Coffeehouse" (PhD diss., Michigan State University, 2011).

35. Stephen Gilbert Brown and Sidney I. Dobrin, eds., *Ethnography Unbound: From Theory Shock to Critical Praxis* (Albany: State University of New York Press, 2004), 1.

36. Stephen Gilbert Brown, "Beyond Theory Shock: Ethos, Knowledge, and Power in Critical Ethnography," in *Ethnography Unbound: From Theory Shock to Critical Praxis,* ed. Stephen Gilbert Brown and Sidney I. Dobrin (Albany: State University of New York Press, 2004), 300.

37. Bruce Horner, "Critical Ethnography, Ethics, and Work: Rearticulating Labor," in *Ethnography Unbound: From Theory Shock to Critical Praxis,* ed. Stephen Gilbert Brown and Sidney I. Dobrin (Albany: State University of New York Press, 2004), 31.

38. Physical anthropology, which is closely allied with medical science, is an exception, and complex technical studies in physical anthropology did contribute to anthropology's growing scientific reputation in the late nineteenth and early twentieth centuries. Yet within the four fields of anthropology (cultural anthropology, linguistic anthropology, physical anthropology, and archaeology), cultural anthropology became predominant by the 1920s and required the fewest technical apparatus compared to the other three fields.

39. Otis T. Mason, "What Is Anthropology?," in *The Saturday Lectures,* 25–43 (Washington, DC: Judd and Detweiler, 1882), 26.

40. Levine, *The Amateur and the Professional,* 30.

41. Franz Boas, "The Foundation of a National Anthropological Society," *Science* 15, no. 386 (1902): 805.

42. Donald Fisher, *Fundamental Development of the Social Sciences: Rockefeller Philanthropy and the United States Social Science Research Council* (Ann Arbor: University of Michigan Press, 1993); Fisher, "Rockefeller Philanthropy and the Rise of Social Anthropology," *Anthropology Today* 2, no. 1 (1986): 5–8; George W. Stocking Jr., "Philanthropoids and Vanishing Cultures: Rockefeller Funding and the End of the Museum Era in Anglo-American Anthropology," in *Objects and Others: Essays on Museums and Material Culture,* ed. George W. Stocking Jr. (Madison: University of Wisconsin Press, 1985), 112–45.

43. Londa Schiebinger, *Has Feminism Changed Science?* (Cambridge, MA: Harvard University Press, 2001), 5.

44. On Boas's antiracism and his importance as a political, profeminist, and prohuman rights figure, see Marshall Hyatt, *Franz Boas, Social Activist: The Dynamics of Ethnicity* (New York: Greenwood, 1990); Julia E. Liss, "Diasporic Identities: The Science and Politics of Race in the Work of Franz Boas and W. E. B. Du Bois, 1894–1919," *Cultural Anthropology* 13, no. 2 (1998): 127–66; George W. Stocking Jr., ed., *The Shaping of American Anthropology, 1883–1911: A Franz Boas Reader* (New York: Basic Books, 1974). For a particularly vehement defense, see Herbert S. Lewis, "The Passion of Franz Boas," *American Anthropologist* 103, no. 2 (2001): 447–67.

45. Sandra Harding, ed., *The "Racial" Economy of Science: Toward a Democratic Future* (Bloomington: Indiana University Press, 1993).

46. See Fine-Dare, *Grave Injustice;* MariJo Moore, ed., *Genocide of the Mind: New Native American Writing* (New York: Nation Books, 2003); Devon A. Mihesuah, *American Indians: Stereotypes and Realities* (Atlanta: Clarity Press, 2009); Mark Rifkin, *When Did Indians Become Straight? Kinship, the History of Sexuality, and Native Sovereignty* (New York: Oxford University Press, 2011); Mark Rifkin, *The Erotics of Sovereignty: Queer Native Writing in the Era of Self-Determination* (Minneapolis: University of Minnesota Press, 2012); Tisa Joy Wenger, *We Have a Religion: The 1920s Pueblo Indian Dance Controversy and American Religious Freedom* (Chapel Hill: University of North Carolina Press, 2009); David E. Wilkins and K. Tsianina Lomawaima, *Uneven Ground: American Indian Sovereignty and Federal Law* (Norman: University of Oklahoma Press, 2001).

47. Lee D. Baker, *Anthropology and the Racial Politics of Culture* (Durham, NC: Duke University Press, 2010); Michel-Rolph Trouillot, *Global Transformations: Anthropology and the Modern World* (New York: Palgrave Macmillan, 2003).

48. Kurt Spellmeyer, "Travels to the Heart of the Forest: Dilettantes, Professionals, and Knowledge," *College English* 56, no. 7 (1994): 791.

49. Scott Lyons, "Rhetorical Sovereignty: What Do American Indians Want from Writing?," *College Composition and Communication* 51, no. 3 (2000): 449–50. Lisa King, "Speaking Sovereignty and Communicating Change: Rhetorical Sovereignty and the Inaugural Exhibits at the NMAI," *American Indian Quarterly* 35, no. 1 (2011): 75–103, notes that sovereignty in Native American communities has been "linked to self-determination, land rights, cultural integrity, self-governance, treaty rights, and cultural revitalization, though it is not limited to these" (77). The linked concepts of sovereignty and rhetorical sovereignty are articulated in Lyons, "Rhetorical Sovereignty"; Jessica Enoch, *Refiguring Rhetorical Education: Women Teaching African American, Native American, and Chicano/a Students, 1865–1911* (Carbondale: Southern Illinois University Press, 2008); Malea Powell, "Rhetorics of Survivance: How American Indians *Use* Writing," *College Composition and Communication* 53, no. 3 (2002): 396–434.

50. Gerald Vizenor, ed., *Survivance: Narratives of Native Presence* (Lincoln: University of Nebraska Press, 2008), 1.

51. Catherine F. Schryer, "The Lab vs. the Clinic: Sites of Competing Genres," in *Genre and the New Rhetoric,* ed. Aviva Freedman and Peter Medway (London: Taylor and Francis, 1994), 105–24; Carolyn R. Miller, "Genre as Social Action," *Quarterly Journal of Speech* 70, no. 2 (1984): 151–67.

52. Catherine F. Schryer, "Walking a Fine Line: Writing Negative Letters in an Insurance Company," *Journal of Business and Technical Communication* 14, no. 4 (2000): 450.

53. Amy J. Devitt, *Writing Genres* (Carbondale: Southern Illinois University Press, 2004), 139–40.

54. Ibid.; JoAnne Yates and Wanda J. Orlikowski, "Genre Systems: Structuring Interaction through Communicative Norms," *Journal of Business Communication* 39, no. 1 (2002): 13–35; Charles Bazerman, Joseph Little, and Teri Chavkin, "The Production of Information for Genred Activity Spaces: Informational Motives and Consequences of the Environmental Impact Statement," *Written Communication* 20, no. 4 (2003): 455–77; Dorothy A. Winsor, *Writing Power: Communication in an Engineering Center* (Albany: State University of New York Press, 2003).

55. Anthony Paré, "Genre and Identity: Individuals, Institutions, and Ideology," in *The Rhetoric and Ideology of Genre,* ed. Richard M. Coe, Lorelei Lingard, and Tatiana Teslenko, 57–71 (Cresskill, NJ: Hampton, 2002), 59.

56. Brent Henze, "Emergent Genres in Young Disciplines: The Case of Ethnological Science," *Technical Communication Quarterly* 13, no. 4 (2004): 393–421; Donna J. Kain, "Constructing Genre: A Threefold Typology," *Technical Communication Quarterly* 14, no. 4 (2005): 375–409.

57. Anis Bawarshi, "The Genre Function," *College English* 62, no. 3 (2000): 335–60; Carolyn Berkenkotter and Thomas Huckin, "Rethinking Genre from a Sociocognitive Perspective," *Written Communication* 10, no. 4 (1993): 475–509; Coe, Lingard, and Teslenko, *Rhetoric and Ideology of Genre;* Jennifer Schacker, "Unruly Tales: Ideology, Anxiety, and the Regulation of Genre," *Journal of American Folklore* 120, no. 478 (2007): 381–400.

58. Thomas Helscher, "The Subject of Genre," in *Genre and Writing: Issues, Arguments, Alternatives,* ed. Wendy Bishop and Hans Ostrom (Portsmouth, NH: Boynton/Cook, 1997), 29.

59. Carol Berkenkotter, *Patient Tales: Case Histories and the Uses of Narrative in Psychiatry* (Columbia: University of South Carolina Press, 2008), 3; Jordynn Jack, *Science on the Home Front: American Women Scientists in World War II* (Urbana: University of Illinois Press, 2009), 7.

60. Berkenkotter, *Patient Tales,* 3

61. In his analysis of artistic creation, Becker reflects this dimension of contemporary genre theory in his argument that the unconventional must always be articulated through the conventional; see Howard S. Becker, *Art Worlds* (Berkeley and Los Angeles: University of California Press, 1982).

62. Devitt, *Writing Genres,* 146.

63. Schryer, "Walking a Fine Line," 450.

64. Aviva Freedman and Peter Medway, "Locating Genre Studies: Antecedents and Prospects," in *Genre and the New Rhetoric,* ed. Aviva Freedman and Peter Medway (London: Taylor and Francis, 1994), 11, 12.

65. This point is made by Clifford Geertz, *Works and Lives: The Anthropologist as Author* (Stanford, CA: Stanford University Press, 1988), 1–17. An entire cohort

of late-twentieth-century anthropologists examined the textual construction of anthropological authority; see Ruth Behar, *Translated Woman: Crossing the Border with Esperanza's Story* (Boston: Beacon Press, 1993); Ruth Behar, *The Vulnerable Observer: Anthropology That Breaks Your Heart* (Boston: Beacon Press, 1996); Ruth Behar and Deborah Gordon, eds., *Women Writing Culture* (Berkeley and Los Angeles: University of California Press, 1995); James Clifford, "On Ethnographic Authority," *Representations* 1, no. 2 (1983): 118–46; James Clifford and George Marcus, eds., *Writing Culture: The Poetics and Politics of Ethnography* (Berkeley and Los Angeles: University of California Press, 1986); John B. Gatewood, "A Short Typology of Ethnographic Genres: Or Ways to Write about Other Peoples," *Anthropology and Humanism Quarterly* 9, no. 4 (1984): 5–10; Martyn Hammersley, "The Rhetorical Turn in Ethnography," *Social Science Information* 32, no. 1 (1993): 23–37; Marc Manganaro, "Textual Play, Power, and Cultural Critique: An Orientation to Modernist Anthropology," in *Modernist Anthropology: From Fieldwork to Text* (Princeton, NJ: Princeton University Press, 1990); George E. Marcus, "Rhetoric and the Ethnographic Genre in Anthropological Research," *Current Anthropology* 21, no. 4 (1980): 507–10; George E. Marcus and Dick Cushman, "Ethnographies as Texts," *Annual Review of Anthropology* 11 (1982): 25–69; George E. Marcus and Michael M. J. Fischer, *Anthropology as Cultural Critique: An Experimental Moment in the Human Sciences* (Chicago: University of Chicago Press, 1999); Paul Rabinow, *Reflections on Fieldwork in Morocco* (Berkeley and Los Angeles: University of California Press, 1977); Renato Rosaldo, "Where Objectivity Lies: The Rhetoric of Anthropology," in *The Rhetoric of the Human Sciences: Language and Argument in Scholarship and Public Affairs,* ed. John S. Nelson, Allan Megill, and Donald N. McCloskey (Madison: University of Wisconsin Press, 1987), 87–110; Kamala Visweswaran, *Fictions of Feminist Ethnography* (Minneapolis: University of Minnesota Press, 1994). For one recent attempt to reclaim the epistemological authority of fieldwork experiences, felt to be eroded by such examinations, see John Borneman and Abdellah Hammoudi, eds., *Being There: The Fieldwork Encounter and the Making of Truth* (Berkeley and Los Angeles: University of California Press, 2009).

66. Geertz, *Works and Lives,* 10.

67. On the representation of space in the creation of ethnographic authority, see especially James Clifford, "Spatial Practices: Fieldwork, Travel, and the Disciplining of Anthropology," in *Anthropological Locations: Boundaries and Grounds of a Field Science,* ed. Akhil Gupta and James Ferguson (Berkeley and Los Angeles: University of California Press, 1997), 185–222; Johannes Fabian, *Time and the Other: How Anthropology Makes Its Object* (New York: Columbia University Press, 1983); Robert J. Thornton, "'Imagine Yourself Set Down . . . ': Mach, Frazer, Conrad, Malinowski, and the Role of Imagination in Ethnography," *Anthropology Today* 1, no. 5 (1985): 7–14; Robert J. Thornton, "The Rhetoric of Ethnographic Holism," *Cultural Anthropology* 3, no. 3 (1988): 285–303.

68. Matti Bunzl, "Boas, Foucault, and the 'Native Anthropologist': Notes Toward a Neo-Boasian Anthropology," *American Anthropologist* 106, no. 3 (2004): 435.

69. Clifford, "Spatial Practices," 206.

70. Peter Pels, "The Anthropology of Colonialism: Culture, History, and the Emergence of Western Governmentality," *Annual Review of Anthropology* 26 (1997): 165.

71. Behar, *Vulnerable Observer,* 9.

72. Nathan Stormer, "Addressing the Sublime: Space, Mass Representation, and the Unpresentable," *Critical Studies in Media Communication* 21, no. 3 (2004): 214.

73. Carole Blair and Neil Michel, "Reproducing Civil Rights Tactics: The Rhetorical Performances of the Civil Rights Memorial," *Rhetoric Society Quarterly* 30, no. 2 (2000): 31–55; Greg Dickinson, "Joe's Rhetoric: Starbucks and the Spatial Rhetoric of Authenticity," *Rhetoric Society Quarterly* 32, no. 4 (2002): 5–28; Peter Ehrenhaus, "The Vietnam Veterans Memorial: An Invitation to Argument," *Journal of the American Forensic Association* 25, no. 2 (1988): 54–64; Victoria J. Gallagher, "Memory as Social Action: Cultural Projection and Generic Form in Civil Rights Memorials," in *New Approaches to Rhetoric,* ed. Patricia A. Sullivan and Steven R. Goldzwig (Thousand Oaks, CA: Sage, 2004), 149–71; Tamar Katriel, "Sites of Memory: Discourses of the Past in Israeli Pioneering Settlement Museums," *Quarterly Journal of Speech* 80, no. 1 (1994): 1–20.

74. Jessica Enoch, "A Woman's Place Is in the School: Rhetorics of Gendered Space in Nineteenth-Century America," *College English* 70, no. 3 (2008): 275–95; Nan Johnson, *Gender and Rhetorical Space in American Life, 1866–1910* (Carbondale: Southern Illinois University Press, 2002).

75. Jordynn Jack, "Space, Time, Memory: Gendered Recollections of Wartime Los Alamos," *Rhetoric Society Quarterly* 37, no. 3 (2007): 229–50; Catherine F. Schryer, "Genre Time/Space: Chronotopic Strategies in the Experimental Article," *JAC: Journal of Advanced Composition* 19, no. 1 (1999): 81–89.

76. Lisa Flores, "Creating Discursive Space through a Rhetoric of Difference: Chicana Feminists Craft a Homeland," *Quarterly Journal of Speech* 82, no. 2 (1996): 142–56; Roxanne Mountford, "On Gender and Rhetorical Space," *Rhetoric Society Quarterly* 30, no. 1 (2001): 41–71; Susan E. Wood, *The Freedom of the Streets: Work, Citizenship, and Sexuality in a Gilded-Age City* (Chapel Hill: University of North Carolina Press, 2005).

77. See Visweswaran, " 'Wild West' Anthropology." The murder of Henrietta Schmerler, a young white Columbia graduate student, during her field research among the Apache in 1931 prompted sensational news stories and reenergized discussions about whether fieldwork was safe for women; see Nancy Howell, "Human Hazards of Fieldwork," in *Ethnographic Fieldwork: An Anthropological Reader,* ed. Antonius C. G. M. Robben and Jeffrey A. Sluka (Malden, MA: Wiley-Blackwell, 2007), 234–44. For anthropologists' response to the murder, see Ruth Benedict to

Boas, 28 July 1931 and 26 Dec. 1931, Franz Boas Papers; Gladys Reichard to Boas, 26 July 1931 and 24 Aug. 1931, Franz Boas Papers.

78. Elsie Clews Parsons to Alfred Kroeber, 26 March 1929, Parsons Papers.

79. Edward Sapir to Elsie Clews Parsons, 27 March 1929, Parsons Papers.

80. Shepherd Krech, in *The Ecological Indian: Myth and History* (New York: Norton, 2000), notes that portrayals of space have been historically significant in relation to Native American communities in particular, as Native Americans are repeatedly associated with pristine landscapes, corrupt reservations, or with land-based spirituality and environmentalism.

81. Henri Lefebvre, *The Production of Space,* trans. Donald Nicholson-Smith (Oxford: Blackwell, 1991), 83.

1. Ethnographic Monographs: Genre Change and Rhetorical Scarcity

1. Otis T. Mason, "What Is Anthropology?," *The Saturday Lectures,* 25–43 (Washington, DC: Judd and Detweiler, 1882), 25, 26, 42.

2. Anita Newcomb McGee, "Historical Sketch of the Women's Anthropological Society of America. Read at the Annual Reception, February 25, 1889," in *Organization and Historical Sketch of the Women's Anthropological Society of America,* 16–22 (Washington, DC: Women's Anthropological Society of America, 1889), 19.

3. Mason, "What Is Anthropology?" 37.

4. Bronislaw Malinowski, *Argonauts of the Western Pacific: An Account of Native Enterprise and Adventure in the Archipelagoes of Melanesian New Guinea* (1922; repr., Prospect Heights, IL: Waveland Press, 1984), xv.

5. On "salvage anthropology," see Jerome W. Gruber, "Ethnographic Salvage and the Shaping of Anthropology," *American Anthropologist* 72, no. 6 (1970): 1289–99. For critiques of the practice of salvage anthropology, see Johannes Fabian, *Time and the Other: How Anthropology Makes Its Object* (New York: Columbia University Press, 1983); Patrick Wolfe, *Settler Colonialism and the Transformation of Anthropology: The Politics and Poetics of an Ethnographic Event* (London: Cassell, 1999).

6. Malinowski, *Argonauts,* xv.

7. Ibid., xv.

8. George W. Stocking Jr., "Paradigmatic Traditions in the History of Anthropology," in *The Ethnographer's Magic and Other Essays in the History of Anthropology* (Madison: University of Wisconsin Press, 1992), 342.

9. See Peter T. Manicas, "The Social Science Disciplines: The American Model," in *Discourses on Society: The Shaping of the Social Science Disciplines,* ed. Peter Wagner, Bjorn Wittrock, and Richard Whitley, 45–71 (Dordrecht: Kluwer, 1991); Helga Nowotny, "Knowledge for Certainty: Poverty, Welfare Institutions, and the Institutionalization of Social Science," in Wagner, Wittrock, and Whitley, *Discourses on Society,* 23–41.

10. Margaret W. Rossiter, *Women Scientists in America: Struggles and Strategies to 1940* (Baltimore: Johns Hopkins University Press, 1982), 63, 73.

11. Alfred Kroeber to Elsie Clews Parsons, 13 April 1929, Elsie Clews Parsons Papers, American Philosophical Society, Philadelphia.

12. Donald Fisher, *Fundamental Development of the Social Sciences: Rockefeller Philanthropy and the United States Social Science Research Council* (Ann Arbor: University of Michigan Press, 1993), 13–14; George W. Stocking Jr., "Franz Boas and the Founding of the American Anthropological Association," *American Anthropologist* 62, no. 1 (1960): 1–17.

13. Though this book primarily discusses American anthropology, several scholars have noted strong parallels between anthropology in the British functionalist and American culturalist traditions after 1920; see, for instance, Henrika Kuklick, "The British Tradition," in Kuklick, *A New History of Anthropology,* ed. Henrika Kuklick, 52–78 (Malden, MA: Wiley-Blackwell, 2008); Stocking, "Paradigmatic Traditions," 342–61. Robert Thornton, "Narrative Ethnography in Africa, 1850–1920: The Creation and Capture of an Appropriate Domain for Anthropology," *Man* 18, no. 3 (1983): 502–20, writes that in Britain,

> the monograph was physically presented in a way distinctly different from the missionary reportage [of Africa] that preceded and accompanied it. The authors of the first monographs . . . sought to justify ethnography as truly scientific. Under the influence of European intellectual and moral concerns, on the one hand, and the response of the newly literate Africans, their students and clients, on the other, ethnographic writing was transformed into an abstracted discourse on a restricted realm of experience, formally defined and conventionally presented. It functioned consequently as symbolic capital that at once permitted rationalization of a particular form of administrative practice and provided the basis for the emergence of a new profession. (509)

14. Clifford Geertz, *Works and Lives: The Anthropologist as Author* (Stanford, CA: Stanford University Press, 1988), 75.

15. See Dilip Gaonkar, "The Idea of Rhetoric in the Rhetoric of Science," in *Rhetorical Hermeneutics: Invention and Interpretation in the Age of Science,* ed. Alan G. Gross and William M. Keith, 25–85 (Albany: State University of New York Press, 1997); Jenny Edbauer, "Unframing Models of Public Distribution: From Rhetorical Situation to Rhetorical Ecologies," *Rhetoric Society Quarterly* 35, no. 4 (2005): 5–24.

16. Dorothy A. Winsor, "Ordering Work: Blue-Collar Literacy and the Political Nature of Genre," *Written Communication* 17, no. 2 (2000): 156.

17. Aviva Freedman and Peter Medway, "Locating Genre Studies: Antecedents and Prospects," in *Genre and the New Rhetoric,* ed. Aviva Freedman and Peter Medway, 2–19 (London: Taylor and Francis, 1994), 14.

18. Charles Alan Taylor, *Defining Science: A Rhetoric of Demarcation* (Madison: University of Wisconsin Press, 1996), 5.

19. Mason, "What Is Anthropology?," 26, 42.

20. Catherine F. Schryer, "Records as Genre," *Written Communication* 10, no. 2 (1993): 204; Charles Bazerman, "The Life of Genre, the Life in the Classroom," in *Genre and Writing: Issues, Arguments, Alternatives,* ed. Wendy Bishop and Hans Ostrom, 19–26 (Portsmouth, NH: Boynton/Cook, 1997), 22; Anis Bawarshi, "The Genre Function," *College English* 62, no. 3 (2000): 336.

21. Richard M. Coe, "'An Arousing and Fulfillment of Desires': The Rhetoric of Genre in the Process Era—and Beyond," in Freedman and Medway, *Genre and the New Rhetoric,* 185; on "restrictive curbs," see Jane Danielewicz, "Personal Genres, Public Voices," *College Composition and Communication* 59, no. 3 (2008): 427.

22. Catherine F. Schryer, "The Lab vs. the Clinic: Sites of Competing Genres," in Freedman and Medway, *Genre and the New Rhetoric,* 108.

23. Joseph Little, "Achieving Objectivity through Genred Activity: A Case Study," *Journal of Technical Writing and Communication* 37, no. 1 (2007): 75–94.

24. Carol Berkenkotter and Thomas N. Huckin, "Rethinking Genre from a Sociocognitive Perspective," *Written Communication* 10, no. 4 (1993): 476.

25. Dorothy A. Winsor, *Writing Power: Communication in an Engineering Center* (Albany, NY: State University of New York Press, 2003), 10.

26. This trajectory has been documented extensively by historians of anthropology. See especially Donald Collier and Harry Tschopik Jr., "The Role of Museums in American Anthropology," *American Anthropologist* 56, no. 5 (1954): 768–79; Fisher, *Fundamental Development;* Regna Darnell, *And Along Came Boas: Continuity and Revolution in Americanist Anthropology* (Philadelphia: John Benjamins, 1998); George W. Stocking Jr., "Ideas and Institutions in American Anthropology: Thoughts toward a History of the Interwar Years," in *Selected Papers from the American Anthropologist, 1921–1945,* ed. George W. Stocking Jr., 1–74 (Washington, DC: American Anthropological Association, 1976); Thomas C. Patterson, *A Social History of Anthropology in the United States* (New York: Berg, 2001).

27. Regna Darnell, "The Professionalization of American Anthropology: A Case Study in the Sociology of Knowledge," *Social Science Information* 10, no. 2 (1971): 87.

28. Anthropological traditions in France, Germany, and Great Britain developed along different lines, resulting in a distinct institutional context for American anthropology. French anthropology, for instance, developed ethnographic fieldwork much later than other anthropological traditions, while German anthropology had its origins in studies of European folklore and retained a much greater emphasis on museum studies of material culture than did anthropology elsewhere. Although the heterogeneity of early practitioners that I recount below is to some degree shared among all these national anthropological traditions, the institutional association of

American anthropology with settler-colonialist administration of Native American populations through the Department of the Interior and the Bureau of American Ethnology gives a particular shape to professional anthropology as it developed in the United States context. See Henrika Kuklick, *The Savage Within: The Social History of British Anthropology, 1885–1945* (Cambridge: Cambridge University Press, 1991); H. Glenn Penny and Matti Bunzl, eds., *Worldly Provincialism: German Anthropology in the Age of Empire* (Ann Arbor: University of Michigan Press, 2003); H. Glenn Penny, "Traditions in the German Language," in Kuklick, *A New History of Anthropology,* 79–95; H. Glenn Penny, *Objects of Culture: Ethnology and Ethnographic Museums in Imperial Germany* (Chapel Hill: University of North Carolina Press, 2002); Fredrik Barth, Andre Gingrich, Robert Parkin, and Sydel Silverman, *One Discipline, Four Ways: British, German, French, and American Anthropology* (Chicago: University of Chicago Press, 2005); Adam Kuper, *Anthropology and Anthropologists: The Modern British School,* 3rd ed. (London: Routledge, 1996).

29. Frederica de Laguna, "The Development of Anthropology," in *Selected Papers from the American Anthropologist, 1888–1920,* 2nd ed., ed. Frederica de Laguna and A. I. Hallowell, 101–14 (Lincoln: University of Nebraska Press, 2002), 103.

30. Ibid., 104.

31. Leslie White, "Lewis Henry Morgan: His Life and His Researches," in *The Indian Journals, 1859–1862,* by Lewis Henry Morgan, ed. Leslie White, 1–15 (New York: Dover, 1993), 3.

32. Frederick S. Dellenbaugh, "Memorial to John Wesley Powell," *American Anthropologist* 20, no. 4 (1918): 432–36.

33. Brent Henze, "Emergent Genres in Young Disciplines: The Case of Ethnological Science," *Technical Communication Quarterly* 13, no. 4 (2004): 394.

34. De Laguna, "The Development of Anthropology," 104.

35. Don D. Fowler, *A Laboratory for Anthropology: Science and Romanticism in the American Southwest, 1846–1930* (Albuquerque: University of New Mexico Press, 2000); Donald Worster, *A River Running West: The Life of John Wesley Powell* (Oxford: Oxford University Press, 2001).

36. Darnell, *And Along Came Boas,* 125–26.

37. Patterson, *Social History of Anthropology,* 36.

38. Collier and Tschopik, "The Role of Museums," 771; see also Regna Darnell, "The Emergence of Academic Anthropology at the University of Pennsylvania," *Journal of the History of the Behavioral Sciences* 6, no. 1 (1970): 80–92; Nancy J. Parezo, ed., *Hidden Scholars: Women Anthropologists and the Native American Southwest* (Albuquerque: University of New Mexico Press, 1993); Fowler, *Laboratory for Anthropology,* 220–46.

39. Aleš Hrdlička, *Physical Anthropology: Its Scope and Aims; Its History and Present Status in the United States* (Philadelphia: Wistar Institute of Anatomy and Biology, 1919).

40. Collier and Tschopik, "The Role of Museums," 772.

41. Patterson, *Social History of Anthropology,* 50.

42. Rossiter, *Women Scientists in America,* 157.

43. Sources for these figures vary somewhat in the absolute number of awarded doctorates they identify, depending on how broadly or narrowly they constitute anthropology as a field, but all chart a similar pattern of gradual increase from 1900 to 1920 and much more rapid increase from 1920 to 1940. See Jay H. Bernstein, "First Recipients of Anthropological Doctorates in the United States, 1891–1930," *American Anthropologist* 104, no. 2 (2002): 551–64; Patterson, *Social History of Anthropology.* On the particular importance of Columbia University in awarding doctorates to women, see Rossiter, *Women Scientists in America,* 150–52.

44. See Darnell, *And Along Came Boas;* Stocking, "Franz Boas"; Richard Handler, "Boasian Anthropology and the Critique of American Culture," *American Quarterly* 42, no. 2 (1990): 252–73; Herbert S. Lewis, "Passion of Franz Boas," *American Anthropologist* 103, no. 2 (2001): 447–67; Julia E. Liss, "Diasporic Identities: The Science and Politics of Race in the Work of Franz Boas and W. E. B. DuBois, 1894–1919," *Cultural Anthropology* 13, no. 2 (1998): 127–66.

45. Patterson, *Social History of Anthropology,* 73.

46. Robert C. Bannister, *Sociology and Scientism: The American Quest for Objectivity, 1880–1940* (Chapel Hill: University of North Carolina Press, 1987), 4; Helene Silverberg, "Introduction: Toward a Gendered Social Science History," in *Gender and American Social Science: The Formative Years,* ed. Helene Silverberg, 3–32 (Princeton, NJ: Princeton University Press, 1998); Manicas, "The Social Science Disciplines."

47. Stocking, "Ideas and Institutions," 9–13.

48. Fisher, *Fundamental Development;* George W. Stocking Jr., "Philanthropoids and Vanishing Cultures: Rockefeller Funding and the End of the Museum Era in Anglo-American Anthropology," in *Objects and Others: Essays on Museums and Material Culture,* ed. George W. Stocking Jr. (Madison: University of Wisconsin Press, 1985), 112–45.

49. Pliny Earle Goddard to Alfred Tozzer, 7 Mar. 1917, American Anthropological Association Records, National Anthropological Archives, Suitland, MD.

50. See Clark Wissler to Alfred Tozzer, 23 and 29 May 1919, 9 June 1919, 20 and 29 Sept. 1919; Pliny Earle Goddard to Tozzer, 23 May 1919, 8 July 1919; Tozzer to Wissler, 11 Aug. 1919, 26 Sept. 1919; Wissler to Executive Committee of the AAA, 25 Aug. 1919; Alfred Kroeber to Wissler, 18 Sept. 1919; W. V. Bingham to Tozzer, 28 Nov. 1919. For complaints about the process undertaken to determine the NRC delegates and responses from the officers responsible for the vote, see Aleš Hrdlička to Wissler, 23 June 1919; W. H. Holmes to Wissler, 23 June 1919, 3 Sept. 1919; Wissler to Goddard, June 1919, 17 Sept. 1919; W. C. Farabee to Wissler, 4 Sept. 1919; Franz Boas to Tozzer, 6 Sept. 1919; Alice Fletcher to Wissler, n.d., 10

Sept. 1919; Wissler to Fletcher, 6 Sept. 1919; Neil M. Judd to Wissler, 10 and 12 Sept. 1919; Wissler to Judd, 11 Sept. 1919; M. H. Seville to Wissler, 12 Sept. 1919; H. Newell Wardle to Wissler, 12 Sept. 1919; Holmes to Executive Council of AAA, 12 Sept. 1919; Wissler to Holmes, 20 Sept. 1919. All letters from American Anthropological Association Records, National Anthropological Archives, Suitland, MD.

51. See Wissler to Kidder, 8 Feb. 1926, 15 Apr. 1926; Wissler to Hrdlička, 16 Mar. 1926; Hrdlička to Wissler, 22 and 26 Mar. 1926, 8 Apr. 1926; Hrdlička to Boas, 22 and 26 Mar. 1926, 8 Apr. 1926; Hrdlička to Kidder, 8 Apr. 1926; Edwin R. A. Seligman to Kidder, 28 May 1926; Kidder to the Executive Committee of the AAA, n.d.; Seligman, "Report on the Project of the Encyclopaedia of the Social Sciences," n.d. Additional efforts requiring coordination of the AAA membership with other constituencies include the American Year Book article concerning "Constituent Societies and Their Representatives" (Spier to Hrdlička, 22 Mar. 1926), the new Encyclopaedia Britannica, which first included an entry on the AAA after 1927 (Rollins to Hallowell, 24 Oct. 1927), and new interdisciplinary institutes, such as the Institute for Research in Tropical America (Hrdlička to Kidder, 3 Apr. 1926). All letters from American Anthropological Association Records, National Anthropological Archives, Suitland, MD

52. See Jerry Gershenhorn, *Melville J. Herskovits and the Racial Politics of Knowledge* (Lincoln: University of Nebraska Press, 2004); Lewis, "Passion of Franz Boas." Boas's inclusiveness is an important part of his legacy in American anthropology; his work in support of students of anthropology who were Jewish, people of color, women, or otherwise marginalized made anthropology a different discipline than it otherwise would have been. But this inclusiveness on Boas's part was connected to—not in contrast with—his determination to increase the proportion of highly trained, credentialed anthropologists and to minimize the role of amateurs in the field, making his commitment to scientific professionalization similar to Malinowski's. See Stocking, "Franz Boas"; Gelya Frank, "Jews, Multiculturalism, and Boasian Anthropology," *American Anthropologist* 99, no. 4 (1997): 731–45.

53. Lewis, "Passion of Franz Boas"; Frank, "Jews, Multiculturalism."

54. Nancy J. Parezo and Don D. Fowler, *Anthropology Goes to the Fair: The 1904 Louisiana Purchase Exposition* (Lincoln: University of Nebraska Press, 2007), 379.

55. Anthropology's historians have studied the pre- and protoprofessional development of the discipline extensively. Collier and Tschopik's classic article, "The Role of Museums in American Anthropology," identifies 1920 as the year the discipline shifted from museum-based to university-based anthropology; see also Stocking, "Ideas and Institutions," and A. I. Hallowell, "The Beginnings of American Anthropology," in de Laguna, *Selected Papers, 1888–1920*, 1–90. Both divide American anthropology into pre-1920 and post-1920 phases.

56. To identify monographs for analysis, I consulted all works published in anthropological series by the departments and museums where American anthro-

pology was first established, including the Columbia University Contributions to Anthropology, the University of California Publications in American Archaeology and Ethnology, the University of Chicago Series in Anthropology, the University of Washington Publications in Anthropology, the Anthropological Papers of the American Museum of Natural History, and the Field Columbian Museum Anthropological Series. Because the nascent professionalization of late-nineteenth-century anthropology was largely enabled by government-sponsored field expeditions, I also analyzed governmental publication series, including the Bureau of American Ethnology's *Reports* and *Bulletins* series. Additionally, monographs published outside of any regular series were identified by searching book reviews and review essays from the *American Anthropologist* (including all volumes from 1888 to 1945), the *Journal of American Folklore* (1888 to 1945), and *Man* (1901 to 1945); texts referred to as monographs by early anthropologists were included in my analyses.

57. Bernstein, for instance, defines monographs primarily by length (longer than journal articles but shorter than books) and mode of publication (in an ongoing series).

58. Frank Spencer, "The Rise of Academic Physical Anthropology in the United States (1880–1980): A Historical Overview," *American Journal of Physical Anthropology* 56, no. 4 (1981): 353–64.

59. Virginia Kerns, *Scenes from the High Desert: Julian Steward's Life and Theory* (Urbana: University of Illinois Press, 2003), 18.

60. Fowler, *Laboratory for Anthropology,* 113.

61. Frank Hamilton Cushing, *Outlines of Zuni Creation Myths* (Washington, DC: Government Printing Office, 1896), 327.

62. James Mooney, *The Ghost Dance Religion and the Sioux Outbreak of 1890* (Washington, DC: Government Printing Office, 1896), 654.

63. Ibid., 657.

64. Kenneth Burke, "Four Master Tropes," *Kenyon Review* 3, no. 4 (1941): 428.

65. Albert S. Gatschet, *A Migration Legend of the Creek Indians, with a Linguistic, Historic, and Ethnographic Introduction* (1884; repr., New York: AMS Press, 1969), 9.

66. Ibid., 11.

67. Franz Boas, *The Social Organization and Secret Societies of the Kwakiutl Indians* (Washington, DC: Government Printing Office, 1897), 317.

68. Through their creation of a spatial repository, early anthropologists reveal the "extraordinary obsession of scientists with papers, prints, diagrams, archives, abstracts, and curves on graph paper" that Latour describes as a key to scientific domination in "Visualisation and Cognition." Latour argues that it is by mustering agreement through a "cascade" of inscribed visualizations—lists, maps, cataloged collections of objects, linguistic diagrams, genealogical charts, photographs, account books, and all the other "immutable mobiles"—that "the few may dominate the many." See Bruno Latour, "Visualisation and Cognition: Drawing Things To-

gether," in *Representation in Scientific Practice,* ed. Michael Lynch and Steve Woolgar, 19–68 (Cambridge, MA: MIT Press, 1990), 54.

69. See Darnell, *And Along Came Boas;* Melville J. Herskovits, *Franz Boas: The Science of Man in the Making* (New York: Scribner, 1953); George W. Stocking Jr., ed., *The Shaping of American Anthropology, 1883–1911: A Franz Boas Reader* (New York: Basic Books, 1974).

70. A small subset of early monograph writers did *not* rely upon some form of fieldwork, but performed analyses of physical specimens or material artifacts using other methods of statistical and historical analysis.

71. Leo J. Frachtenberg, *Lower Umpqua Texts and Notes on the Kusan Dialects* (New York: Columbia University Press), 1914.

72. Certainly some early anthropologists did attain competence in the languages spoken by the communities they studied; however, very few anthropologists in the prewar period considered competence in an indigenous language a requirement for effective fieldwork.

73. Malinowski, *Argonauts,* xvi–xvii.

74. Malinowski's portrayal of himself in isolation has been disputed, particularly since the publication of his field diaries in 1967; see Phyllis Kaberry, "Malinowski's Contribution to Field-Work Methods and the Writing of Ethnography," in *Man and Culture: An Evaluation of the Work of Bronislaw Malinowski,* ed. Raymond Firth (London: Routledge and Kegan Paul, 1957), 71–91; George W. Stocking Jr., "Maclay, Kubary, Malinowski: Archetypes from the Dreamtime of Anthropology," in *Colonial Situations: Essays on the Contextualization of Ethnographic Knowledge,* ed. George W. Stocking Jr., 9–74 (Madison: University of Wisconsin Press, 1991); George W. Stocking, Jr., "The Ethnographer's Magic: Fieldwork in British Anthropology from Tylor to Malinowski," in *Observers Observed: Essays on Ethnographic Fieldwork,* ed. George W. Stocking Jr., 70–120 (Madison: University of Wisconsin Press, 1983); Michael W. Young, *Malinowski: Odyssey of an Anthropologist, 1884–1920* (New Haven, CT: Yale University Press, 2004).

75. Robert Redfield, *Tepoztlán, A Mexican Village: A Study of Folk Life* (Chicago: University of Chicago Press, 1930), vii; Margaret Mead, *Coming of Age in Samoa: A Psychological Study of Primitive Youth for Western Civilization* (1928; repr., New York: Morrow Quill Paperbacks, 1973), 10; Hortense Powdermaker, *Life in Lesu: The Study of a Melanesian Society in New Ireland* (New York: Norton, 1933), 15; Marian W. Smith, *The Puyallup-Nisqually* (New York: Columbia University Press, 1940), xi; Horace Miner, *St. Denis: A French-Canadian Parish* (Chicago: University of Chicago Press, 1939), vii; Wendell C. Bennett and Robert M. Zingg, *The Tarahumara: An Indian Tribe of Northern Mexico* (Chicago: University of Chicago Press, 1935), vii.

76. Ralph Linton, *The Tanala: A Hill Tribe of Madagascar* (Chicago: Field Museum of Natural History, 1933), 15; Malinowski, *Argonauts,* 12–13; John Alden

Mason, *Archaeology of Santa Marta Colombia: The Tairona Culture, Part 1: Report on Field Work* (Chicago: Field Museum of Natural History, 1931), 16–17, 20.

77. Mead, *Coming of Age,* 10.

78. Miner, *St. Denis,* vii; Bennett and Zingg, *Tarahumara,* x; Bennett and Zingg, *Tarahumara,* xv.

79. Malinowski, *Argonauts,* 6.

80. Letters exchanged among anthropologists, especially those held in the Elsie Clews Parsons Papers and the Franz Boas Papers at the American Philosophical Society and in the Records of the American Anthropological Association at the National Anthropological Archives, corroborate the arguments of scholars such as Talal Asad and Gary Wilder regarding anthropologists' embeddedness in structures of colonial administration. See Talal Asad, *Anthropology and the Colonial Encounter* (New York: Ithaca Press, 1973); Gary Wilder, "Colonial Ethnology and Political Rationality in French West Africa," *History and Anthropology* 14, no. 3 (2003): 219–52.

81. See Stocking, "Maclay, Kubary, Malinowski"; Stocking, "Ethnographer's Magic"; Young, *Malinowski;* Kamala Visweswaran, *Fictions of Feminist Ethnography* (Minneapolis: University of Minnesota Press, 1994).

82. Burke, "Four Master Tropes," 427.

83. Malinowski, *Argonauts,* xvi.

84. Mead, *Coming of Age,* 11.

85. Redfield, *Tepoztlán,* 20, 16.

86. Malinowski, *Argonauts,* 8–9.

87. Jan Golinski, *Science as Public Culture: Chemistry and Enlightenment in Britain, 1760–1820* (New York: Cambridge University Press, 1992), 10.

88. See Sidonie Smith, "Autobiographical Manifestos," in *Women, Autobiography, Theory: A Reader,* ed. Sidonie Smith and Julia Watson (Madison: University of Wisconsin Press, 1998), 433–40; Cristina Kirklighter, *Traversing the Democratic Borders of the Essay* (Albany: State University of New York Press, 2002).

89. Elsie Clews Parsons, ed., *American Indian Life by Several of Its Students* (1922; repr., Lincoln: University of Nebraska Press, 1967), 1.

2. *Field Autobiographies*: Rhetorical Recruitment and Embodied Ethnography

1. Ann Axtell Morris, *Digging in the Southwest* (New York: Doubleday/Junior Literary Guild, 1933), 13, 19.

2. Gladys Reichard to Ann Axtell Morris, 5 Dec. 1932, Morris Family Collections, Bayfield, CO; hereafter cited as Morris Family Collections.

3. Suzanne Le-May Sheffield, *Women and Science: Social Impact and Interaction* (New Brunswick, NJ: Rutgers University Press, 2005), 145–46.

4. Mary M. Lay, *The Rhetoric of Midwifery: Gender, Knowledge, and Power* (New Brunswick, NJ: Rutgers University Press, 2000).

5. Jordynn Jack, *Science on the Home Front: American Women Scientists in World War II* (Urbana: University of Illinois Press, 2009), 16.

6. See Margaret W. Rossiter, *Women Scientists in America: Struggles and Strategies to 1940* (Baltimore: Johns Hopkins University Press, 1982); Wini Warren, *Black Women Scientists in the United States* (Bloomington: Indiana University Press, 1999); Londa Schiebinger, *Has Feminism Changed Science?* (Cambridge, MA: Harvard University Press, 2001); Ira E. Harrison and Faye V. Harrison, eds., *African-American Pioneers in Anthropology* (Urbana: University of Illinois Press, 1998).

7. Rossiter, *Women Scientists in America,* 159.

8. Edward Sapir to Leslie White, 15 Mar. 1928, qtd. in Maria Lepowsky, "Charlotte Gower and the Subterranean History of Anthropology," in *Excluded Ancestors, Inventible Traditions: Essays toward a More Inclusive History of Anthropology,* ed. Richard Handler, 123–70 (Madison: University of Wisconsin Press, 2000), 141. See also Desley Deacon, *Elsie Clews Parsons: Inventing Modern Life* (Chicago: University of Chicago Press, 1997), 268. For a synopsis of the constraints that curtailed the influence of white women and people of color in early-twentieth-century professional anthropology, see Louise Lamphere, "Unofficial Histories: A Vision of Anthropology from the Margins," *American Anthropologist* 106, no. 1 (2004): 126–39.

9. Ruth Bunzel to Elsie Clews Parsons, 16 July 1934, Elsie Clews Parsons Papers, American Philosophical Society, Philadelphia; hereafter cited as Parsons Papers.

10. Ibid.

11. Lepowsky, "Charlotte Gower," 131–32.

12. Ruth Underhill to Franz Boas, 1935, Franz Boas Papers, American Philosophical Society, Philadelphia; hereafter cited as Boas Papers.

13. Underhill to Boas, 2 Sept. 1936, Boas Papers.

14. Underhill to Boas, undated, Boas Papers.

15. Deacon, *Elsie Clews Parsons,* 269.

16. Bunzel to Parsons, 16 July 1934, Parsons Papers.

17. Reichard to Morris, 5 Dec. 1932, Morris Family Collections.

18. Bunzel to Parsons, 16 July 1934, Parsons Papers.

19. Wendy Sharer, "Genre Work: Expertise and Advocacy in the Early Bulletins of the U.S. Women's Bureau," *Rhetoric Society Quarterly* 33, no. 1 (2003): 5–32.

20. Brent Henze, "Emergent Genres in Young Disciplines: The Case of Ethnological Science," *Technical Communication Quarterly* 13, no. 4 (2004): 396.

21. Caren Kaplan, "Resisting Autobiography: Out-Law Genres and Transnational Feminist Subjects," in *Women, Autobiography, Theory: A Reader,* ed. Sidonie Smith and Julia Watson (Madison: University of Wisconsin Press, 1998).

22. Evidence of this public interest can be seen in the surge in publication of career-related texts for women during this period, as vocational guides, vocational surveys, and career-advice manuals targeting women and girls proliferated. For examples of such texts, see Elizabeth Kemper Adams, *Women Professional Workers:*

A Study Made for the Women's Educational and Industrial Union (New York: Chautauqua, 1921); Virginia MacMakin Collier, *Marriage and Careers: A Study of One Hundred Women Who Are Wives, Mothers, Homemakers and Professional Workers* (New York: The Channel Bookshop, 1926); Beatrice Doerschuk, *Women in the Law: An Analysis of Training, Practice, and Salaried Positions* (New York: Bureau of Vocational Information, 1920); Doerschuk, *Statistical Work: A Study of Opportunities for Women* (New York: Bureau of Vocational Information, 1921); Catherine Filene, *Careers for Women* (New York: Houghton Mifflin, 1920); Filene, *Careers for Women: New Ideas, New Methods, New Opportunities to Fit a New World,* rev. ed. (Boston: Houghton Mifflin, 1934); Grace Hutchins, *Women Who Work* (New York: International Publishers, 1934); Miriam Simons Leuck, *Fields of Work for Women,* 3rd ed. (New York: Appleton-Century, 1938); Frances Maule, *She Strives to Conquer* (New York: Funk and Wagnalls, 1934); Maule, *Girl with a Paycheck: How She Lands It—Holds It—Makes It Grow* (New York: Harper and Brothers, 1941); Anne Hendry Morrison, *Women and Their Careers: A Study of 306 Women in Business and the Professions* (New York: National Federation of Business and Professional Women's Clubs, 1934); Catharine Oglesby, *Business Opportunities for Women,* 3rd ed. (New York: Harper and Brothers, 1937); Frances Perkins, *Vocations for the Trained Woman: Opportunities Other Than Teaching* (New York: Longman, Green, 1921); Adah Pierce, *Vocations for Women* (New York: Macmillan, 1933); *Training for the Professions and Allied Occupations: Facilities Available to Women in the United States* (New York: Bureau of Vocational Information, 1924); Mattie Lloyd Wooten, *Classified List of Vocations and Professions for Trained Women* (Denton: Texas State College for Women, 1931).

23. For examples, see Margaret Anderson, *My Thirty Years' War: An Autobiography* (New York: Knopf, 1930); Josephine Baker, *Fighting for Life* (New York: Macmillan, 1939); Ethel Sturges Dummer, *Why I Think So: The Autobiography of a Hypothesis* (Chicago: Clarke-McElroy, 1937); Adelaide Lisetta Fries, *The Road to Salem* (Chapel Hill: University of North Carolina Press, 1944); Wanda Gag, *Growing Pains* (New York: Coward McCann, 1940); Alice Hamilton, *Exploring the Dangerous Trades: The Autobiography of Alice Hamilton, M.D.* (New York: Little, Brown, 1943); Clara Louise Kellogg, *Memoirs of an American Prima Donna* (New York: G. P. Putnam's Sons, 1913); Mary Knight, *On My Own* (New York: Macmillan, 1938); Irene Kuhn, *Assigned to Adventure* (New York: Grosset and Dunlap, 1938); Elizabeth Marbury, *My Crystal Ball: Reminiscences* (New York: Boni and Liveright, 1923); Beryl Markham, *West with the Night* (New York: Houghton Mifflin, 1942); Hortense Odlum, *A Woman's Place: The Autobiography of Hortense Odlum* (New York: Scribner, 1939); Josephine de Mott Robinson, *The Circus Lady* (New York: Thomas Crowell, 1926); Elizabeth Shepley Sergeant, *Shadow-Shapes: The Journal of a Wounded Woman* (New York: Houghton Mifflin, 1920); Rosalie Slaughter Morton, *A Woman Surgeon* (New York: Frederick A. Stokes, 1937); Ida M. Tarbell, *All in the Day's Work: An Autobiography* (New York: Macmillan, 1939);

Marie Zakrzewska, *A Woman's Quest,* ed. Agnes Vietor (New York: D. Appleton, 1924).

24. Gladys A. Reichard, *Spider Woman* (1934; repr., Glorieta, NM: Rio Grande Press, 1968), 279.

25. Morris, *Digging in the Southwest,* 12–13.

26. Reichard, *Spider Woman,* 108–09.

27. Nathan S. Atkinson, David Kaufer, and Suguru Ishizaki, "Presence and Global Presence in Genres of Self-Presentation: A Framework for Comparative Analysis," *Rhetoric Society Quarterly* 38, no. 4 (2008): 357–84.

28. Morris, *Digging in the Southwest,* 15.

29. Reichard, *Spider Woman,* 107.

30. As narratives recounting embodied acts of research, field autobiographies are linked to travel narratives, an early genre out of which professional anthropological discourse developed. Historians have shown not only the close epistemic and institutional association between eighteenth- and nineteenth-century travel narratives and the development of anthropology as a scientific discipline, but also the significance of travel writing as a discourse *against* which twentieth-century anthropologists identified themselves. See Erwin H. Ackerknecht, "George Foster, Alexander von Humboldt, and Ethnology," *Isis* 46, no. 2 (1955): 83–95; George E. Marcus and Dick Cushman, "Ethnographies as Texts," *Annual Review of Anthropology* 11 (1982): 27; Mary Louise Pratt, *Imperial Eyes: Travel Writing and Transculturation* (London: Routledge, 1992), 63–65; Robert J. Thornton, "Narrative Ethnography in Africa, 1850–1920: The Creation and Capture of an Appropriate Domain for Anthropology," *Man* 18, no. 3 (1983): 502–20; Valerie Wheeler, "Travelers' Tales: Observations on the Travel Book and Ethnography," *Anthropological Quarterly* 59, no. 2 (1986): 52–63. Wheeler notes that anthropologists "sought dissociation from the unscientific traveler who was an amateur, a dilettante, and even a novelist," and many maintain a "nonspecific antipathy toward any similarity drawn between the traveler and the ethnographer" (54).

Field autobiographies, which developed in the 1920s and 1930s *after* anthropology's successful efforts to distinguish ethnography from travel writing, are distinct from travel narratives insofar as they are focused not on travel but on *work,* specifically within the context of a professional undertaking. In travel writing, the reader partially gains a vicarious experience and receives an implicit invitation to undertake the same travel; field autobiographies craft a strong professional frame around the depicted experience, suggesting that one's invitation to undertake these experiences is garnered *through* professional participation.

31. The effort to contain Ann Morris's work *within* the work of her husband continued to some degree, despite the independent publication of her field autobiographies. John Meriam, head of the Carnegie Institution that funded Earl and Ann's excavations in the Yucatan, recommended to Ann that she be careful to

ensure that *Digging in Yucatan* would be published only *after* Earl's book (John Meriam to Ann Axtell Morris, 2 Jan. 1930, Morris Family Collections). In addition, Ann's only reviewer in a scholarly publication treats *Digging in Yucatan* as a "second volume [which] should be read after the first," namely Earl Morris's *Temple of the Warriors,* "into which it dovetails perfectly." See James A. Robertson, review of *The Temple of the Warriors* by Earl H. Morris and *Digging in Yucatan* by Ann Axtell Morris, *Hispanic American Historical Review* 14, no. 3 (1934): 349.

32. In considering the related issues of innovation, recurrence, and genre change, it is important to note that the effects of a particular genre performance are neither ensured by nor limited to a writer's purposes or intentions. Instead, effects of small-scale changes may accumulate—or fail to do so—regardless of writers' intentions, and it can be difficult to predict the effects of any particular innovation or to reconstruct the complex of forces by which genres emerge, materialize, change, combine, and dissolve over time. In relation to the (vexing) issues of agency in genre change, see Carolyn R. Miller, "Do Genres Evolve?" keynote presentation at Genre 2012 Conference, Ottawa, Ontario, 27 June 2012; Risa Applegarth, "Rhetorical Scarcity: Spatial and Economic Inflections on Genre Change," *College Composition and Communication* 63, no. 3 (2012): 453–83; Dylan B. Dryer, "Taking Up Space: On Genre Systems as Geographies of the Possible," *JAC: A Journal of Composition Theory* 28, nos. 3–4 (2008): 503–34.

33. Kathleen Jamieson's concept of antecedent genres has been widely used to understand the role that a powerful genre can play in influencing future rhetorical performances, even in rhetorical situations that exist at a significant remove from the genre's development; see Kathleen M. Jamieson, "Antecedent Genre as Rhetorical Constraint," *Quarterly Journal of Speech* 61, no. 4 (1975): 406–15; recent uses of Jamieson's work to articulate the momentum that antecedent genres carry forward include Elizabeth G. Maurer, "'Working Consensus' and the Rhetorical Situation: The Homeless Blogs Negotiation of Public Meta-Genre," in *Genres in the Internet: Issues in the Theory of Genre,* ed. Janet Giltrow and Dieter Stein, 113–42 (Amsterdam: John Benjamins, 2009); and Carolyn R. Miller and Dawn Shepherd, "Questions for Genre Theory from the Blogosphere," in Giltrow and Stein, *Genres in the Internet,* 263–90. On the capacity of genre-based innovations to pressure assumptions embedded in prior genres, see Risa Applegarth, "Genre, Location, and Mary Austin's *Ethos,*" *Rhetoric Society Quarterly* 41, no. 1 (2011): 41–63; and Laurie McNeill, "Teaching an Old Genre New Tricks: The Diary on the Internet," *Biography* 26, no. 1 (2003): 24–47.

34. Helen Ferris to Morris, 1 May 1931, Morris Family Collections.

35. "Finding America's Past," review of *Digging in the Southwest* by Ann Axtell Morris, *New York Times Book Review,* 19 Nov. 1933, 23.

36. Ruth Benedict, review of *Digging in Yucatan* by Ann Axtell Morris, *New York Herald Tribune,* 31 May 1931, 9.

37. Ann Axtell Morris to Dorothy Bryan, 18 Mar. 1933, Morris Family Collections. Morris sailed to France to study at the American School of Prehistoric Archaeology after graduating from Smith College with a bachelor's degree in history in 1922.

38. Ann's initial involvement in the Chichen Itza project was as a nanny for Sylvanus Morley's daughter and as a chaperone for Morley's unmarried secretary and bookkeeper, Edith Bayles. Inga Calvin, personal correspondence, 27 July 2008. In *Digging in Yucatan,* Morris omits discussion of her nanny and chaperone duties.

39. Earl H. Morris, Jean Charlot, and Ann Axtell Morris, *The Temple of the Warriors at Chichen Itza, Yucatan* (Washington, DC: Carnegie Institution of Washington, 1931).

40. This situation was unfortunately common among early married scientists; see Rossiter, *Women Scientists in America;* Nancy J. Parezo, "Anthropology: The Welcoming Science," in *Hidden Scholars: Women Anthropologists and the Native American Southwest,* ed. Nancy J. Parezo, 3–37 (Albuquerque: University of New Mexico Press, 1993). Louise Lamphere suggests that Reichard was successful in earning a faculty position in part *because* she was unmarried and thus was perceived by Boas as having a greater need for an institutional position; see Louise Lamphere, "Gladys Reichard among the Navajo," *Frontiers: A Journal of Women's Studies* 12, no. 3 (1992): 79–115.

41. Nedra Reynolds, "Ethos as Location: New Sites for Understanding Discursive Authority," *Rhetoric Review* 11, no. 2 (1993): 325.

42. Ann Axtell Morris, *Digging in Yucatan* (New York: Doubleday/Junior Literary Guild, 1931), 153.

43. Ibid., 154.

44. Morris's contemporary reviewers consistently represented her as an expert in her own right; see "Books," *Washington Post,* 4 Nov. 1933, 12; Anne T. Eaton, "New Children's Books," review of *Digging in the Southwest* by Ann Axtell Morris, *New York Times Book Review,* 10 Dec. 1933, 16; "Story Book Lady," *Washington Post,* 31 Dec. 1933, SP3. Later, in their 1968 biography of Earl Morris, Florence Cline Lister and Robert H. Lister overlook Ann Morris's field training and portray her—contrary to her self-representation in her field autobiographies—as disgusted by fieldwork, repulsed by mummies, and, when she becomes ill, shirking her duties as a mother and thus disrupting her husband's legitimate archaeological work; see Lister and Lister, *Earl Morris and Southwestern Archaeology* (Albuquerque: University of New Mexico Press, 1968), 116, 140, 167, 169.

45. Morris, *Digging in Yucatan,* 8.

46. Morris, *Digging in the Southwest,* 38.

47. Ibid., 19.

48. Ibid., 20–22.

49. "Finding America's Past," review of *Digging in the Southwest* by Ann Axtell Morris, *New York Times Book Review* 19 Nov. 1933, 23.

50. Eaton, "New Children's Books," 16. *Digging in Yucatan* is identified in the National Council of Teachers of English publication, the *English Journal,* in 1933 as a book that should be taught to junior high school students to promote "international-mindedness" and "international good will"; see Ruth Barnes, "Developing International-Mindedness in Junior High School," *English Journal* 22, no. 6 (1933): 476–81.

51. Morris, *Digging in the Southwest,* 11.

52. Ibid., 11.

53. Ibid., 17.

54. Nancy J. Parezo and Margaret A. Hardin, "In the Realm of the Muses," in *Hidden Scholars: Women Anthropologists and the Native American Southwest,* ed. Nancy J. Parezo, 270–93 (Albuquerque: University of New Mexico Press, 1993), 285; Hilary Lynn Chester, "Frances Eliza Babbitt and the Growth of Professionalism of Women in Archaeology," in *New Perspectives on the Origins of Americanist Archaeology,* ed. David L. Browman and Stephen Williams (Tuscaloosa: University of Alabama Press, 2002), 164–84.

55. Morris, *Digging in the Southwest,* 12.

56. Ibid., figs. 11 (opp. p. 48), 28 (opp. p. 124).

57. Morris, *Digging in Yucatan,* fig. 25 (opp. p. 164).

58. Morris, *Digging in the Southwest,* fig. 26 (opp. p. 117); Morris, *Digging in Yucatan,* fig. 21 (opp. p. 140).

59. Morris, *Digging in the Southwest,* figs. 30 (opp. p. 125), 3 (opp. p. 16).

60. Morris, *Digging in Yucatan,* 6.

61. Parezo and Hardin, "In the Realm of the Muses," 284–91.

62. Morris, *Digging in the Southwest,* 22, 19, 18, 23.

63. Carolyn R. Miller, "Rhetorical Communities: The Cultural Basis of Genre," in *Genre and the New Rhetoric,* ed. Aviva Freedman and Peter Medway, 67–78 (London: Taylor and Francis, 1994), 73.

64. Sylvanus Morley, Report, Carnegie Institution of Washington, *Year Book* 24 (Washington: Carnegie Institution, July 1924–June 1925), 247.

65. Jean Charlot, the professional artist employed to copy excavated murals, earned two hundred dollars a month for his work; Ann earned seventy-five dollars a month for her work as an artist on the same project. Inga Calvin, Lecture, Museum of the University of Colorado, Boulder, CO, 1 Mar. 2007.

66. Ann Axtell Morris to Dorothy Bryan, 18 Mar. 1933, Morris Family Collections.

67. Reichard to Boas, 18 May 1919, Boas Papers.

68. Boas to Reichard, 11 June 1919, Boas Papers.

69. On Reichard's career, still largely obscured in histories of the discipline, see

Esther Schiff Goldfrank, "Gladys Amanda Reichard, 1893–1955," *Journal of American Folklore* 69, no. 271 (1956): 53–54; Lamphere, "Gladys Reichard"; Catherine J. Lavender, *Scientists and Storytellers: Feminist Anthropologists and the Construction of the American Southwest* (Albuquerque: University of New Mexico Press, 2006); Eleanor Leacock, "Gladys Amanda Reichard," in *Women Anthropologists: A Biographical Dictionary,* ed. Ute Gacs, Aisha Khan, Jerrie McIntyre, and Ruth Weinberg, 303–09 (New York: Greenwood Press, 1988); William H. Lyon, "Gladys Reichard at the Frontiers of Navajo Culture," *American Indian Quarterly* 13, no. 2 (1989): 137–63. Because degrees at Columbia were not conferred until the dissertation had been published, it was not unusual for a student to complete all the degree requirements and, if fortunate, begin a teaching position before her degree was awarded, as Reichard did.

70. Gladys Reichard, *Melanesian Design: A Study of Style in Wood and Tortoiseshell Carving* (New York: Columbia University Press, 1933). *Melanesian Design* won the 1932 A. Cressy Morrison Prize in natural science from the New York Academy of Sciences.

71. Reichard to Morris, 5 Dec. 1932, Morris Family Collections.

72. Ibid.

73. Reichard, *Spider Woman,* 1.

74. Ibid., 2.

75. Bronislaw Malinowski, *Argonauts of the Western Pacific: An Account of Native Enterprise and Adventure in the Archipelagoes of Melanesian New Guinea* (1922; repr., Prospect Heights, IL: Waveland Press, 1984), 3.

76. Vincent Crapanzano, "Hermes' Dilemma: The Masking of Subversion in Ethnographic Description," in *Writing Culture: The Poetics and Politics of Ethnography,* ed. James Clifford and George Marcus, 51–76 (Berkeley and Los Angeles: University of California Press, 1986), 69.

77. Malinowski, *Argonauts,* 57.

78. Crapanzano, "Hermes' Dilemma," 53.

79. Reichard, *Spider Woman,* 101.

80. Ibid., 184–86.

81. Ibid., 208.

82. Ibid., 3, 72, 90, 128, 162; quotes at 13.

83. Ibid., 90.

84. Ibid., 3.

85. Crapanzano, "Hermes' Dilemma," 53.

86. Lessie Jo Frazier, "Genre, Methodology and Feminist Practice: Gladys Reichard's Ethnographic Voice," *Critique of Anthropology* 13, no. 4 (1993): 364.

87. Reichard, *Spider Woman,* 14.

88. Ibid., 17.

89. Ibid., 17–18.

90. Ibid., 18.

91. Catherine F. Schryer, "Genre and Power: A Chronotopic Analysis," in *The Rhetoric and Ideology of Genre: Strategies for Stability and Change,* ed. Richard M. Coe, Lorelei Lingard, and Tatiana Teskenko, 73–102 (Cresskill, NJ: Hampton Press, 2002); Schryer, "Genre Time/Space: Chronotopic Strategies in the Experimental Article," *JAC: A Journal of Composition Theory* 19, no. 1 (1999): 81–89; Jordynn Jack, "Chronotopes: Forms of Time in Rhetorical Argument," *College English* 69, no. 1 (2006): 52–73.

92. Reichard, *Spider Woman,* 204.

93. Ibid., 85–87.

94. Ibid., 145.

95. Ibid., 2.

96. Ibid., 3.

97. Malinowski, *Argonauts,* 5.

98. Robert Redfield, *Tepoztlán, a Mexican Village: A Study of Folk Life* (Chicago: University of Chicago Press, 1930), 17.

99. Ibid., 17.

100. Reichard, *Spider Woman,* 14.

101. Redfield, *Tepoztlán,* 21.

102. Ann Axtell Morris to Dorothy Bryan, 18 Mar. 1933, Morris Family Collections.

103. Alice Ruth Bruce, "I Aim to Be—,"*Washington Post,* 19 Sept. 1937, PY2.

104. Anne Freadman, "Anyone for Tennis?," in *Genre in the New Rhetoric,* ed. Aviva Freedman and Peter Medway, 43–66 (London: Taylor and Francis, 1994); Freadman, "The Traps and Trappings of Genre Theory," *Applied Linguistics* 33, no. 5 (2012): 560.

105. Jacqueline Jones Royster, "Disciplinary Landscaping, or Contemporary Challenges in the History of Rhetoric," *Philosophy and Rhetoric* 36, no. 2 (2003): 149.

106. Cynthia Huff, ed., *Women's Life Writing and Imagined Communities* (London: Routledge, 2005), 7.

107. Helene Silverberg, "Introduction: Toward a Gendered Social Science History," in *Gender and American Social Science: The Formative Years,* ed. Helene Silverberg, 3–32 (Princeton, NJ: Princeton University Press, 1998), 23.

3. *Folklore Collections*: Professional Positions and Situated Representations

1. Franz Boas to Ella Cara Deloria, 27 Nov. 1935, 23 Feb. 1938, and 1 June 1938, Franz Boas Papers, American Philosophical Society, Philadelphia.

2. Ella Cara Deloria to Franz Boas, 1932, Boas Papers.

3. See Matti Bunzl, "Boas, Foucault, and the 'Native Anthropologist': Notes toward a Neo-Boasian Anthropology," *American Anthropologist* 106, no. 3 (2004):

435–42; María Eugenia Cotera, *Native Speakers: Ella Deloria, Zora Neale Hurston, Jovita Gonzalez, and the Poetics of Culture* (Austin: University of Texas Press, 2008); Dell Hymes, "The Use of Anthropology: Critical, Political, Personal," in *Reinventing Anthropology*, ed. Dell Hymes, 3–79 (New York: Pantheon Books, 1972); Kirin Narayan, "How Native Is a 'Native' Anthropologist?" *American Anthropologist* 95, no. 3 (1993): 671–86; Kath Weston, "The Virtual Anthropologist," in *Anthropological Locations: Boundaries and Grounds of a Field Science*, ed. Akhil Gupta and James Ferguson, 163–84 (Berkeley and Los Angeles: University of California Press, 1997).

4. As Cotera explains, "Dakota" was used in early ethnolinguistic studies to refer to tribes that spoke one of three related dialects: Dakota (Santee), Lakota (Teton), and Nakota (Yankton); these distinct but related dialects are now typically referred to as D/L/Nakota. The term "Sioux" referred to the larger group of plains tribes that belonged to the same linguistic family. Deloria "claimed fluency in all three dialects" and preferred the more precise term "Dakota" over the more general term, Sioux (Cotera, *Native Speakers*, 236). I follow Deloria's practice throughout this chapter.

5. Dorothy A. Winsor, "Genre and Activity Systems: The Role of Documentation in Maintaining and Changing Engineering Activity Systems," *Written Communication* 16, no. 2 (1999): 200–24.

6. Amy J. Devitt, *Writing Genres* (Carbondale: Southern Illinois University Press, 2004), 159.

7. Anthony Paré, "Genre and Identity: Individuals, Institutions, and Ideology," in *The Rhetoric and Ideology of Genre: Strategies for Stability and Change*, ed. Richard M. Coe, Lorelei Lingard, and Tatiana Teskenko, 57–71 (Cresskill, NJ: Hampton Press, 2002), 59.

8. Franz Boas, *Race, Language, and Culture* (Chicago: University of Chicago Press, 1940), 28–59, 60–75.

9. Boas, *Race, Language, and Culture*, 642.

10. Bunzl, "Boas, Foucault," 437. Bunzl writes that Boas believed the true task of anthropology was to investigate *all* human cultures and all forms of human variation, yet he admitted that investigation of literate groups had already been undertaken by fields such as history and philology; for this reason, "Boas stressed that this 'limitation of the field' was 'more or less accidental,' a function of the fact that 'other sciences occupied part of the ground before the development of modern anthropology'" (437, quoting Boas, "Anthropology," in *A Franz Boas Reader: The Shaping of American Anthropology, 1883–1911*, ed. George W. Stocking Jr. [Chicago: University of Chicago Press, 1974], 269).

11. Cotera, *Native Speakers*, 28.

12. Darnell suggests that the involvement of the Boasians in the *Journal of American Folk-Lore (JAFL)* was largely because this publication was less strongly controlled by the Washington anthropologists who opposed Boas and resisted his

influence in the discipline. See Regna Darnell, "American Anthropology and the Development of Folklore Scholarship: 1890–1920," *Journal of the Folklore Institute* 10, nos. 1–2 (1973): 33–34.

13. Charles Briggs and Richard Bauman, "'The Foundation of All Future Researches': Franz Boas, George Hunt, Native American Texts, and the Construction of Modernity," *American Quarterly* 51, no. 3 (1999): 483.

14. Otis T. Mason, "The Natural History of Folk-Lore," *Journal of American Folklore* 4, no. 13 (1891): 100.

15. Ibid., 99.

16. Ibid., 101.

17. Darnell, "American Anthropology," 26–27.

18. The decontextualized collection of folklore may seem to contradict Boas's investment in historical research. In fact, Boas's folklore research mirrors his statistical analyses in his physical anthropological work, insofar as each research practice accumulates numerous data points to identify larger patterns. Boas's many publications that merely record texts for later analysis treat such texts as data points that would form the basis for (much later) analyses of distribution, variation, and historical change in language, myth, religion, and other dimensions of cultural practice.

19. Franz Boas, *Bella Bella Texts* (New York: Columbia University Press, 1928), 151.

20. Some critique of decontextualized folklore was voiced in Raglan's review of Boas's later collection, *Bella Bella Tales,* which remarks that readers "are told nothing of the Bella Bella, not even where they live." See Lord Raglan [FitzRoy Richard Somerset], review of *Bella Bella Tales, Man* 34 (Apr. 1934): 63.

21. Ruth Benedict, *Tales of the Cochiti Indians* (Washington, DC: Government Printing Office, 1931), 130.

22. Ibid., 130n32.

23. John P. Harrington, *Karuk Indian Myths* (Washington, DC: Government Printing Office, 1932), 11.

24. Roger M. Keesing, "Kwaio Women Speak: The Micropolitics of Autobiography in a Solomon Island Society," *American Anthropologist* 87, no. 1 (1985): 37.

25. Pliny Earle Goddard, *Jicarilla Apache Texts* (New York: Trustees of the American Museum of Natural History, 1911), 42.

26. Ibid., 206.

27. Ibid., 206.

28. Benedict, *Tales of the Cochiti,* ix.

29. Frank G. Speck, *Catawba Texts* (New York: Columbia University Press, 1934), xi.

30. Elsie Clews Parsons, *Tewa Tales* (New York: American Folk-Lore Society, 1926), 6.

31. Elsie Clews Parsons, *Taos Pueblo* (Menasha, WI: American Anthropological

Association, 1936). Also see Catherine J. Lavender, *Scientists and Storytellers: Feminist Anthropologists and the Construction of the American Southwest* (Albuquerque: University of New Mexico Press, 2006), 61–65.

32. Benedict, *Tales of the Cochiti*, ix.

33. John R. Swanton, *Myths and Tales of the Southeastern Indians* (Washington, DC: Government Printing Office, 1929), 1.

34. Benedict, *Tales of the Cochiti*, 51n17.

35. Speck, *Catawba Texts*, 32.

36. Ibid., 12.

37. Ibid., 31.

38. Benedict, *Tales of the Cochiti*, 74n9.

39. Speck, *Catawba Texts*, xi–xiii.

40. Boas, *Bella Bella Texts*, ix.

41. Speck, *Catawba Texts*, x. That Speck was himself not fluent appears to him an insignificant barrier, as when he notes that "a short collection of texts was taken by me from Mrs. Owl's dictation without prior knowledge on my part of the grammatical structure of the language" (x).

42. Ibid., x, xiv.

43. Ibid., x.

44. Swanton, *Myths and Tales*, 2.

45. Mikhail Bakhtin, *The Dialogic Imagination: Four Essays,* trans. Caryl Emerson and Michael Holquist (Austin: University of Texas Press, 1981).

46. Catherine F. Schryer, "Walking a Fine Line: Writing Negative Letters in an Insurance Company," *Journal of Business and Technical Communication* 14, no. 4 (2000): 459.

47. Jerome W. Gruber, "Ethnographic Salvage and the Shaping of Anthropology," *American Anthropologist* 72, no. 6 (1970): 1289–99.

48. Cotera, *Native Speakers*, 31.

49. Bunzl, "Boas, Foucault," 438.

50. Ibid., 438.

51. Ella Cara Deloria to Martha Beckwith, 11 Nov. 1926, Boas Papers.

52. Boas to Deloria, 6 Apr. 1927, Boas Papers.

53. Boas to Deloria, 28 Sept. 1927, Boas Papers.

54. Boas to Deloria, 13 Nov. 1929; Deloria to Boas, 1 Nov. 1929, Boas Papers.

55. Deloria to Boas, 10 Oct. 1934; Deloria to Boas, 11 Nov. 1935, Boas Papers.

56. Deloria to Boas, 10 Nov. 1929 and 26 Nov. 1927, Boas Papers.

57. Benedict to Boas, 30 June 1932, and Deloria to Boas, 11 July 1932, Boas Papers.

58. Although both writers deployed "resistant rhetorical strategies" in their many published and unpublished texts, "by 1928 Hurston had distanced herself from Boas and Columbia University" and corresponded with Boas far less frequently

than did Deloria as each conducted her field research (Cotera, *Native Speakers*, 25, 74).

59. Hurston was born in Notasulga, Alabama, in 1891; her family moved shortly afterward to Eatonville, Florida, the small all-black town where Hurston grew up and to which she returned during her first fieldwork expedition in 1927. Hurston gave varying information about her birth year at points throughout her life, repeatedly suggesting that she was younger than she was. On Hurston's financial difficulties and her struggle late in her life to find publishers, see Carla Kaplan, introduction to *Zora Neale Hurston: A Life in Letters,* ed. Carla Kaplan, 12–32 (New York: Doubleday, 2002); Marjorie Pryse, "Introduction: Zora Neale Hurston, Alice Walker, and the 'Ancient Power' of Black Women," in *Conjuring: Black Women, Fiction, and Literary Tradition,* ed. Marjorie Pryse and Hortense Spillers, 1–24 (Bloomington: Indiana University Press, 1985); Alice Walker, "Zora Neale Hurston: A Cautionary Tale and Partisan View," in Robert Hemenway, *Zora Neale Hurston: A Literary Biography*, xi–xviii (Urbana: University of Illinois Press, 1980).

60. Walker, "Zora Neale Hurston"; Pryse, "Introduction"; quote from Robert Hemenway, foreword to *Zora Neale Hurston: A Life in Letters* (New York: Doubleday, 2002), 4.

61. Zora Neale Hurston to Franz Boas, 8 June [1930], Boas Papers.

62. Although Boas encouraged Hurston in her pursuit of the PhD, he elsewhere expressed reservations about the employment prospects of students of color in anthropology. He wrote to Booker T. Washington in 1904 to seek advice about "a young gentleman, Mr. J. E. Aggerey, of Livingstone College, Salisbury, N.C. [who] desires to study anthropology at Columbia University. He is a full-blood negro . . . I very much hesitate to advise the young man to take up his work, because I fear that it would be very difficult after he has completed his studies to find a place. On the other hand, it might be possible for him to study for two or three years and take his degree of master of arts, and then to obtain a position in one of the schools for his people" (Boas to Washington, 30 Nov. 1904, Boas Papers).

63. Paré, "Genre and Identity," 60.

64. Quoted in Raymond J. Demallie, introduction to *Dakota Texts* by Ella Cara Deloria (Lincoln: University of Nebraska Press, 2006), ix.

65. Deloria to Boas, 21 Aug. 1928, Boas Papers.

66. Janet L. Finn, "Walls and Bridges: Cultural Mediation and the Legacy of Ella Deloria," *Frontiers: A Journal of Women Studies* 21, no. 3 (2000): 163.

67. Ella Cara Deloria, *Dakota Texts* (1932; repr. Lincoln: University of Nebraska Press, 2006), 14, 123.

68. Ibid., 17, 99, 19.

69. Ibid., 11, 68, 128.

70. Ibid., 17, 40, 165, 28.

71. Ibid., 43, 136, 139.

72. Finn, "Walls and Bridges," 174.

73. Deloria, *Dakota Texts,* xxv, xxvi, 50, xxv.

74. Speck, *Catawba Texts,* xiv.

75. Deloria, *Dakota Texts,* 7, 75.

76. Ibid., 14.

77. Ibid., 45.

78. Ibid., xxvi.

79. Ella Cara Deloria, *Speaking of Indians* (1944; repr. Lincoln: University of Nebraska Press, 1998), 84.

80. Finn, "Walls and Bridges," 168.

81. Deloria, *Dakota Texts,* 251.

82. Ibid., 176, 187, 277.

83. Hurston to Boas, 20 Aug. 1934, Boas Papers.

84. Boas to Hurston, 12 Sept. 1934, Boas Papers. *Mules and Men* did appear with a preface from Boas. Carla Kaplan points out that this preface praises Hurston "for breaking through the 'feather-bed resistance' [to outsiders] that, *as* an anthropologist, she has identified—in this same book—as one of the most important traits of black culture" (Kaplan, *Zora Neale Hurston,* 51).

85. D. A. Boxwell, "'Sis Cat' as Ethnographer: Self-Presentation and Self-Inscription in Zora Neale Hurston's *Mules and Men,*" *African American Review* 26, no. 4 (1992): 609.

86. Zora Neale Hurston, *Mules and Men* (New York: Lippincott, 1935), 74, 75.

87. Ibid., 40–42, 45, 49, 50.

88. Ibid., 31.

89. Ibid., 33, 34, 38.

90. Ibid., 9–10. Although Hurston's work to inscribe African American dialect in *Mules and Men* strikes some contemporary readers as jarring, this visual and phonetic disruption was part of her political commitment to respecting African American vernacular language and folk culture; see John Edgar Wideman, foreword to *Every Tongue Got to Confess: Negro Folk-Tales from the Gulf States* by Zora Neale Hurston (New York: Perennial, 2002), xi–xx.

91. Zora Neale Hurston, "Characteristics of Negro Expression," in *Negro: An Anthology,* ed. Nancy Cunard, 24–31 (New York: F. Ungar, 1934), 27.

92. Hurston, *Mules and Men,* 11–13, 15.

93. Ibid., 50–51.

94. Ibid., 65.

95. Ibid., 65.

96. Ibid., 69, 70.

97. Boxwell, "'Sis Cat' as Ethnographer," 612. Once Hurston is taken up by this new community, her responsibilities and relationships extend in more directions than simply acquiring tales. She remarks that once she managed "to prove that I was their kind," after that, her car "was everybody's car" (*Mules and Men,* 70); being

accepted carries with it expectations of community membership, such as sharing possessions and accepting relations of reciprocity. Hurston ultimately makes the people of Polk County into her collaborators, bringing them into the project by holding a "lying contest" that becomes a community party.

98. Jordynn Jack, *Science on the Home Front: American Women Scientists in World War II* (Urbana: University of Illinois Press, 2009).

4. *Ethnographic Novels*: Educational Critiques and Rhetorical Trajectories

1. Elsie Clews Parsons, ed., *American Indian Life by Several of Its Students* (1922; repr., Lincoln: University of Nebraska Press, 1967), 2. Also see Gretchen M. Bataille, ed., *Native American Representations: First Encounters, Distorted Images, and Literary Appropriations* (Lincoln: University of Nebraska Press, 2001); Robert F. Berkhofer Jr., *The White Man's Indian: Images of the American Indian from Columbus to the Present* (New York: Vintage, 1979); Philip J. Deloria, *Playing Indian* (New Haven, CT: Yale University Press, 1998); Vine Deloria Jr., *Custer Died for Your Sins* (1969; repr., Norman: University of Oklahoma Press, 1988).

2. Alanson Skinner, "Little-Wolf Joins the Medicine Lodge," in *American Indian Life by Several of Its Students,* ed. Elsie Clews Parsons, 63–74 (1922; repr., Lincoln: University of Nebraska Press, 1967), 63.

3. Parsons, *American Indian Life,* 1.

4. See Desley Deacon, *Elsie Clews Parsons: Inventing Modern Life* (Chicago: University of Chicago Press, 1997); Louis A. Hieb, "Elsie Clews Parsons in the Southwest," in *Hidden Scholars: Women Anthropologists and the Native American Southwest,* ed. Nancy J. Parezo (Albuquerque: University of New Mexico Press, 1993), 63–75; Gladys Reichard, "Elsie Clews Parsons," *Journal of American Folklore* 56, no. 219 (1943): 45–48; Rosemary Lévy Zumwalt, *Wealth and Rebellion: Elsie Clews Parsons, Anthropologist and Folklorist* (Urbana: University of Illinois Press, 1992).

5. Barbara T. Gates and Ann B. Shteir, eds., *Natural Eloquence: Women Reinscribe Science* (Madison: University of Wisconsin Press, 1997); Suzanne Le-May Sheffield, *Women and Science: Social Impact and Interaction* (New Brunswick, NJ: Rutgers University Press, 2005).

6. Jeanne Fahnestock, "Accommodating Science: The Rhetorical Life of Scientific Facts," *Written Communication* 3, no. 3 (1986): 275–96; Greg Myers, "Discourse Studies of Scientific Popularizations: Questioning the Boundaries," *Discourse Studies* 5, no. 2 (2003): 265–79.

7. Wendy Sharer, "Genre Work: Expertise and Advocacy in the Early Bulletins of the U.S. Women's Bureau," *Rhetoric Society Quarterly* 33, no. 1 (2003): 5–32; Anthony Paré, "Genre and Identity: Individuals, Institutions, and Ideology," in *The Rhetoric and Ideology of Genre: Strategies for Stability and Change,* ed. Richard M. Coe, Lorelei Lingard, and Tatiana Teskenko, 57–71 (Cresskill, NJ: Hampton Press, 2002).

8. Parsons, *American Indian Life,* 2. Although these writers' investment in the

act of knowledge-making varies—and certainly differs from that of monograph writers—I suggest below that pervasive attestations to fieldwork experience mark these texts collectively as claiming epistemic status, using the discursive tools of professional anthropology to do so. Similarly, reviews in scholarly and popular periodicals that characterize ethnographic novels as accurate, trustworthy, and scientifically informed further bolster the texts' knowledge-making status.

9. Ethnographic novels written by professional anthropologists or, in some cases, by writers who claimed that their fiction portrayed a Native community accurately because of their firsthand field research, include Oliver La Farge, *Laughing Boy* (Boston: Houghton Mifflin, 1929), and *The Enemy Gods* (Boston: Houghton Mifflin, 1937); Frances Gillmor, *Windsinger* (New York: Minton, Balch, 1930); Margaret Smith, *Hopi Girl* (Stanford, CA: Stanford University Press, 1931); Robert Gessner, *Broken Arrow* (New York: Farrar and Rinehart, 1933); John Joseph Mathews, *Sundown* (1934; repr., Norman: University of Oklahoma Press, 1988); D'Arcy McNickle, *The Surrounded* (New York: Dodd, Mead, 1936); John Louw Nelson, *Rhythm for Rain* (Boston: Houghton Mifflin, 1937); Gladys Reichard, *Dezba, Woman of the Desert* (New York: J. J. Augustin, 1939); and Ruth Underhill, *Hawk Over Whirlpools* (New York: J. J. Augustin, 1940). Ella Deloria also wrote her ethnographic novel *Waterlily* during the 1930s, but could not find a publisher for the book, which was published posthumously in 1988 by the University of Nebraska Press. Of these texts, some were written by practicing, credentialed anthropologists such as La Farge, Reichard, and Underhill, all of whom earned advanced degrees in anthropology, pursued funded field research, and published other anthropological texts in genres more central to their discipline. Others were written by amateur anthropologists who emphasized their firsthand access to Native communities to authorize their texts as knowledge, such as Gillmor, Smith, Gessner, and Nelson, who completed research within those communities through semiofficial arrangements. Mathews and McNickle both legitimated the ethnographic quality of their work through their insider status as members of the Native communities they represented in fiction; McNickle and Deloria had anthropological training as well.

10. Sharer, "Genre Work," 8.

11. Gregory Clark and S. Michael Halloran, "Transformations of Public Discourse in Nineteenth-Century America," in *Oratorical Culture in Nineteenth-Century America,* ed. Gregory Clark and S. Michael Halloran, 1–28 (Carbondale: Southern Illinois University Press, 1993), 25.

12. Sharer, "Genre Work," 8.

13. K. Tsianina Lomawaima, *They Called It Prairie Light: The Story of Chilocco Indian School* (Lincoln: University of Nebraska Press, 1995), xi.

14. The complex repercussions of federal off-reservation boarding school programs have been examined by many scholars; see especially David Wallace Adams, *Education for Extinction: American Indians and the Boarding School Experience, 1875–*

1928 (Lawrence: University of Kansas Press, 1995); Brenda J. Child, *Boarding School Seasons: American Indian Families, 1900–1940* (Lincoln: University of Nebraska Press, 1998); Jacqueline Fear-Segal, *White Man's Club: Schools, Race, and the Struggle of Indian Acculturation* (Lincoln: University of Nebraska Press, 2007); Frederick E. Hoxie, *A Final Promise: The Campaign to Assimilate the Indians, 1880–1920* (Lincoln: University of Nebraska Press, 1984); K. Tsianina Lomawaima, "Domesticity in the Federal Indian Schools: The Power of Authority over Mind and Body," *American Ethnologist* 20, no. 2 (1993): 227–40; Lomawaima, *They Called It Prairie Light;* Scott Lyons, "The Left Side of the Circle: American Indians and Progressive Politics," in *Radical Relevance: Essays toward a Scholarship of the Whole Left,* ed. Steven Rosendale and Laura Gray Rosendale, 69–84 (New York: State University of New York Press, 2005); Joel Pfister, *Individuality Incorporated: Indians and the Multicultural Modern* (Durham, NC: Duke University Press, 2004); Malea Powell, "Rhetorics of Survivance: How American Indians *Use* Writing," *College Composition and Communication* 53, no. 3 (2002): 396–434; Clifford E. Trafzer, Jean A. Keller, and Lorene Sisquoc, eds., *Boarding School Blues: Revisiting American Indian Educational Experiences* (Lincoln: University of Nebraska Press, 2006).

15. Lewis Meriam et al., *The Problem of Indian Administration* (Baltimore: Johns Hopkins University Press, 1928), 605.

16. Ibid., 314–39. Although the writers of the Meriam Report assumed that these failings were due to mismanagement by administrators who lacked sufficient expertise, scholars in Native American studies rightly interpret these practices as contributing to the implicit goal of late-nineteenth-century Indian policy: the eradication of indigenous people. See Adams, *Education for Extinction;* Child, *Boarding School Seasons;* Mark Rifkin, *When Did Indians Become Straight? Kinship, the History of Sexuality, and Native Sovereignty* (New York: Oxford University Press, 2011).

17. Meriam, *Problem of Indian Administration,* 32, 33, 403.

18. George E. Marcus and Michael M. J. Fischer, *Anthropology as Cultural Critique: An Experimental Moment in the Human Sciences,* 2nd ed. (Chicago: University of Chicago Press, 1999), 23. Throughout this chapter, my use of the term "realist" refers specifically to this characterization from Marcus and Fischer of the mechanism by which anthropological discourse establishes its accuracy and insists upon its mimetic relation to an observed empirical world. By "realist," then, I mean accounts that provide abundant descriptive detail after the manner of classic ethnographic discourse.

19. Ibid., 22.

20. George E. Marcus and Dick Cushman, "Ethnographies as Texts," *Annual Review of Anthropology* 11 (1982): 29.

21. Nelson, *Rhythm for Rain,* viii; Gillmor, *Windsinger,* v.

22. Smith, *Hopi Girl,* 28.

23. These descriptions of artisanal processes in texts aimed at popular audiences

also emphasize the labor-intensive steps involved in the production of indigenous arts, reinforcing the authenticity and thus the value of highly coveted objects such as Hopi pots and Navajo rugs.

24. R. R. Marrett, review of *American Indian Life by Several of Its Students,* ed. Elsie Clews Parsons, *American Anthropologist* 25, no. 2 (1923): 266.

25. Gladys Reichard, review of *Laughing Boy* by Oliver La Farge, *Journal of American Folk-Lore* 44, no. 171 (1931): 121–22.

26. John Adair, review of *Dezba, Woman of the Desert* by Gladys A. Reichard, *American Anthropologist* 42, no. 3 (1940): 500.

27. "Miscellaneous Brief Reviews," review of *Dezba, Woman of the Desert* by Gladys Reichard, *New York Times,* 14 May 1939, 17.

28. Marcus and Cushman note that "the exclusion of individual characters from the realist ethnography probably accounts, more than any other single factor, for the dry, unreadable tone of such texts" ("Ethnographies as Texts," 32).

29. Martha Gruening, "The Indian's Tragedy," review of *Broken Arrow* by Robert Gessner, *Nation* 137, no. 3565 (1933): 518; Eda Lou Walton, "The Lives and the Legends of the Hopi Indians," review of *Rhythm for Rain* by John Louw Nelson, *New York Times Book Review,* 2 May 1937, 9.

30. Oliver La Farge, "Return of the Native," review of *Hawk Over Whirlpools* by Ruth Murray Underhill, *Saturday Review of Literature,* 14 Dec. 1940, 10; La Farge, "The Realistic Story of an Indian Youth," review of *Sundown* by John Joseph Mathews, *Saturday Review of Literature,* 24 Nov. 1934, 309.

31. Smith, *Hopi Girl,* ix.

32. Reichard, *Dezba,* 13.

33. Ibid., 13.

34. Gessner, *Broken Arrow,* 165–66.

35. Gillmor, *Windsinger,* 66; Reichard, *Dezba,* 58.

36. Gessner, *Broken Arrow,* 170.

37. McNickle, *The Surrounded,* 186, 189, 191.

38. Ibid., 171.

39. Underhill, *Hawk Over Whirlpools,* 57.

40. Ibid., 60.

41. Gillmor, *Windsinger,* 66.

42. Gessner, *Broken Arrow,* 169; Underhill, *Hawk Over Whirlpools,* 59.

43. Gessner, *Broken Arrow,* 165–66, 175–77.

44. Parsons, *American Indian Life,* 1.

45. Catherine Maria Sedgwick, *Hope Leslie; or, Early Times in the Massachusetts* (New York: Harper and Brothers, 1842); Lydia Maria Child, *Hobomok: A Tale of Early Times* (Boston: Cummings, Hilliard, 1824).

46. La Farge, *Laughing Boy,* 179.

47. Nelson, *Rhythm for Rain,* ix–x.

48. Ibid., x.

49. Ibid., ix.

50. Gladys Reichard to Elsie Clews Parsons, 25 Feb. 1934, Elsie Clews Parsons Papers, American Philosophical Society, Philadelphia.

51. Reichard to Franz Boas, 17 July 1934, Franz Boas Papers, American Philosophical Society, Philadelphia.

52. Ibid.; Reichard to Boas, 4 July 1934, Boas Papers.

53. Reichard to Boas, 29 July 1934, Boas Papers.

54. Reichard to Parsons, 9 Sept. 1934, Parsons Papers.

55. Reichard to Boas, 17 July 1934, Boas Papers.

56. Reichard to Boas, 29 July 1934, Boas Papers; Reichard to Parsons, 9 Sept. 1934, Parsons Papers.

57. "Miscellaneous," 17.

58. See Adams, *Education for Extinction;* Child, *Boarding School Seasons;* Pfister, *Individuality Incorporated.*

59. Reichard, *Dezba,* 25, 60, 60–61.

60. Ibid., 61.

61. Ibid., 59.

62. Ibid., 62–63.

63. Child, *Boarding School Seasons,* 69–81; Lomawaima, *They Called It Prairie Light,* 66–72.

64. Reichard, *Dezba,* 64.

65. Ibid., 63.

66. See Lomawaima, *They Called It Prairie Light;* Child, *Boarding School Seasons.* Reichard, *Dezba,* 65.

67. Reichard, *Dezba,* 73.

68. Ibid., 129–30, 141.

69. Ibid., 69.

70. James Clifford, "On Ethnographic Authority," *Representations* 1, no. 2 (1983): 142.

71. Joseph Jay Tobin, "Visual Anthropology and Multivocal Ethnography: A Dialogical Approach to Japanese Preschool Class Size," *Dialectical Anthropology* 13, no. 2 (1989): 173.

72. Reichard, *Dezba,* 130–31.

73. Ibid., 131–32.

74. Ibid., 134.

75. Ibid., 134–35.

76. Ibid., 140.

77. Ibid., 138–39.

Conclusion: Rhetorical Archaeology

1. Richard Leo Enos, "The Archaeology of Women in Rhetoric: Rhetorical Sequencing as a Research Method for Historical Scholarship," *Rhetoric Society Quarterly* 32, no. 1 (2002): 66.

2. Jacqueline Jones Royster, *Traces of a Stream: Literacy and Social Change among African American Women* (Pittsburgh: University of Pittsburgh Press, 2000), 282, 6.

3. Amy J. Devitt, Anis Bawarshi, and Mary Jo Reiff, "Materiality and Genre in the Study of Discourse Communities," *College English* 65, no. 5 (2003): 542.

4. Amy J. Devitt, *Writing Genres* (Carbondale: Southern Illinois University Press, 2004), 214.

5. David R. Russell, "Rethinking Genre in School and Society: An Activity Theory Analysis," *Written Communication* 14, no. 4 (1997): 513.

6. Devitt, *Writing Genres,* 218.

7. Scholarship on rhetorical agency is extraordinarily extensive; I articulate here a middle-ground position developed in sympathy with the accounts of agency found in Marilyn M. Cooper, "Rhetorical Agency as Emergent and Enacted," *College Composition and Communication* 62, no. 3 (2011): 420–49; Jenny Edbauer, "Unframing Models of Public Distribution: From Rhetorical Situation to Rhetorical Ecologies," *Rhetoric Society Quarterly* 35, no. 4 (2005): 5–24; and Dylan B. Dryer, "Taking Up Space: On Genre Systems as Geographies of the Possible," *JAC: A Journal of Composition Theory* 28, nos. 3–4 (2008): 503–34.

8. Anne Freadman, "Uptake," in *Rhetoric and Ideology of Genre: Strategies for Stability and Change,* ed. Richard M. Coe, Lorelei Lingard, and Tatiana Teskenko, 39–53 (Cresskill, NJ: Hampton Press, 2002), 40.

9. Anne Freadman, "The Traps and Trappings of Genre Theory," *Applied Linguistics* 33, no. 5 (2012): 560.

10. Jessica Enoch and Jordynn Jack, "Remembering Sappho: New Perspectives on Teaching (and Writing) Women's Rhetorical History," *College English* 73, no. 5 (2011): 534.

11. Carolyn R. Miller, "Genre as Social Action," *Quarterly Journal of Speech* 70, no. 2 (1984): 163; Kathleen M. Jamieson, "Antecedent Genre as Rhetorical Constraint," *Quarterly Journal of Speech* 61, no. 4 (1975): 406.

12. See Carolyn R. Miller and Dawn Shepherd, "Blogging as Social Action: A Genre Analysis of the Weblog," in *Into the Blogosphere: Rhetoric, Community, and Culture of Weblogs,* ed. Laura J. Gurak, Smiljana Antonijevic, Laurie Johnson, Clancy Ratliff, and Jessica Reyman (N.p, 2004); Richard M. Coe, "The New Rhetoric of Genre: Writing Political Briefs," in *Genre in the Classroom: Multiple Perspectives,* ed. Ann M. Johns, 197–207 (Mahwah, NJ: Lawrence Erlbaum Associates, 2002) 198; Alan G. Gross, Joseph E. Harmon, and Michael S. Reidy, *Communicating Sci-*

ence: *The Scientific Article from the Seventeenth Century to the Present* (Oxford: Oxford University Press, 2002), 15; Laurie McNeill, "Genre under Construction: The Diary on the Internet," *Language @ Internet* 2 (2005); Susan C. Herring, Lois Ann Scheidt, Sabrina Bonus, and Elijah Wright, "Bridging the Gap: A Genre Analysis of Weblogs," in *Proceedings of the 37th Hawaii International Conference on System Sciences,* 1–11 (Los Alamitos: IEEE Press, 2004), 2.

13. Catherine F. Schryer, "Records as Genre," *Written Communication* 10, no. 2 (1993): 208. See also Dwight Atkinson, "The Evolution of Medical Research Writing from 1735 to 1985: The Case of the *Edinburgh Medical Journal*," *Applied Linguistics* 13, no. 4 (1992): 337–74; Dwight Atkinson, *Scientific Discourse in Sociohistorical Context: The Philosophical Transactions of the Royal Society of London, 1675–1975* (Mahwah, NJ: Lawrence Erlbaum Associates, 1999); Charles Bazerman, *Shaping Written Knowledge: The Genre and Activity of the Experimental Article in Science* (Madison: University of Wisconsin Press, 1988); Carol Berkenkotter and Thomas N. Huckin, *Genre Knowledge in Disciplinary Communication: Cognition/Culture/Power* (Mahwah, NJ: Lawrence Erlbaum Associates, 1995); Sharon D. Downey, "The Evolution of the Rhetorical Genre of Apologia," *Western Journal of Communication* 57, no. 1 (1993): 42–64; JoAnne Yates and Wanda J. Orlikowski, "Genres of Organizational Communication: A Structurational Approach to Studying Communication and Media," *Academy of Management Review* 17, no. 2 (1992): 299–326; Miller and Shepherd, "Blogging as Social Action"; Carol Berkenkotter, "Genre Evolution? The Case for a Diachronic Perspective," in *Advances in Discourse Studies,* ed. Vijay K. Bhatia, John Flowerdew, and Rodney H. Jones, 178–91 (London: Routledge, 2008); Gross, Harmon, and Reidy, *Communicating Science,* 2002.

14. Carolyn R. Miller, "Do Genres Evolve?" Keynote presentation, Genre 2012 Conference, Ottawa, Ontario, 27 June 2012. Although scientific studies have rendered a more sophisticated model of evolution in recent years, its popular use— which I would suggest is what many scholars in rhetoric are drawing upon for their terms—persists primarily in the idea similar to the "minimal model" that Miller advocates: that variations occur at random; that selection pressures render some of these variations valuable for survival; that surviving traits are heritable.

15. Miller, "Do Genres Evolve?"

16. Daniel C. Dennett, *Darwin's Dangerous Idea: Evolution and the Meanings of Life* (New York: Simon and Schuster, 1995), 308. The mindless nature of this algorithmic process is precisely what Dennett identifies as "Darwin's dangerous idea," namely, that "the algorithmic level *is* the level that best accounts for the speed of the antelope, the wing of the eagle, the shape of the orchid, the diversity of species, and all the other occasions for wonder in the world of nature" (59). Most importantly for my critique of evolutionary language in genre studies, Dennett reminds us that, as an algorithmic explanation, evolution *requires* the absence of (human or divine)

agency: "no matter how impressive the products of an algorithm, the underlying process always consists of nothing but a set of individually mindless steps succeeding each other without the help of any intelligent supervision" (59).

17. Aviva Freedman and Peter Medway, "Locating Genre Studies: Antecedents and Prospects," in *Genre and the New Rhetoric,* ed. Aviva Freedman and Peter Medway, 1–19 (London: Taylor and Francis, 1994).

18. Ibid., 12.

19. Coe, "The New Rhetoric of Genre," 198.

20. Gross, Harmon, and Reidy, *Communicating Science,* 219.

21. Dryer, "Taking Up Space," 504.

Bibliography

Archival Materials

American Anthropological Association Records. National Anthropological Archives, Suitland, MD.

Ann Axtell Morris Papers. Elizabeth Ann Morris and the Morris Family Collections. Bayfield, CO. Held privately by Inga Calvin.

Elsie Clews Parsons Papers. American Philosophical Society, Philadelphia.

Franz Boas Papers. American Philosophical Society, Philadelphia.

Gladys Reichard Papers. Museum of Northern Arizona. Flagstaff, AZ.

Books and Articles

Ackerknecht, Erwin H. "George Foster, Alexander von Humboldt, and Ethnology." *Isis* 46, no. 2 (1955): 83–95.

Adair, John. Review of *Dezba, Woman of the Desert,* by Gladys A. Reichard. *American Anthropologist* 42, no. 3 (1940): 500–01.

Adams, David Wallace. *Education for Extinction: American Indians and the Boarding School Experience, 1875–1928.* Lawrence: University of Kansas Press, 1995.

Adams, Elizabeth Kemper. *Women Professional Workers: A Study Made for the Women's Educational and Industrial Union.* New York: Chautauqua, 1921.

Alexander, Hartley. "Francis La Flesche." *American Anthropologist* 35, no. 2 (1933): 328–31.

Amsden, Charles. Review of *Spider Woman: A Story of Navajo Weavers and Chanters,* by Gladys A. Reichard. *American Anthropologist* 37 (1935): 497.

Anderson, Margaret. *My Thirty Years' War: An Autobiography.* New York: Knopf, 1930.

"Ann Axtell Morris." *American Antiquity* 11, no. 2 (1945): 117.

Applegarth, Risa. "Genre, Location, and Mary Austin's *Ethos*." *Rhetoric Society Quarterly* 41, no. 1 (2011): 41–63.

———. "Rhetorical Scarcity: Spatial and Economic Inflections on Genre Change." *College Composition and Communication* 63, no. 3 (2012): 453–83.

Asad, Talal. *Anthropology and the Colonial Encounter.* New York: Ithaca Press, 1973.

———. "From the History of Colonial Anthropology to the Anthropology of Western Hegemony." In *Colonial Situations: Essays on the Contextualization of Ethnographic Knowledge,* edited by George W. Stocking Jr., 314–24. Madison: University of Wisconsin Press, 1991.

Atkinson, Dwight. "The Evolution of Medical Research Writing from 1735 to 1985: The Case of the *Edinburgh Medical Journal.*" *Applied Linguistics* 13, no. 4 (1992): 337–74.

———. *Scientific Discourse in Sociohistorical Context: The Philosophical Transactions of the Royal Society of London, 1675–1975.* Mahwah, NJ: Lawrence Erlbaum Associates, 1999.

Atkinson, Nathan S., David Kaufer, and Suguru Ishizaki. "Presence and Global Presence in Genres of Self-Presentation: A Framework for Comparative Analysis." *Rhetoric Society Quarterly* 38, no. 4 (2008): 357–84.

Baker, Josephine. *Fighting for Life.* New York: Macmillan, 1939.

Baker, Lee D. *Anthropology and the Racial Politics of Culture.* Durham, NC: Duke University Press, 2010.

Bakhtin, Mikhail. *The Dialogic Imagination: Four Essays.* Translated by Caryl Emerson and Michael Holquist. Austin: University of Texas Press, 1981.

———. *Speech Genres and Other Late Essays.* Edited by Michael Holquist and Caryl Emerson. Translated by Vern W. McGee. Austin: University of Texas Press, 1986.

Bandelier, Adolf. *The Delight Makers.* 1890. Reprint, New York: Dodd, Mead, 1917.

Banner, Lois W. *Intertwined Lives: Margaret Mead, Ruth Benedict, and Their Circle.* New York: Knopf, 2003.

Bannister, Robert C. *Sociology and Scientism: The American Quest for Objectivity, 1880–1940.* Chapel Hill: University of North Carolina Press, 1987.

Barnes, Ruth. "Developing International-Mindedness in Junior High School." *English Journal* 22, no. 6 (1933): 476–81.

Barth, Fredrik, Andre Gingrich, Robert Parkin, and Sydel Silverman. *One Discipline, Four Ways: British, German, French, and American Anthropology.* Chicago: University of Chicago Press, 2005.

Bataille, Gretchen M., ed. *Native American Representations: First Encounters, Distorted Images, and Literary Appropriations.* Lincoln: University of Nebraska Press, 2001.

Bawarshi, Anis. *Genre and the Invention of the Writer: Reconsidering the Place of Invention in Composition.* Logan: Utah State University Press, 2003.

———. "The Genre Function." *College English* 62, no. 3 (2000): 335–60.

Bazerman, Charles. "The Life of Genre, the Life in the Classroom." In *Genre and Writing: Issues, Arguments, Alternatives,* edited by Wendy Bishop and Hans Ostrom, 19–26. Portsmouth, NH: Boynton/Cook, 1997.

———. *Shaping Written Knowledge: The Genre and Activity of the Experimental Article in Science.* Madison: University of Wisconsin Press, 1988.

Bazerman, Charles, Joseph Little, and Teri Chavkin. "The Production of Information for Genred Activity Spaces: Informational Motives and Consequences of the Environmental Impact Statement." *Written Communication* 20, no. 4 (2003): 455–77.

Becker, Howard S. *Art Worlds.* Berkeley and Los Angeles: University of California Press, 1982.

Becker, M. L. Review of *Digging in Yucatan* by Ann Axtell Morris. *Outlook* 158, no. 6 (10 June 1931): 183.

Behar, Ruth. *Translated Woman: Crossing the Border with Esperanza's Story.* Boston: Beacon Press, 1993.

————. *The Vulnerable Observer: Anthropology That Breaks Your Heart.* Boston: Beacon Press, 1996.

Behar, Ruth, and Deborah Gordon, eds. *Women Writing Culture.* Berkeley and Los Angeles: University of California Press, 1995.

Benedict, Ruth. *Tales of the Cochiti Indians.* Washington, DC: Government Printing Office, 1931.

Bennett, Wendell C., and Robert M. Zingg. *The Tarahumara: An Indian Tribe of Northern Mexico.* Chicago: University of Chicago Press, 1935.

Berkenkotter, Carol. "Genre Evolution? The Case for a Diachronic Perspective." In *Advances in Discourse Studies,* edited by Vijay K. Bhatia, John Flowerdew, and Rodney H. Jones, 178–91. London: Routledge, 2008.

————. *Patient Tales: Case Histories and the Uses of Narrative in Psychiatry.* Columbia: University of South Carolina Press, 2008.

Berkenkotter, Carol, and Thomas N. Huckin. *Genre Knowledge in Disciplinary Communication: Cognition/Culture/Power.* Mahwah, NJ: Lawrence Erlbaum Associates, 1995.

————. "Rethinking Genre from a Sociocognitive Perspective." *Written Communication* 10, no. 4 (1993): 475–509.

Berkhofer, Robert F., Jr. *The White Man's Indian: Images of the American Indian from Columbus to the Present.* New York: Vintage, 1979.

Berman, Judith. "George Hunt and the Kwak'wala Texts." *Anthropological Linguistics* 36, no. 4 (1994): 482–514.

Bernstein, Jay H. "First Recipients of Anthropological Doctorates in the United States, 1891–1930." *American Anthropologist* 104, no. 2 (2002): 551–64.

Biolsi, Thomas. "Bringing the Law Back In: Legal Rights and the Regulation of Indian-White Relations on Rosebud Reservation." *Current Anthropology* 36, no. 4 (1995): 543–71.

Biolsi, Thomas, and Larry J. Zimmerman. *Indians and Anthropologists: Vine Deloria, Jr. and the Critique of Anthropology.* Tucson: University of Arizona Press, 1997.

Bishop, Wendy. *Something Old, Something New: College Writing Teachers and Classroom Change.* Carbondale: Southern Illinois University Press, 1990.

Blair, Carole, and Neil Michel. "Reproducing Civil Rights Tactics: The Rhetorical Performances of the Civil Rights Memorial." *Rhetoric Society Quarterly* 30, no. 2 (2000): 31–55.

Bledstein, Burton. *The Culture of Professionalism: The Middle Class and the Development of Higher Education in America.* New York: Norton, 1978.

Boas, Franz. "Anthropologic Miscellanea." *American Anthropologist* 11, no. 1 (1909): 137–39.

———. *Bella Bella Tales.* New York: American Folk-Lore Society/G. E. Stechert, 1932.

———. *Bella Bella Texts.* New York: Columbia University Press, 1928.

———. "The Foundation of a National Anthropological Society." *Science* 15, no. 386 (1902): 804–09.

———. *Kathlamet Texts.* Washington, DC: Government Printing Office, 1901.

———. *Kutenai Tales.* Smithsonian Institution. Bureau of American Ethnology Bulletin 59. Washington, DC: Government Printing Office, 1918.

———. *Race, Language, and Culture.* Chicago: University of Chicago Press, 1940.

———. "Report on the Academic Teaching of Anthropology." *American Anthropologist* 21, no. 1 (1919): 41–48.

———. *The Social Organization and Secret Societies of the Kwakiutl Indians.* Washington, DC: Government Printing Office, 1897.

Boas, Franz, and George Hunt. *Kwakiutl Texts.* New York: G. E. Stechert, 1905.

———. *Kwakiutl Texts, Second Series.* New York: G. E. Stechert, 1906.

"Books in Brief." Review of *Digging in Yucatan. Nation* 134 (20 Jan. 1932): 80.

Bordewich, Fergus. *Killing the White Man's Indian: Reinventing Native Americans at the End of the Twentieth Century.* New York: Doubleday, 1996.

Borneman, John, and Abdellah Hammoudi, eds. *Being There: The Fieldwork Encounter and the Making of Truth.* Berkeley and Los Angeles: University of California Press, 2009.

Boxwell, D. A. "'Sis Cat' as Ethnographer: Self-Presentation and Self-Inscription in Zora Neale Hurston's *Mules and Men.*" *African American Review* 26, no. 4 (1992): 605–17.

"Brief Notices." Review of *Spider Woman: A Story of Navajo Weavers and Chanters,* by Gladys A. Reichard. *Quarterly Review of Biology* 10, no. 3 (1935): 348.

Briggs, Charles, and Richard Bauman. "'The Foundation of All Future Researches': Franz Boas, George Hunt, Native American Texts, and the Construction of Modernity." *American Quarterly* 51, no. 3 (1999): 479–528.

Brown, Stephen Gilbert. "Beyond Theory Shock: Ethos, Knowledge, and Power in Critical Ethnography." In *Ethnography Unbound: From Theory Shock to Critical Praxis,* edited by Stephen Gilbert Brown and Sidney I. Dobrin, 299–315. Albany: State University of New York Press, 2004.

Brown, Stephen Gilbert, and Sidney I. Dobrin, eds. *Ethnography Unbound: From Theory Shock to Critical Praxis.* Albany: State University of New York Press, 2004.

Bunzel, Ruth. *The Pueblo Potter: A Study of Creative Imagination in Primitive Art.* New York: Columbia University Press, 1929.

Bunzl, Matti. "Boas, Foucault, and the 'Native Anthropologist': Notes toward a Neo-Boasian Anthropology." *American Anthropologist* 106, no. 3 (2004): 435–42.

Burgess, Amy. "Doing Time: An Exploration of Timescapes in Literacy Learning and Research." *Language and Education* 24, no. 5 (2010): 353–65.

Burke, Kenneth. "Four Master Tropes." *Kenyon Review* 3, no. 4 (1941): 421–38.

Calvin, Inga. Lecture. Museum of the University of Colorado. Boulder, 1 Mar. 2007.

———. Personal correspondence. 27 July 2008.

Chester, Hilary Lynn. "Frances Eliza Babbitt and the Growth of Professionalism of Women in Archaeology." In *New Perspectives on the Origins of Americanist Archaeology,* edited by David L. Browman and Stephen Williams, 164–84. Tuscaloosa: University of Alabama Press, 2002.

Child, Brenda J. *Boarding School Seasons: American Indian Families, 1900–1940.* Lincoln: University of Nebraska Press, 1998.

Child, Lydia Maria. *Hobomok: A Tale of Early Times.* Boston: Cummings, Hilliard, 1824.

Cintron, Ralph. *Angels' Town: Chero Ways, Gang Life, and Rhetorics of the Everyday.* Boston: Beacon Press, 1997.

———. "Wearing a Pith Helmet at a Sly Angle; or, Can Writing Researchers Do Ethnography in a Postmodern Era?" *Written Communication* 10, no. 3 (1993): 371–412.

Clark, Gregory, and S. Michael Halloran. "Transformations of Public Discourse in Nineteenth-Century America." In *Oratorical Culture in Nineteenth-Century America,* edited by Gregory Clark and S. Michael Halloran, 1–28. Carbondale: Southern Illinois University Press, 1993.

Clemente, Angeles, Michael James Higgins, and William Michael Sughrua. "'I Don't Find Any Privacy Around Here': Ethnographic Encounters with Local Practices of Literacy in the State Prison of Oaxaca." *Language and Education* 25, no. 6 (2011): 491–513.

Clifford, James. "On Ethnographic Authority." *Representations* 1, no. 2 (1983): 118–46.

———. "Spatial Practices: Fieldwork, Travel, and the Disciplining of Anthropology." In *Anthropological Locations: Boundaries and Grounds of a Field Science,* edited by Akhil Gupta and James Ferguson, 185–222. Berkeley and Los Angeles: University of California Press, 1997.

Clifford, James, and George Marcus, eds. *Writing Culture: The Poetics and Politics of Ethnography.* Berkeley and Los Angeles: University of California Press, 1986.

Coe, Richard M. "'An Arousing and Fulfillment of Desires': The Rhetoric of Genre in the Process Era—and Beyond." In *Genre and the New Rhetoric,* edited by Aviva Freedman and Peter Medway, 181–90. London: Taylor and Francis, 1994.

———. "The New Rhetoric of Genre: Writing Political Briefs." In *Genre in the*

Classroom: Multiple Perspectives, edited by Ann M. Johns, 197–207. Mahwah, NJ: Lawrence Erlbaum Associates, 2002.

Coe, Richard M., Lorelei Lingard, and Tatiana Teslenko, eds. *The Rhetoric and Ideology of Genre.* Cresskill, NJ: Hampton, 2002.

Cole, Sally. Introduction to *The City of Women,* by Ruth Landes. Albuquerque: University of New Mexico Press, 1994.

———. *Ruth Landes: A Life in Anthropology.* Lincoln: University of Nebraska Press, 2003.

Collier, Donald, and Harry Tschopik Jr. "The Role of Museums in American Anthropology." *American Anthropologist* 56, no. 5 (1954): 768–79.

Collier, Virginia MacMakin. *Marriage and Careers: A Study of One Hundred Women Who Are Wives, Mothers, Homemakers and Professional Workers.* New York: The Channel Bookshop, 1926.

Cooper, Marilyn M. "Rhetorical Agency as Emergent and Enacted." *College Composition and Communication* 62, no. 3 (2011): 420–49.

Cotera, María Eugenia. *Native Speakers: Ella Deloria, Zora Neale Hurston, Jovita Gonzalez, and the Poetics of Culture.* Austin: University of Texas Press, 2008.

Crapanzano, Vincent. "Hermes' Dilemma: The Masking of Subversion in Ethnographic Description." In *Writing Culture: The Poetics and Politics of Ethnography,* edited by James Clifford and George Marcus, 51–76. Berkeley and Los Angeles: University of California Press, 1986.

———. *Tuhami: Portrait of a Moroccan.* Chicago: University of Chicago Press, 1985.

Cushing, Frank Hamilton. *Outlines of Zuni Creation Myths.* Washington, DC: Government Printing Office, 1896.

Cushman, Ellen. *The Struggle and the Tools: Oral and Literate Strategies in an Inner-City Community.* Albany: State University of New York Press, 1998.

Danielewicz, Jane. "Personal Genres, Public Voices." *College Composition and Communication* 59, no. 3 (2008): 420–50.

Darnell, Regna. "American Anthropology and the Development of Folklore Scholarship: 1890–1920." *Journal of the Folklore Institute* 10, nos. 1–2 (1973): 23–39.

———. *. And Along Came Boas: Continuity and Revolution in Americanist Anthropology.* Philadelphia: John Benjamins, 1998.

———. "The Emergence of Academic Anthropology at the University of Pennsylvania." *Journal of the History of the Behavioral Sciences* 6, no. 1 (1970): 80–92.

———. "History of Anthropology in Historical Perspective." *Annual Review of Anthropology* 6 (1977): 399–417.

———. "North American Traditions in Anthropology: The Historiographic Baseline." In *A New History of Anthropology,* edited by Henrika Kuklick, 35–51. Malden, MA: Wiley-Blackwell, 2008.

———. "The Professionalization of American Anthropology: A Case Study in the Sociology of Knowledge." *Social Science Information* 10, no. 2 (1971): 83–103.

Deacon, Desley. *Elsie Clews Parsons: Inventing Modern Life.* Chicago: University of Chicago Press, 1997.

de Laguna, Frederica. "The Development of Anthropology." In *Selected Papers from the American Anthropologist, 1888–1920,* 2nd ed., edited by Frederica de Laguna, 101–14. Lincoln: University of Nebraska Press, 2002.

de Laguna, Frederica, ed. *Selected Papers from the American Anthropologist, 1888–1920.* 2nd ed. Lincoln: University of Nebraska Press, 2002.

Dellenbaugh, Frederick S. "Memorial to John Wesley Powell." *American Anthropologist* 20, no. 4 (1918): 432–36.

Deloria, Ella Cara. *Dakota Texts.* 1932. Reprint, Lincoln: University of Nebraska Press, 2006.

———. *Speaking of Indians.* 1944. Reprint, Lincoln: University of Nebraska Press, 1998.

———. *Waterlily.* Lincoln: University of Nebraska Press, 1988.

Deloria, Philip J. *Playing Indian.* New Haven, CT: Yale University Press, 1998.

Deloria, Vine, Jr. *Custer Died for Your Sins.* 1969. Reprint, Norman: University of Oklahoma Press, 1988.

Demallie, Raymond J. Introduction to *Dakota Texts,* by Ella Cara Deloria. Lincoln: University of Nebraska Press, 2006.

Dennett, Daniel C. *Darwin's Dangerous Idea: Evolution and the Meanings of Life.* New York: Simon and Schuster, 1995.

Devitt, Amy J. *Writing Genres.* Carbondale: Southern Illinois University Press, 2004.

Devitt, Amy J., Anis Bawarshi, and Mary Jo Reiff. "Materiality and Genre in the Study of Discourse Communities." *College English* 65, no. 5 (2003): 541–58.

Dickinson, Greg. "Joe's Rhetoric: Starbucks and the Spatial Rhetoric of Authenticity." *Rhetoric Society Quarterly* 32, no. 4 (2002): 5–28.

Doerschuk, Beatrice. *Statistical Work: A Study of Opportunities for Women.* New York: Bureau of Vocational Information, 1921.

———. *Women in the Law: An Analysis of Training, Practice, and Salaried Positions.* New York: Bureau of Vocational Information, 1920.

Dorsey, George A. *The Cheyenne.* Chicago: Field Columbian Museum, 1905.

Downey, Sharon D. "The Evolution of the Rhetorical Genre of Apologia." *Western Journal of Communication* 57, no. 1 (1993): 42–64.

Dryer, Dylan B. "Taking Up Space: On Genre Systems as Geographies of the Possible." *JAC: A Journal of Composition Theory* 28, nos. 3–4 (2008): 503–34.

Dummer, Ethel Sturges. *Why I Think So: The Autobiography of a Hypothesis.* Chicago: Clarke-McElroy, 1937.

"Earl Halstead Morris, 1889–1956." Obituary. *American Anthropologist* 59, no. 3 (1957): 521–23.

Edbauer, Jenny. "Unframing Models of Public Distribution: From Rhetorical Situation to Rhetorical Ecologies." *Rhetoric Society Quarterly* 35, no. 4 (2005): 5–24.

Ehrenhaus, Peter. "The Vietnam Veterans Memorial: An Invitation to Argument." *Journal of the American Forensic Association* 25, no. 2 (1988): 54–64.

Enoch, Jessica. *Refiguring Rhetorical Education: Women Teaching African American, Native American, and Chicano/a Students, 1865–1911.* Carbondale: Southern Illinois University Press, 2008.

———. "A Woman's Place Is in the School: Rhetorics of Gendered Space in Nineteenth-Century America." *College English* 70, no. 3 (2008): 275–95.

Enoch, Jessica, and Jordynn Jack. "Remembering Sappho: New Perspectives on Teaching (and Writing) Women's Rhetorical History." *College English* 73, no. 5 (2011): 518–37.

Enos, Richard Leo. "The Archaeology of Women in Rhetoric: Rhetorical Sequencing as a Research Method for Historical Scholarship." *Rhetoric Society Quarterly* 32, no. 1 (2002): 65–79.

Fabian, Johannes. *Time and the Other: How Anthropology Makes Its Object.* New York: Columbia University Press, 1983.

Fahnestock, Jeanne. "Accommodating Science: The Rhetorical Life of Scientific Facts." *Written Communication* 3, no. 3 (1986): 275–96.

Fawcett, Melissa Jayne. *Medicine Trail: The Life and Lessons of Gladys Tantaquidgeon.* Tucson: University of Arizona Press, 2000.

Fear-Segal, Jacqueline. *White Man's Club: Schools, Race, and the Struggle of Indian Acculturation.* Lincoln: University of Nebraska Press, 2007.

Filene, Catherine. *Careers for Women.* Boston: Houghton Mifflin, 1920.

———. *Careers for Women: New Ideas, New Methods, New Opportunities to Fit a New World.* Rev. ed. Boston: Houghton Mifflin, 1934.

Fine-Dare, Kathleen. *Grave Injustice: The American Indian Repatriation Movement and NAGPRA.* Lincoln: University of Nebraska Press, 2002.

Finn, Janet L. "Walls and Bridges: Cultural Mediation and the Legacy of Ella Deloria." *Frontiers: A Journal of Women Studies* 21, no. 3 (2000): 158–82.

Fisher, Donald. *Fundamental Development of the Social Sciences: Rockefeller Philanthropy and the United States Social Science Research Council.* Ann Arbor: University of Michigan Press, 1993.

———. "Rockefeller Philanthropy and the Rise of Social Anthropology." *Anthropology Today* 2, no. 1 (1986): 5–8.

Fisher, Lillian Estelle. Review of *Spider Woman: A Story of Navajo Chanters and Weavers,* by Gladys A. Reichard. *Mississippi Valley Historical Review* 22, no. 2 (1935): 312–13.

Fletcher, Alice Cunningham. *The Hako: A Pawnee Ceremony.* Bureau of American Ethnology. 22nd Annual Report, 1900–1901. Washington, DC: Government Printing Office, 1904.

Flores, Lisa. "Creating Discursive Space through a Rhetoric of Difference: Chicana Feminists Craft a Homeland." *Quarterly Journal of Speech* 82, no. 2 (1996): 142–56.

Fowler, Don D. *A Laboratory for Anthropology: Science and Romanticism in the American Southwest, 1846–1930.* Albuquerque: University of New Mexico Press, 2000.

Frachtenberg, Leo J. *Lower Umpqua Texts and Notes on the Kusan Dialects.* New York: Columbia University Press, 1914.

Frank, Gelya. "Jews, Multiculturalism, and Boasian Anthropology." *American Anthropologist* 99, no. 4 (1997): 731–45.

Frazier, Lessie Jo. "Genre, Methodology and Feminist Practice: Gladys Reichard's Ethnographic Voice." *Critique of Anthropology* 13, no. 4 (1993): 363–78.

Freadman, Anne. "Anyone for Tennis?" In *Genre in the New Rhetoric,* edited by Aviva Freedman and Peter Medway, 43–66. London: Taylor and Francis, 1994.

———. "The Traps and Trappings of Genre Theory." *Applied Linguistics* 33, no. 5 (2012): 544–63.

———. "Uptake." In *The Rhetoric and Ideology of Genre: Strategies for Stability and Change,* edited by Richard M. Coe, Lorelei Lingard, and Tatiana Teskenko, 39–53. Cresskill, NJ: Hampton Press, 2002.

Freedman, Aviva, and Peter Medway. "Locating Genre Studies: Antecedents and Prospects." In *Genre and the New Rhetoric,* edited by Aviva Freedman and Peter Medway, 1–19. London: Taylor and Francis, 1994.

Freedman, Aviva, and Peter Medway, eds. *Genre and the New Rhetoric.* London: Taylor and Francis, 1994.

Fries, Adelaide Lisetta. *The Road to Salem.* Chapel Hill: University of North Carolina Press, 1944.

Gacs, Ute, Aisha Khan, Jerrie McIntyre, and Ruth Weinberg, eds. *Women Anthropologists: A Biographical Dictionary.* New York: Greenwood Press, 1988.

Gag, Wanda. *Growing Pains.* New York: Coward McCann, 1940.

Gallagher, Victoria J. "Memory as Social Action: Cultural Projection and Generic Form in Civil Rights Memorials." In *New Approaches to Rhetoric,* edited by Patricia A. Sullivan and Steven R. Goldzwig, 149–71. Thousand Oaks, CA: Sage, 2004.

Gaonkar, Dilip. "The Idea of Rhetoric in the Rhetoric of Science." In *Rhetorical Hermeneutics: Invention and Interpretation in the Age of Science,* edited by Alan G. Gross and William M. Keith, 25–85. Albany: State University of New York Press, 1997.

Gates, Barbara T., and Ann B. Shteir, eds. *Natural Eloquence: Women Reinscribe Science.* Madison: University of Wisconsin Press, 1997.

Gatewood, John. B. "A Short Typology of Ethnographic Genres; or, Ways to Write about Other Peoples." *Anthropology and Humanism Quarterly* 9, no. 4 (1984): 5–10.

Gatschet, Albert S. "The Klamath Indians of Southwestern Oregon." *Contributions to North American Ethnology,* vol. 1, parts 1 and 2. Washington, DC: Government Printing Office, 1890.

———. *A Migration Legend of the Creek Indians, with a Linguistic, Historic, and Ethnographic Introduction.* 1884. Reprint, New York: AMS Press, 1969.

Geertz, Clifford. *Works and Lives: The Anthropologist as Author.* Stanford, CA: Stanford University Press, 1988.

Gershenhorn, Jerry. *Melville J. Herskovits and the Racial Politics of Knowledge.* Lincoln: University of Nebraska Press, 2004.

Gessner, Robert. *Broken Arrow.* New York: Farrar and Rinehart, 1933.

Gieryn, Thomas F. *Cultural Boundaries of Science: Credibility on the Line.* Chicago: University of Chicago Press, 1999.

Gillmor, Frances. *Windsinger.* New York: Minton, Balch, 1930.

Giltrow, Janet, and Dieter Stein, eds. *Genres in the Internet: Issues in the Theory of Genre.* Amsterdam: John Benjamins, 2009.

Goddard, Pliny Earle. *Hupa Texts.* Berkeley and Los Angeles: University of California Press, 1903–1904.

———. *Jicarilla Apache Texts.* New York: Trustees of the American Museum of Natural History, 1911.

Goldfrank, Esther Schiff. "Gladys Amanda Reichard, 1893–1955." *Journal of American Folklore* 69, no. 271 (1956): 53–54.

Golinski, Jan. *Science as Public Culture: Chemistry and Enlightenment in Britain, 1760–1820.* New York: Cambridge University Press, 1999.

Gordon, Deborah. "Among Women: Gender and Ethnographic Authority of the Southwest, 1930–1960." In *Hidden Scholars: Women Anthropologists and the Native American Southwest,* edited by Nancy J. Parezo, 129–45. Albuquerque: University of New Mexico Press, 1993.

Grek-Martin, Jason. "Vanishing the Haida: George Dawson's Ethnographic Vision and the Making of Settler Space on the Queen Charlotte Islands in the Late Nineteenth-Century." *The Canadian Geographer/Le Géographe canadien* 51, no. 3 (2007): 373–98.

Gross, Alan G., Joseph E. Harmon, and Michael S. Reidy. *Communicating Science: The Scientific Article from the Seventeenth Century to the Present.* Oxford: Oxford University Press, 2002.

Grote, Ellen. "Challenging the Boundaries between School-Sponsored and Vernacular Literacies: Urban Indigenous Teenage Girls Writing in an 'At Risk' Program." *Language and Education* 20, no. 6 (2006): 478–92.

Gruber, Jerome W. "Ethnographic Salvage and the Shaping of Anthropology." *American Anthropologist* 72, no. 6 (1970): 1289–99.

Gruening, Martha. "The Indian's Tragedy." Review of *Broken Arrow,* by Robert Gessner. *Nation* 137, no. 3565 (1933): 518.

Gunther, Erna. *Klallam Ethnography.* Seattle: University of Washington Press, 1927.

———. *Klallam Folk Tales.* Seattle: University of Washington Press, 1925.

Haile, Berard. Review of *Social Life of the Navajo Indians,* by Gladys A. Reichard. *American Anthropologist* 34, no. 4 (1932): 711–17.

Hallowell, A. I. "The Beginnings of American Anthropology." In *Selected Papers from the American Anthropologist, 1888–1920,* edited by Frederica de Laguna, for the Publications Committee of the American Anthropological Association, 1–90. Evanston, IL: Row, Peterson/American Anthropological Association, 1960.

Hamilton, Alice. *Exploring the Dangerous Trades: The Autobiography of Alice Hamilton, M.D.* New York: Little, Brown, 1943.

Hammersley, Martyn. "The Rhetorical Turn in Ethnography." *Social Science Information* 32, no. 1 (1993): 23–37.

Handler, Richard. "Boasian Anthropology and the Critique of American Culture." *American Quarterly* 42, no. 2 (1990): 252–73.

Harding, Sandra, ed. *The "Racial" Economy of Science: Toward a Democratic Future.* Bloomington: Indiana University Press, 1993.

Harrington, John P. *Karuk Indian Myths.* Washington, DC: Government Printing Office, 1932.

Harrison, Ira E., and Faye V. Harrison, eds. *African-American Pioneers in Anthropology.* Urbana: University of Illinois Press, 1999.

Heath, Shirley Brice. *Ways with Words: Language, Life, and Work in Communities and Classrooms.* New York: Cambridge University Press, 1983.

Helscher, Thomas. "The Subject of Genre." In *Genre and Writing: Issues, Arguments, Alternatives,* edited by Wendy Bishop and Hans Ostrom, 27–36. Portsmouth, NH: Boynton/Cook, 1997.

Hemenway, Robert. Foreword to *Zora Neale Hurston: A Life in Letters,* by Zora Neale Hurston, edited by Carla Kaplan, 1–6. New York: Doubleday, 2002.

———. *Zora Neale Hurston: A Literary Biography.* Urbana: University of Illinois Press, 1980.

Henze, Brent. "Emergent Genres in Young Disciplines: The Case of Ethnological Science." *Technical Communication Quarterly* 13, no. 4 (2004): 393–421.

———. "Scientific Definition in Rhetorical Formations: Race as "Permanent Variety" in James Cowles Pritchard's Ethnology." *Rhetoric Review* 23, no. 4 (2004): 311–31.

Herring, Susan C., Lois Ann Scheidt, Sabrina Bonus, and Elijah Wright. "Bridging the Gap: A Genre Analysis of Weblogs." In *Proceedings of the 37th Hawaii International Conference on System Sciences,* 1–11. Los Alamitos: IEEE Press, 2004.

Herskovits, Melville. *Franz Boas: The Science of Man in the Making.* New York: Scribner, 1953.

Hertzberg, Hazel. "Nationality, Anthropology, and Pan-Indianism in the Life of Arthur C. Parker." *Proceedings of the American Philosophical Society* 123, no. 1 (1979): 47–72.

Hieb, Louis A. "Elsie Clews Parsons in the Southwest." In *Hidden Scholars: Women Anthropologists and the Native American Southwest,* edited by Nancy J. Parezo, 63–75. Albuquerque: University of New Mexico Press, 1993.

Hinsley, Curtis. *Savages and Scientists: The Smithsonian Institution and the Development of American Anthropology, 1846–1910.* Washington, DC: Smithsonian Institution, 1981.

Hoefel, Roseanne. "'Different by Degree': Ella Cara Deloria, Zora Neale Hurston, and Franz Boas Contend with Race and Ethnicity." *American Indian Quarterly* 25, no. 2 (2001): 181–202.

Horner, Bruce. "Critical Ethnography, Ethics, and Work: Rearticulating Labor." In *Ethnography Unbound: From Theory Shock to Critical Praxis,* edited by Stephen Gilbert Brown and Sidney I. Dobrin, 13–34. Albany: State University of New York Press, 2004.

Hough, Walter. "Alice Cunningham Fletcher." *American Anthropologist* 25, no. 2 (1923): 254–58.

———. "Otis Tufton Mason." *American Anthropologist* 10, no. 4 (1908): 661–67.

Howell, Nancy. "Human Hazards of Fieldwork." In *Ethnographic Fieldwork: An Anthropological Reader,* edited by Antonius C. G. M. Robben and Jeffrey A. Sluka, 234–44. Malden, MA: Wiley-Blackwell, 2007.

Hoxie, Frederick E. *A Final Promise: The Campaign to Assimilate the Indians, 1880–1920.* Lincoln: University of Nebraska Press, 1984.

Hrdlička, Aleš. *Physical Anthropology: Its Scope and Aims; Its History and Present Status in the United States.* Philadelphia: Wistar Institute of Anatomy and Biology, 1919.

———. *Physiological and Medical Observations among the Indians of Southwestern United States and Northern New Mexico.* Bureau of American Ethnology. 34th Annual Report. Washington, DC: Government Printing Office, 1908. 1–460.

Huff, Cynthia, ed. *Women's Life Writing and Imagined Communities.* London: Routledge, 2005.

Hurston, Zora Neale. "Characteristics of Negro Expression." In *Negro: An Anthology,* edited by Nancy Cunard, 24–31. New York: F. Ungar, 1934.

———. *Mules and Men.* New York: Lippincott, 1935.

———. *Tell My Horse.* New York: Lippincott, 1938.

———. *Zora Neale Hurston: A Life in Letters.* Edited by Carla Kaplan. New York: Doubleday, 2002.

Hutchins, Grace. *Women Who Work.* New York: International Publishers, 1934.

Hutto, David. "When Professional Biologists Write: An Ethnographic Study with Pedagogical Implications." *Technical Communication Quarterly* 12, no. 2 (2003): 207–23.

Hyatt, Marshall. *Franz Boas, Social Activist: The Dynamics of Ethnicity.* New York: Greenwood, 1990.

Hymes, Dell. "The Use of Anthropology: Critical, Political, Personal." In *Reinventing Anthropology,* edited by Dell Hymes, 3–82. New York: Pantheon Books, 1972.

Irwin-Williams, Cynthia. "Women in the Field: The Role of Women in Archaeology before 1960." In *Women of Science: Righting the Record,* edited by Gabriela Kass-Simon, Patricia Farnes, and Deborah Nash, 1–41. Bloomington: Indiana University Press, 1990.

Jack, Jordynn. "Chronotopes: Forms of Time in Rhetorical Argument." *College English* 69, no. 1 (2006): 52–73.

———. *Science on the Home Front: American Women Scientists in World War II.* Urbana: University of Illinois Press, 2009.

———. "Space, Time, Memory: Gendered Recollections of Wartime Los Alamos." *Rhetoric Society Quarterly* 37, no. 3 (2007): 229–50.

Jamieson, Kathleen M. "Antecedent Genre as Rhetorical Constraint." *Quarterly Journal of Speech* 61, no. 4 (1975): 406–15.

Johnson, Amber Lauren. "'We Don't Just Write to Write, We Write to Be Free': A Rhetorical Ethnography of Spoken Word in Los Angeles." PhD diss., Pennsylvania State University, 2006.

Johnson, Nan. *Gender and Rhetorical Space in American Life, 1866–1910.* Carbondale: Southern Illinois University Press, 2002.

"John Wesley Powell." *American Anthropologist* 4, no. 3 (1902): 564–65.

Kaberry, Phyllis. "Malinowski's Contribution to Field-Work Methods and the Writing of Ethnography." In *Man and Culture: An Evaluation of the Work of Bronislaw Malinowski,* edited by Raymond Firth, 71–91. London: Routledge and Kegan Paul, 1957.

Kain, Donna J. "Constructing Genre: A Threefold Typology." *Technical Communication Quarterly* 14, no. 4 (2005): 375–409.

Kaplan, Caren. "Resisting Autobiography: Out-Law Genres and Transnational Feminist Subjects." In *Women, Autobiography, Theory: A Reader,* edited by Sidonie Smith and Julia Watson, 208–16. Madison: University of Wisconsin Press, 1998.

Kaplan, Carla, ed. *Zora Neale Hurston: A Life in Letters.* New York: Doubleday, 2002.

Kass-Simon, Gabriela, Patricia Farnes, and Deborah Nash, eds. *Women of Science: Righting the Record.* Bloomington: Indiana University Press, 1990.

Katriel, Tamar. "Sites of Memory: Discourses of the Past in Israeli Pioneering Settlement Museums." *Quarterly Journal of Speech* 80, no. 1 (1994): 1–20.

Keesing, Roger M. "Kwaio Women Speak: The Micropolitics of Autobiography in a Solomon Island Society." *American Anthropologist* 87, no. 1 (1985): 27–39.

Kehoe, Alice. "Revisionist Anthropology: Aboriginal North America." *Current Anthropology* 22, no. 5 (1981): 503–17.

Kellogg, Clara Louise. *Memoirs of an American Prima Donna.* New York: G.P. Putnam's Sons, 1913.

Kerns, Virginia. *Scenes from the High Desert: Julian Steward's Life and Theory.* Champaign: University of Illinois Press, 2003.

King, Lisa. "Speaking Sovereignty and Communicating Change: Rhetorical Sovereignty and the Inaugural Exhibits at the NMAI." *American Indian Quarterly* 35, no. 1 (2011): 75–103.

Kirklighter, Cristina. *Traversing the Democratic Borders of the Essay.* Albany: State University of New York Press, 2002.

Knight, Mary. *On My Own.* New York: Macmillan, 1938.

Krech, Shepard, III. *The Ecological Indian: Myth and History.* New York: Norton, 2000.

Kroeber, Alfred L. "Decorative Symbolism of the Arapaho." *American Anthropologist* 3, no. 2 (1901): 308–36.

Kuhn, Irene. *Assigned to Adventure.* New York: Grosset and Dunlap, 1938.

Kuklick, Henrika. "The British Tradition." In *A New History of Anthropology,* edited by Henrika Kuklick, 52–78. Malden, MA: Blackwell, 2008.

———. Introduction to *A New History of Anthropology,* edited by Henrika Kuklick, 1–17. Malden, MA: Blackwell, 2008.

———. *The Savage Within: The Social History of British Anthropology, 1885–1945.* Cambridge: Cambridge University Press, 1991.

Kuklick, Henrika, ed. *A New History of Anthropology.* Malden, MA: Blackwell, 2008.

Kuper, Adam. *Anthropology and Anthropologists: The Modern British School.* 3rd ed. London: Routledge, 1996.

La Farge, Oliver. *The Enemy Gods.* Boston: Houghton Mifflin, 1937.

———. *Laughing Boy.* Boston: Houghton Mifflin, 1929.

LaFrance, Michelle, and Melissa Nichols. "Institutional Ethnography as Materialist Framework for Writing Program Research and the Faculty-Staff Work Standpoints Project." *College Composition and Communication* 64, no. 1 (2012): 130–50.

Lamphere, Louise. "Feminist Anthropology: The Legacy of Elsie Clews Parsons." *American Ethnologist* 16, no. 3 (1989): 518–33.

———. "Gladys Reichard among the Navajo." *Frontiers: A Journal of Women's Studies* 12, no. 3 (1992): 79–115.

———. "Unofficial Histories: A Vision of Anthropology from the Margins." *American Anthropologist* 106, no. 1 (2004): 126–39.

Laquintano, Timothy. "Sustained Authorship: Digital Writing, Self-Publishing, and the eBook." PhD diss., University of Wisconsin at Madison, 2010.

Latour, Bruno. "Visualisation and Cognition: Drawing Things Together." In

Representation in Scientific Practice, edited by Michael Lynch and Steve Woolgar, 19–68. Cambridge, MA: MIT Press, 1990.

Lavender, Catherine J. *Scientists and Storytellers: Feminist Anthropologists and the Construction of the American Southwest.* Albuquerque: University of New Mexico Press, 2006.

Lay, Mary M. *The Rhetoric of Midwifery: Gender, Knowledge, and Power.* New Brunswick, NJ: Rutgers University Press, 2000.

Leacock, Eleanor. "Gladys Amanda Reichard." In *Women Anthropologists: A Biographical Dictionary,* edited by Ute Gacs, Aisha Khan, Jerrie McIntyre, and Ruth Weinberg, 303–09. New York: Greenwood Press, 1988.

Lefebvre, Henri. *The Production of Space.* Translated by Donald Nicholson-Smith. Oxford: Blackwell, 1991.

Le-May Sheffield, Suzanne. *Women and Science: Social Impact and Interaction.* New Brunswick, NJ: Rutgers University Press, 2005.

Lepowsky, Maria. "Charlotte Gower and the Subterranean History of Anthropology." In *Excluded Ancestors, Inventible Traditions: Essays toward a More Inclusive History of Anthropology,* edited by Richard Handler, 123–70. Madison: University of Wisconsin Press, 2000.

Leuck, Miriam Simons. *Fields of Work for Women.* 3rd ed. New York: Appleton-Century, 1938.

Levine, Philippa. *The Amateur and the Professional: Antiquarians, Historians and Archaeologists in Victorian England, 1838–1886.* Cambridge: Cambridge University Press, 1986.

Lewis, Herbert S. "The Passion of Franz Boas." *American Anthropologist* 103, no. 2 (2001): 447–67.

Lillis, Theresa. "Ethnography as Method, Methodology, and 'Deep Theorizing': Closing the Gap between Text and Context in Academic Writing Research." *Written Communication* 25, no. 3 (2008): 353–88.

Lindquist, Julie. *A Place to Stand: Politics and Persuasion in a Working Class Bar.* London: Oxford University Press, 2002.

Linton, Ralph. *The Tanala: A Hill Tribe of Madagascar.* Chicago: Field Museum of Natural History, 1933.

Liss, Julia E. "Diasporic Identities: The Science and Politics of Race in the Work of Franz Boas and W. E. B. DuBois, 1894–1919." *Cultural Anthropology* 13, no. 2 (1998): 127–66.

Lister, Florence Cline, and Robert H. Lister. *Earl Morris and Southwestern Archaeology.* Albuquerque: University of New Mexico Press, 1968.

Little, Joseph. "Achieving Objectivity through Genred Activity: A Case Study." *Journal of Technical Writing and Communication* 37, no. 1 (2007): 75–94.

Lomawaima, K. Tsianina. "Domesticity in the Federal Indian Schools: The Power of Authority over Mind and Body." *American Ethnologist* 20, no. 2 (1993): 227–40.

———. *They Called It Prairie Light: The Story of Chilocco Indian School.* Lincoln: University of Nebraska Press, 1994.

Lurie, Nancy O. "Epilogue." In *Irredeemable America: The Indians' Estate and Land Claims,* edited by Imre Sutton, 363–82. Albuquerque: University of New Mexico Press, 1985.

———. "Women in Early Anthropology." In *Pioneers of American Anthropology,* edited by June Helm, 29–81. Seattle: University of Washington Press, 1966.

Lyon, William H. "Gladys Reichard at the Frontiers of Navajo Culture." *American Indian Quarterly* 13, no. 2 (1989): 137–63.

Lyons, Scott. "The Left Side of the Circle: American Indians and Progressive Politics." In *Radical Relevance: Essays toward a Scholarship of the Whole Left,* edited by Steven Rosendale and Laura Gray Rosendale, 69–84. New York: State University of New York Press, 2005.

———. "Rhetorical Sovereignty: What Do American Indians Want from Writing?" *College Composition and Communication* 51, no. 3 (2000): 447–68.

Malinowski, Bronislaw. *Argonauts of the Western Pacific: An Account of Native Enterprise and Adventure in the Archipelagoes of Melanesian New Guinea.* 1922. Reprint, Prospect Heights, IL: Waveland Press, 1984.

———. *A Diary in the Strict Sense of the Term.* London: Routledge and Kegan Paul, 1967.

———. Review of *Coming of Age in Samoa,* by Margaret Mead. *Pacific Affairs* 2, no. 4 (1929): 225–26.

Manganaro, Marc. "Textual Play, Power, and Cultural Critique: An Orientation to Modernist Anthropology." *Modernist Anthropology: From Fieldwork to Text.* Princeton, NJ: Princeton University Press, 1990.

Manicas, Peter T. "The Social Science Disciplines: The American Model." In *Discourses on Society: The Shaping of the Social Science Disciplines,* edited by Peter Wagner, Bjorn Wittrock, and Richard Whitley, 45–71. Dordrecht: Kluwer, 1991.

Marbury, Elizabeth. *My Crystal Ball: Reminiscences.* New York: Boni and Liveright, 1923.

Marcus, George E. "Rhetoric and the Ethnographic Genre in Anthropological Research." *Current Anthropology* 21, no. 4 (1980): 507–10.

Marcus, George E., and Dick Cushman. "Ethnographies as Texts." *Annual Review of Anthropology* 11 (1982): 25–69.

Marcus, George E., and Michael M. J. Fischer. *Anthropology as Cultural Critique: An Experimental Moment in the Human Sciences.* 2nd ed. Chicago: University of Chicago Press, 1999.

Mark, Joan. "Francis La Flesche: The American Indian as Anthropologist." *Isis* 73, no. 4 (1982): 496–510.

Markham, Beryl. *West with the Night*. New York: Houghton Mifflin, 1942.

Marrett, R. R. Review of *American Indian Life by Several of Its Students*, edited by Elsie Clews Parsons. *American Anthropologist* 25, no. 2 (1923): 266–69.

Mason, John Alden. *Archaeology of Santa Marta Colombia: The Tairona Culture. Part 1: Report on Field Work*. Chicago: Field Museum of Natural History, 1931.

Mason, Otis T. "The Natural History of Folk-Lore." *Journal of American Folklore* 4, no. 13 (1891): 97–105.

———. "What Is Anthropology?" *The Saturday Lectures*, 25–43. Washington, DC: Judd and Detweiler, 1882.

Mathews, John Joseph. *Sundown*. 1934. Reprint, Norman: University of Oklahoma Press, 1988.

Maule, Frances. *Girl with a Paycheck: How She Lands It—Holds It—Makes It Grow*. New York: Harperand Brothers, 1941.

———. *She Strives to Conquer*. New York: Funk and Wagnalls, 1935.

Maurer, Elizabeth G. "'Working Consensus' and the Rhetorical Situation: The Homeless Blogs Negotiation of Public Meta-Genre." In *Genres in the Internet: Issues in the Theory of Genre*, edited by Janet Giltrow and Dieter Stein, 113–42. Amsterdam: John Benjamins, 2009.

McGee, Anita Newcomb. "Historical Sketch of the Women's Anthropological Society of America. Read at the Annual Reception, February 25, 1889." In *Organization and Historical Sketch of the Women's Anthropological Society of America*, 16–22. Washington, DC: Women's Anthropological Society of America, 1889.

McNeill, Laurie. "Genre Under Construction: The Diary on the Internet." *Language @ Internet* 2 (2005).

McNickle, D'Arcy. *The Surrounded*. 1936. Reprint, Albuquerque: University of New Mexico Press, 1997.

Mead, Margaret. *Coming of Age in Samoa: A Psychological Study of Primitive Youth for Western Civilization*. 1928. Reprint, New York: Morrow Quill Paperbacks, 1973.

———. Introduction to *The Golden Age of Anthropology*, edited by Margaret Mead and Ruth Bunzel, 1–12. New York: George Braziller, 1960.

Mehos, Donna C. "Colonial Commerce and Anthropological Knowledge: Dutch Ethnographic Museums in the European Context." In *A New History of Anthropology*, edited by Henrika Kuklick, 173–90. Malden, MA: Blackwell, 2008.

Meriam, Lewis, et al. *The Problem of Indian Administration*. Baltimore: Johns Hopkins University Press, 1928.

Mihesuah, Devon A. *American Indians: Stereotypes and Realities*. 1996. Reprint, Atlanta: Clarity Press, 2009.

Mihesuah, Devon A., ed. *The Repatriation Reader: Who Owns American Indian Remains?* Lincoln: University of Nebraska Press, 2000.

Milburn, Maureen. "The Politics of Possession: Louis Shotridge and the Tlingit

Collections of the University of Pennsylvania Museum." PhD diss., University of British Columbia, 1997.

Miller, Carolyn R. "Do Genres Evolve?" Keynote presentation, Genre 2012 Conference. Ottawa, Ontario, 27 June 2012.

———. "Genre as Social Action." *Quarterly Journal of Speech* 70, no. 2 (1984): 151–67.

———. "Rhetorical Community: The Cultural Basis of Genre." In *Genre and the New Rhetoric,* edited by Aviva Freedman and Peter Medway, 67–78. London: Taylor and Francis, 1994.

Miller, Carolyn R., and Dawn Shepherd. "Blogging as Social Action: A Genre Analysis of the Weblog." In *Into the Blogosphere: Rhetoric, Community, and Culture of Weblogs,* edited by Laura J. Gurak, Smiljana Antonijevic, Laurie Johnson, Clancy Ratliff, and Jessica Reyman. N.p, 2004.

———. "Questions for Genre Theory from the Blogosphere." In *Genres in the Internet: Issues in the Theory of Genre,* edited by Janet Giltrow and Dieter Stein, 263–90. Amsterdam: John Benjamins, 2009.

Miner, Horace. *St. Denis: A French-Canadian Parish.* Chicago: University of Chicago Press, 1939.

Mooney, James. *The Ghost Dance Religion and the Sioux Outbreak of 1890.* Washington, DC: Government Printing Office, 1896.

———. *Myths of the Cherokee.* Bureau of American Ethnology, Nineteenth Annual Report, 1897–1898. Washington, DC: Government Printing Office, 1900.

Moore, MariJo, ed. *Genocide of the Mind: New Native American Writing.* New York: Nation Books, 2003.

Morley, Sylvanus. Report. Carnegie Institution of Washington *Year Book* 24. Washington, DC: Carnegie Institution, 1924–25.

Morris, Ann Axtell. *Digging in the Southwest.* New York: Doubleday/Junior Literary Guild, 1933.

———. *Digging in Yucatan.* New York: Doubleday/Junior Literary Guild, 1931.

———. "Report of Ann Axtell Morris on the Mural Paintings and Painted Reliefs in the Temple of the Chac Mool." Carnegie Institution of Washington *Year Book* 27 (Jul. 1927–Jun. 1928): 297–300.

Morris, Earl H. *The Temple of the Warriors: The Adventure of Exploring and Restoring a Masterpiece of Native American Architecture in the Ruined Maya City of Chichen Itza.* New York: Scribner, 1931.

Morris, Earl H., Jean Charlot, and Ann Axtell Morris. *The Temple of the Warriors at Chichen Itza, Yucatan.* Washington, DC: Carnegie Institution of Washington, 1931.

Morrison, Anne Hendry. *Women and Their Careers: A Study of 306 Women in Business and the Professions.* New York: National Federation of Business and Professional Women's Clubs, 1934.

Mountford, Roxanne. "On Gender and Rhetorical Space." *Rhetoric Society Quarterly* 30, no. 1 (2001): 41–71.

Myers, Greg. "Discourse Studies of Scientific Popularizations: Questioning the Boundaries." *Discourse Studies* 5, no. 2 (2003): 265–79.

———. *Writing Biology: Texts in the Social Construction of Scientific Knowledge.* Madison: University of Wisconsin Press, 1990.

Narayan, Kirin. "How Native Is a 'Native' Anthropologist?" *American Anthropologist* 95, no. 3 (1993): 671–86.

Nelson, John Louw. *Rhythm for Rain.* Boston: Houghton Mifflin, 1937.

Norcini, Marilyn. *Edward Dozier: The Paradox of the American Indian Anthropologist.* Tucson: University of Arizona Press, 2007.

"Notes and News: Ann Axtell Morris." *American Anthropologist* 47, no. 4 (1945): 645.

Nowotny, Helga. "Knowledge for Certainty: Poverty, Welfare Institutions, and the Institutionalization of Social Science." In *Discourses on Society: The Shaping of the Social Science Disciplines,* edited by Peter Wagner, Bjorn Wittrock, and Richard Whitley, 23–41. Dordrecht: Kluwer, 1991.

Odlum, Hortense. *A Woman's Place: The Autobiography of Hortense Odlum.* New York: Scribner, 1939.

Oglesby, Catharine. *Business Opportunities for Women.* 3rd ed. New York: Harper and Brothers, 1937.

Olbrechts, Frans M. Review of *The Pueblo Potter* by Ruth Bunzel. *Journal of American Folklore* 44, no. 173 (1931): 314–16.

Owens, Louis. *Other Destinies: Understanding the American Indian Novel.* Norman: University of Oklahoma Press, 1994.

Paré, Anthony. "Discourse Regulations and the Production of Knowledge." In *Writing in the Workplace: New Research Perspectives,* edited by Rachel Spilka, 111–23. Carbondale: Southern Illinois University Press, 1993.

———. "Genre and Identity: Individuals, Institutions, and Ideology." In *The Rhetoric and Ideology of Genre: Strategies for Stability and Change,* edited by Richard M. Coe, Lorelei Lingard, and Tatiana Teskenko, 57–71. Cresskill, NJ: Hampton Press, 2002.

Paré, Anthony, and Graham Smart. "Observing Genres in Action: Towards a Research Methodology." In *Genre and the New Rhetoric,* edited by Aviva Freedman and Peter Medway, 146–54. London: Taylor and Francis, 1994.

Parezo, Nancy J. "Anthropology: The Welcoming Science." In *Hidden Scholars: Women Anthropologists and the Native American Southwest,* edited by Nancy J. Parezo, 3–37. Albuquerque: University of New Mexico Press, 1993.

Parezo, Nancy J., ed. *Hidden Scholars: Women Anthropologists and the Native American Southwest.* Albuquerque: University of New Mexico Press, 1993.

Parezo, Nancy J., and Don D. Fowler. *Anthropology Goes to the Fair: The 1904 Louisiana Purchase Exposition.* Lincoln: University of Nebraska Press, 2007.

Parezo, Nancy J., and Margaret A. Hardin. "In the Realm of the Muses." In *Hidden Scholars: Women Anthropologists and the Native American Southwest,* edited by Nancy J. Parezo, 270–93. Albuquerque: University of New Mexico Press, 1993.

Parkin, Robert. "The French Speaking Countries." In *One Discipline, Four Ways: British, German, French, and American Anthropology,* by Fredrik Barth, Andre Gingrich, Robert Parkin, and Sydel Silverman, 157–256. Chicago: University of Chicago Press, 2005.

Parsons, Elsie Clews. *Taos Pueblo.* Menasha, WI: American Anthropological Association, 1936.

———. *Tewa Tales.* New York: American Folk-Lore Society, 1926.

Parsons, Elsie Clews, ed. *American Indian Life by Several of Its Students.* 1922. Reprint, Lincoln: University of Nebraska Press, 1967.

Patterson, Thomas C. *A Social History of Anthropology in the United States.* New York: Berg, 2001.

Pels, Peter. "The Anthropology of Colonialism: Culture, History, and the Emergence of Western Governmentality." *Annual Review of Anthropology* 26 (1997): 163–83.

Penny, H. Glenn. "Bastian's Museum: On the Limits of Empiricism and the Transformation of German Ethnology." In *Worldly Provincialism: German Anthropology in the Age of Empire,* edited by H. Glenn Penny and Matti Bunzl, 86–126. Ann Arbor: University of Michigan Press, 2003.

———. *Objects of Culture: Ethnology and Ethnographic Museums in Imperial Germany.* Chapel Hill: University of North Carolina Press, 2002.

———. "Traditions in the German Language." In *A New History of Anthropology,* edited by Henrika Kuklick, 79–95. Malden, MA: Blackwell, 2008.

Penny, H. Glenn, and Matti Bunzl, eds. *Worldly Provincialism: German Anthropology in the Age of Empire.* Ann Arbor: University of Michigan Press, 2003.

Perkins, Frances. *Vocations for the Trained Woman: Opportunities Other Than Teaching.* New York: Longman, Green, 1921.

Pfister, Joel. *Individuality Incorporated: Indians and the Multicultural Modern.* Durham, NC: Duke University Press, 2004.

———. *The Yale Indian: The Education of Henry Roe Cloud.* Durham, NC: Duke University Press, 2009.

Pierce, Adah. *Vocations for Women.* New York: Macmillan, 1933.

Pigg, Stacey. "Embodied Rhetoric in Scenes of Production: The Case of the Coffeehouse." PhD diss., Michigan State University, 2011.

Pinkoski, Marc. "Julian Steward, American Anthropology, and Colonialism." *Histories of Anthropology Annual* 4 (2008): 172–204.

Porter, Joy. *To Be Indian: The Life of Iroquois-Seneca Arthur Caswell Parker.* Norman: University of Oklahoma Press, 2001.

Powdermaker, Hortense. *Life in Lesu: the Study of a Melanesian Society in New Ireland.* New York: Norton, 1933.

Powell, Malea. "Down by the River, or How Susan La Flesche Picotte Can Teach Us about Alliance as a Practice of Survivance." *College English* 67, no. 1 (2004): 38–60.

———. "Rhetorics of Survivance: How American Indians *Use* Writing." *College Composition and Communication* 53, no. 3 (2002): 396–434.

Pratt, Mary Louise. *Imperial Eyes: Travel Writing and Transculturation.* London: Routledge, 1992.

Preston, Jacqueline. "The Fertile Commonplace: Collective Persuasions, Interpretive Acts, and Dialectical Spaces." PhD diss., University of Wisconsin at Madison, 2011.

Pryse, Marjorie. "Introduction: Zora Neale Hurston, Alice Walker, and the 'Ancient Power' of Black Women." In *Conjuring: Black Women, Fiction, and Literary Tradition,* edited by Marjorie Pryse and Hortense Spillers, 1–24. Bloomington: Indiana University Press, 1985.

Rabinow, Paul. *Reflections on Fieldwork in Morocco.* Berkeley and Los Angeles: University of California Press, 1977.

Raglan, Lord. [FitzRoy Richard Somerset.] Review of *Bella Bella Tales. Man* 34 (Apr. 1934): 63.

"Record of American Folk-Lore." *Journal of American Folklore* 18, no. 69 (1905): 144–55.

Redfield, Robert. *The Folk Culture of Yucatan.* Chicago: University of Chicago Press, 1941.

———. *Tepoztlán, a Mexican Village: A Study of Folk Life.* Chicago: University of Chicago Press, 1930.

Reichard, Gladys A. *Dezba, Woman of the Desert.* New York: J. J. Augustin, 1939.

———. "Elsie Clews Parsons." *Journal of American Folklore* 56, no. 219 (Jan.–Mar. 1943): 45–48.

———. *Melanesian Design: A Study of Style in Wood and Tortoiseshell Carving.* New York: Columbia University Press, 1933.

———. *Navajo Shepherd and Weaver.* New York: J. J. Augustin, 1936.

———. Review of *Laughing Boy* by Oliver La Farge. *Journal of American Folk-Lore* 44, no. 171 (1931): 121–22.

———. *Social Life of the Navajo Indians.* New York: Columbia University Press, 1928.

———. *Spider Woman.* 1934. Reprint, Glorieta, NM: Rio Grande Press, 1968.

Reynolds, Nedra. "Ethos as Location: New Sites for Understanding Discursive Authority." *Rhetoric Review* 11, no. 2 (1993): 325–38.

Rideout, Henry Milner. *William Jones: Indian, Cowboy, American Scholar, and Anthropologist in the Field.* New York: Stokes, 1912.

Rifkin, Mark. *The Erotics of Sovereignty: Queer Native Writing in the Era of Self-Determination.* Minneapolis: University of Minnesota Press, 2012.

———. *When Did Indians Become Straight? Kinship, the History of Sexuality, and Native Sovereignty.* New York: Oxford University Press, 2011.

Rivers, William Halse, Albert Jenks, and Sylvanus Morley. *Reports upon the Present Condition and Future Needs of the Science of Anthropology.* Washington, DC: Carnegie Institution of Washington, 1913.

Robertson, James A. Review of *The Temple of the Warriors* by Earl H. Morris and *Digging in Yucatan* by Ann Axtell Morris. *Hispanic American Historical Review* 14, no. 3 (1934): 348–49.

Robinson, Josephine de Mott. *The Circus Lady.* New York: Thomas Crowell, 1926.

Rohner, Richard, ed. *The Ethnography of Franz Boas.* Chicago: University of Chicago Press, 1969.

Rosaldo, Renato. *Culture and Truth: The Remaking of Social Analysis.* Boston: Beacon, 1993.

———. "Where Objectivity Lies: The Rhetoric of Anthropology." In *The Rhetoric of the Human Sciences: Language and Argument in Scholarship and Public Affairs,* edited by John S. Nelson, Allan Megill, and Donald N. McCloskey, 87–110. Madison: University of Wisconsin Press, 1987.

Ross, Dorothy. *The Origins of American Social Science.* Cambridge: Cambridge University Press, 1991.

Rossiter, Margaret W. *Women Scientists in America: Struggles and Strategies to 1940.* Baltimore: Johns Hopkins University Press, 1982.

Rothenberg, Marc. "Organization and Control: Professionals and Amateurs in American Astronomy, 1899–1918." *Social Studies of Science* 11, no. 3 (1981): 305–25.

Royster, Jacqueline Jones. "Disciplinary Landscaping, or Contemporary Challenges in the History of Rhetoric." *Philosophy and Rhetoric* 36, no. 2 (2003): 148–67.

———. *Traces of a Stream: Literacy and Social Change among African American Women.* Pittsburgh: University of Pittsburgh Press, 2000.

Russell, David R. "Rethinking Genre in School and Society: An Activity Theory Analysis." *Written Communication* 14, no. 4 (1997): 504–54.

Schacker, Jennifer. "Unruly Tales: Ideology, Anxiety, and the Regulation of Genre." *Journal of American Folklore* 120, no. 478 (2007): 381–400.

Schiebinger, Londa. *Has Feminism Changed Science?* Cambridge, MA: Harvard University Press, 2001.

Schryer, Catherine F. "Genre and Power: A Chronotopic Analysis." In *The Rhetoric and Ideology of Genre: Strategies for Stability and Change,* edited by Richard M. Coe, Lorelei Lingard, and Tatiana Teskenko, 73–102. Cresskill, NJ: Hampton Press, 2002.

———. "Genre Time/Space: Chronotopic Strategies in the Experimental Article." *JAC: A Journal of Composition Theory* 19, no. 1 (1999): 81–89.

———. "The Lab vs. the Clinic: Sites of Competing Genres." In *Genre and the New Rhetoric,* edited by Aviva Freedman and Peter Medway, 105–24. London: Taylor and Francis, 1994.

———. "Records as Genre." *Written Communication* 10, no. 2 (1993): 200–34.

———. "Walking a Fine Line: Writing Negative Letters in an Insurance Company." *Journal of Business and Technical Communication* 14, no. 4 (2000): 445–97.

Sedgwick, Catherine Maria. *Hope Leslie, or Early Times in Massachusetts.* New York: Harper and Brothers, 1842.

Seitz, David. *Who Can Afford Critical Consciousness? Practicing a Pedagogy of Humility.* Cresskill: Hampton Press, 2004.

Sergeant, Elizabeth Shepley. *Shadow-Shapes: The Journal of a Wounded Woman.* New York: Houghton Mifflin, 1920.

Sharer, Wendy. "Genre Work: Expertise and Advocacy in the Early Bulletins of the U.S. Women's Bureau." *Rhetoric Society Quarterly* 33, no. 1 (2003): 5–32.

Shor, Ira. *When Students Have Power: Negotiating Authority in a Critical Pedagogy.* Chicago: University of Chicago Press, 1997.

Sibeud, Emmanuelle. "The Metamorphosis of Ethnology in France, 1839–1930." In *A New History of Anthropology,* edited by Henrika Kuklick, 96–110. Malden, MA: Blackwell, 2008.

Silverberg, Helene. "Introduction: Toward a Gendered Social Science History." In *Gender and American Social Science: The Formative Years,* edited by Helene Silverberg, 3–32. Princeton, NJ: Princeton University Press, 1998.

Silverman, Sydel. "The United States." In *One Discipline, Four Ways: British, German, French, and American Anthropology,* edited by Fredrik Barth, Andre Gingrich, Robert Parkin, and Sydel Silverman, 257–348. Chicago: University of Chicago Press, 2005.

Singer, Merrill. "Applied Anthropology." In *A New History of Anthropology,* edited by Henrika Kuklick, 327–29. Malden, MA: Blackwell, 2008.

Skinner, Alanson. "Little-Wolf Joins the Medicine Lodge." In *American Indian Life by Several of Its Students,* edited by Elsie Clews Parsons, 63–74. 1922. Reprint, Lincoln: University of Nebraska Press, 1967.

Slaughter Morton, Rosalie. *A Woman Surgeon.* New York: Frederick A. Stokes, 1937.

Smith, Margaret. *Hopi Girl.* Stanford, CA: Stanford University Press, 1931.

Smith, Marian W. *The Puyallup-Nisqually.* New York: Columbia University Press, 1940.

Smith, Sidonie. "Autobiographical Manifestos." In *Women, Autobiography, Theory: A Reader,* edited by Sidonie Smith and Julia Watson, 433–40. Madison: University of Wisconsin Press, 1998.

Smith, Sidonie, and Julia Watson, eds. *Women, Autobiography, Theory: A Reader.* Madison: University of Wisconsin Press, 1998.

Speck, Frank G. *Catawba Texts.* New York: Columbia University Press, 1934.

Spellmeyer, Kurt. "Travels to the Heart of the Forest: Dilettantes, Professionals, and Knowledge." *College English* 56, no. 7 (1994): 788–809.

Spencer, Frank. "The Rise of Academic Physical Anthropology in the United States (1880–1980): A Historical Overview." *American Journal of Physical Anthropology* 56, no. 4 (1981): 353–64.

Spinuzzi, Clay. *Tracing Genres through Organizations: A Sociocultural Approach to Information Design.* Cambridge, MA: MIT Press, 2003.

Starn, Orin. *Nightwatch: The Politics of Protest in the Andes.* Durham, NC: Duke University Press, 1999.

Stocking, George W., Jr. "The Ethnographer's Magic: Fieldwork in British Anthropology from Tylor to Malinowski." In *Observers Observed: Essays on Ethnographic Fieldwork,* edited by George W. Stocking Jr., 70–120. Madison: University of Wisconsin Press, 1983.

———. *The Ethnographer's Magic and Other Essays in the History of Anthropology.* Madison: University of Wisconsin Press, 1992.

———. "Franz Boas and the Founding of the American Anthropological Association." *American Anthropologist* 62, no. 1 (1960): 1–17.

———. "Ideas and Institutions in American Anthropology: Thoughts toward a History of the Interwar Years." In *Selected Papers from the American Anthropologist, 1921–1945,* edited by George W. Stocking Jr., 1–74. Washington, DC: American Anthropological Association, 1976.

———. "Maclay, Kubary, Malinowski: Archetypes from the Dreamtime of Anthropology." In *Colonial Situations: Essays on the Contextualization of Ethnographic Knowledge,* edited by George W. Stocking Jr., 9–74. Madison: University of Wisconsin Press, 1991.

———. "Paradigmatic Traditions in the History of Anthropology." In *The Ethnographer's Magic and Other Essays in the History of Anthropology,* edited by George W. Stocking Jr., 342–61. Madison: University of Wisconsin Press, 1992.

———. "Philanthropoids and Vanishing Cultures: Rockefeller Funding and the End of the Museum Era in Anglo-American Anthropology." In *Objects and Others: Essays on Museums and Material Culture,* edited by George W. Stocking Jr., 112–45. Madison: University of Wisconsin Press, 1985.

———. *Race, Culture, and Evolution: Essays in the History of Anthropology.* 2nd ed. New York: Free Press, 1982.

Stocking, George W., Jr., ed. *Colonial Situations: Essays on the Contextualization of Ethnographic Knowledge.* Madison: University of Wisconsin Press, 1991.

———. *The Shaping of American Anthropology, 1883–1911: A Franz Boas Reader.* New York: Basic Books, 1974.

Stormer, Nathan. "Addressing the Sublime: Space, Mass Representation, and the Unpresentable." *Critical Studies in Media Communication* 21, no. 3 (2004): 212–40.

Swanton, John R. *Myths and Tales of the Southeastern Indians*. Washington, DC: Government Printing Office, 1929.

Tarbell, Ida M. *All in the Day's Work: An Autobiography*. New York: Macmillan, 1939.

Taylor, Brian. "Amateurs, Professionals, and the Knowledge of Archaeology." *British Journal of Sociology* 46, no. 3 (1995): 499–508.

Taylor, Charles Alan. *Defining Science: A Rhetoric of Demarcation*. Madison: University of Wisconsin Press, 1996.

Thornton, Robert J. "'Imagine Yourself Set Down . . .': Mach, Frazer, Conrad, Malinowski, and the Role of Imagination in Ethnography." *Anthropology Today* 1, no. 5 (1985): 7–14.

———. "Narrative Ethnography in Africa, 1850–1920: The Creation and Capture of an Appropriate Domain for Anthropology." *Man* 18, no. 3 (1983): 502–20.

———. "The Rhetoric of Ethnographic Holism." *Cultural Anthropology* 3, no. 3 (1988): 285–303.

Tobin, Joseph Jay. "Visual Anthropology and Multivocal Ethnography: A Dialogical Approach to Japanese Preschool Class Size." *Dialectical Anthropology* 13, no. 2 (1989): 173–87.

Trafzer, Clifford E., Jean A. Keller, and Lorene Sisquoc, eds. *Boarding School Blues: Revisiting American Indian Educational Experiences*. Lincoln: University of Nebraska Press, 2006.

Training for the Professions and Allied Occupations: Facilities Available to Women in the United States. New York: Bureau of Vocational Information, 1924.

Trouillot, Michel-Rolph. *Global Transformations: Anthropology and the Modern World*. New York: Palgrave Macmillan, 2003.

Underhill, Ruth. *The Autobiography of a Papago Woman*. New York: American Anthropological Association, 1936.

———. *Hawk over Whirlpools*. New York: J. J. Augustin, 1940.

Urry, James. "'Notes and Queries on Anthropology' and the Development of Field Methods in British Anthropology, 1870–1920." *Proceedings of the Royal Anthropological Institute of Great Britain and Ireland* (1972): 45–57.

Van Hout, Tom, and Felicitas MacGilchrist. "Framing the News: An Ethnographic View of Business Newswriting." *Text & Talk* 30, no. 2 (Mar. 2010): 169–91.

Vieira, Kate. "Undocumented in a Documentary Society: Textual Borders and Transnational Religious Literacies." *Written Communication* 28, no. 4 (2011): 436–61.

Visweswaran, Kamala. *Fictions of Feminist Ethnography*. Minneapolis: University of Minnesota Press, 1994.

———. "'Wild West' Anthropology and the Disciplining of Gender." In *Gender and*

American Social Science: The Formative Years, edited by Helene Silverberg, 86–123. Princeton, NJ: Princeton University Press, 1998.

Vizenor, Gerald. *Manifest Manners: Postindian Warriors of Survivance.* Hanover, NH: University Press of New England, 1994.

———. *Survivance: Narratives of Native Presence.* Lincoln: University of Nebraska Press, 2008.

Wagner, Peter, Bjorn Wittrock, and Richard Whitley, eds. *Discourses on Society: The Shaping of the Social Science Disciplines.* Dordrecht: Kluwer, 1991.

Walker, Alice. "Zora Neale Hurston: A Cautionary Tale and Partisan View." In *Zora Neale Hurston: A Literary Biography,* by Robert E. Hemenway, xi–xviii. Urbana: University of Illinois Press, 1980.

Warren, Wini. *Black Women Scientists in the United States.* Bloomington: Indiana University Press, 1999.

Weaver, Hilary N. "Indigenous Identity: What Is It, and Who *Really* Has It?" *American Indian Quarterly* 25, no. 2 (2001): 240–55.

Wells, Susan. *Out of the Dead House: Nineteenth-Century Women Physicians and the Writing of Medicine.* Madison: University of Wisconsin Press, 2001.

Wenger, Tisa Joy. *We Have a Religion: The 1920s Pueblo Indian Dance Controversy and American Religious Freedom.* Chapel Hill: University of North Carolina Press, 2009.

Weston, Kath. "The Virtual Anthropologist." In *Anthropological Locations: Boundaries and Grounds of a Field Science,* edited by Akhil Gupta and James Ferguson, 163–84. Berkeley and Los Angeles: University of California Press, 1997.

Wheeler, Valerie. "Travelers' Tales: Observations on the Travel Book and Ethnography." *Anthropological Quarterly* 59, no. 2 (1986): 52–63.

White, Leslie. "Lewis Henry Morgan: His Life and His Researches." In *The Indian Journals, 1859–1862* by Lewis Henry Morgan, edited by Leslie White, 1–15. New York: Dover, 1993.

Wideman, John Edgar. Foreword to *Every Tongue Got to Confess: Negro Folk-Tales from the Gulf States* by Zora Neale Hurston, xi–xx. New York: Perennial, 2002.

Wilder, Gary. "Colonial Ethnology and Political Rationality in French West Africa." *History and Anthropology* 14, no. 3 (2003): 219—52.

Wilkins, David E., and K. Tsianina Lomawaima. *Uneven Ground: American Indian Sovereignty and Federal Law.* Norman: University of Oklahoma Press, 2001.

Willis, William S., Jr. "Skeletons in the Anthropological Closet." In *Reinventing Anthropology,* edited by Dell Hymes, 121–52. New York: Pantheon, 1972.

Winsor, Dorothy A. "Genre and Activity Systems: The Role of Documentation in Maintaining and Changing Engineering Activity Systems." *Written Communication* 16, no. 2 (1999): 200–24.

————. "Ordering Work: Blue-Collar Literacy and the Political Nature of Genre." *Written Communication* 17, no. 2 (2000): 155–84.

————. *Writing Power: Communication in an Engineering Center.* Albany: State University of New York Press, 2003.

Wolfe, Patrick. *Settler Colonialism and the Transformation of Anthropology: The Politics and Poetics of an Ethnographic Event.* London: Cassell, 1999.

Women's Anthropological Society of America. "Organization and Historical Sketch of the Women's Anthropological Society of America." Washington, DC: Women's Anthropological Society of America, 1889.

Wood, Susan E. *The Freedom of the Streets: Work, Citizenship, and Sexuality in a Gilded-Age City.* Chapel Hill: University of North Carolina Press, 2005.

Wooten, Mattie Lloyd. *Classified List of Vocations and Professions for Trained Women.* Denton: Texas State College for Women, 1931.

Worster, Donald. *A River Running West: The Life of John Wesley Powell.* Oxford: Oxford University Press, 2001.

Yates, JoAnne, and Wanda J. Orlikowski. "Genre Systems: Structuring Interaction through Communicative Norms." *Journal of Business Communication* 39, no. 1 (2002): 13–35.

————. "Genres of Organizational Communication: A Structurational Approach to Studying Communication and Media," *Academy of Management Review* 17, no. 2 (1992): 299–326

Young, Michael W. *Malinowski: Odyssey of an Anthropologist, 1884–1920.* New Haven, CT: Yale University Press, 2004.

Zakrzewska, Marie. *A Woman's Quest.* Edited by Agnes Vietor. New York: D. Appleton, 1924.

Zumwalt, Rosemary Lévy. *American Folklore Scholarship: A Dialogue of Dissent.* Bloomington: Indiana University Press, 1988.

————. *Wealth and Rebellion: Elsie Clews Parsons, Anthropologist and Folklorist.* Urbana: University of Illinois Press, 1992.

Index

AAA (American Anthropological Association), 38–39, 42, 115–16
abstraction of storytellers and informants, 106–7, 121–22, 126–29, 147
academic norms, 125–26
activism, 39–40
African American anthropologists, 188n5
African American communities. *See Mules and Men* (Hurston)
agency, rhetorical, 179, 226n7
Aggerey, J. E., 219n62
amateurs in anthropology, 2–3, 13, 26–27, 28, 76
American Anthropological Association (AAA), 38–39, 42, 115–16
American Anthropologist, 35–36, 39, 41, 78, 146
"American Indian," as term, 187n1. *See also* Native Americans
American Indian Life (Parsons), 55, 136–38, 145
American School of Prehistoric Archaeology, 58, 212n37
Angels' Town (Cintron), 10
"Antecedent Genre as Rhetorical Constraint" (Jamieson), 181
antecedent genres, 68, 211n33
Anthropological Society of Washington (ASW), 11, 25–26, 34–35
anthropologists: African American, 188n5; authorization of, 107–9, 122–24, 131–33; Native American, 189n5. *See also specific anthropologists*
anthropology: amateurs in, 2–3, 13,

26–27, 28, 76; British, 5–8, 200n13, 201n28; cultural, 191n19, 194n38; disciplines, precursor, 34–36; discursive norms of, 72–73; field autobiographies' impact on, 68–69, 93–94, 211n32; French, 5–6, 7, 201n28; German, 6, 7, 201n28; institutional setting for, 36–38; internal business of, 38–40; museum-based, 7, 36–37, 204n55; PhDs, 37, 203n43; physical, 191n19, 194n38; practitioners, potential, 25–26; professionalization of, 2–3, 34–40; salvage, 27, 112; scientific status, undermining of, 27–28; social sciences, coordination with other, 39; spy-glass metaphor for, 95, 96, 97–98; subdisciplines of, 6, 191n19, 194n38; university-based, 37–38, 204n55; as welcoming community, 1–2, 3, 58, 76–77
archaeology, rhetorical, 17–18, 175–81, 183–86
Archaeology of Santa Marta Colombia (Mason), 49
Argonauts of the Western Pacific (Malinowski): amateurs in anthropology, 26–27, 28; arrival scene, 80; field methods, 47–48; funding for, 192n26; isolation in fieldwork, 50; roving perspective, 81; scientific methods, 53; spatial synecdoche, 51–52. *See also* Malinowski, Bronislaw
arrival narratives, 80–81
artifacts, genres as, 175–76